THE UPSIDE OF CHRISTIANITY

(Or, Christianity is for Normal People Too)

I0085613

Patricia A. Tauchert

Table of Contents

Contents

Dedicated to my family, the most fun people ever. Love you, mean it.

The Upside
Introduction

This book is written partly out of an urge for self-expression and partly in the hope of encouraging others on a journey that has taken 50 years and counting of my life. I'm still on the path, but I'm better now at seeing the way forward and appreciating the past. There are lots of self-help books out there and lots of books trying to guide people on the path to enlightenment or Christian growth; and most of them don't accomplish much. This book may just be another one. This book may not have an audience at all, it's just something I had to say.

First some background, I am a born-again, evangelical Christian. I'm in church almost every weekend and attend midweek services as often as I can. I've read the Bible around 20 times, I've lost track—and that doesn't count the times I've spent reading the Gospels or the Psalms, or other books of the Bible, and not the whole book. I volunteer, I tithe. I'm one of "those" people. And I've hated church for most of my life.

I've never felt completely comfortable in church and I should be very comfortable. I had perfect attendance until I was a teenager. My whole family went to the same church. We were part of the insider group that scared the new people just a little. My uncles were on the Board, my aunts, mother and grandmother all taught Sunday School. One of my aunts was the church secretary. We were always there; it was as much home as home was. I was saved at age 4, and it stuck. My brother was saved at age 7. I was a little worried that it took him so long to come to the realization that he needed to be washed clean by the blood of Christ--that is how Baptist 12 year olds think. After all I could certainly tell he was a sinner.

Even as children, we knew all the leaders of the church. The pastor was a personal friend of my grandparents and came to visit my sister and me in the hospital when we had our tonsils out. I was about 5. We knew all the ins and out of the building. My sister and I once got into trouble for invading the pastor's office to spin around in his chair. Some of my cousins even crawled up in the rafters to listen in on the pastor's counseling sessions. We were church brats, but I still felt out of place.

The people at church were a little strange. They talked funny. And they were always mad about something. There were a lot of people they didn't like. There were lots of people who weren't there every week and who weren't made to feel welcome when they did come, even though we spent a lot of time talking about how important it was to invite new people. There was a lot of pomp and circumstance. They were very nice people, and they were kind to me, but I felt odd.

There is a reason for that. I was a little odd. I liked the people who didn't come very often. I asked a lot of questions about God and how my teachers were implementing their teachings in their own lives. No one else asked questions—certainly no one else asked retired missionaries if God ever disagreed with what they felt like doing. My mother was not happy about that episode.

The situation did not improve with age. I became a liberal Democrat in 1971. I campaigned for George McGovern, and voted for Hubert Humphrey and Walter Mondale, and I'm proud of it. I voted for Bill Clinton, twice, and I still think he was a good President, despite his lack of respect for his family. I met gays for the first time in college and found I really didn't care. It was the 70's, a lot of people were sleeping with a lot of other people, and it just didn't seem to be any of my business. It still doesn't[1]. None of those opinions were remotely acceptable in the conservative church where I was raised. It was a toss-up whether Democrats or gays were more controversial, but certainly both were heathen. Even I knew better than to ask questions about those subjects. It was a very frustrating church.

I find the church in general, Protestant and Catholic, frustrating on many levels. It often seems unkind, hypocritical and out of touch. The church is probably best known and best described as a social organization for the benefit of its members—a club.

---

[1] For those traditional Christians who point to the "abomination to the Lord" language in the Bible, I won't argue with what the Bible says. I just want to point out that Proverbs 12:22 says that "Lying lips are an abomination to the Lord"; Proverbs 11:1 says that "Dishonest scales are an abomination to the Lord" and Proverbs 16: 5 says, "The proud of heart are an abomination to the Lord." There are numerous references that say worship of another God is an abomination to the Lord. The primary command of Jesus is to "Love one another". We are commanded not to judge one another. I've never married and it is not uncommon for people to assume I must be homosexual. That is rude enough in itself, but as a result of those assumptions, I have some acquaintance with how people treat homosexuals. They are often quite unnecessarily rude without cause; particularly traditional Christians. We don't treat liars and arrogant people with that kind of disdain and contempt. Sometimes we make them pastors. We don't ostracize Buddhists. I think the church needs to get over its preoccupation with homosexuality. It says more about the insecurity of the accusers than it does about homosexuality.

But what I find most troubling about the church is its addiction to sadness. Many people seek out the church when trouble strikes, and that is a good thing. Death, divorce, illness and addiction are powerful motivations for change and to seek out help from a higher power. The vast majority of all adult conversions arise out of traumatic circumstances. The church, for the most part, is good at dealing with trauma. It is good at offering comfort and counsel. Certainly there are exceptions where the church has utterly failed those in need. Women have been told to submit to an abusive or unfaithful husband. AIDS victims have been told they are reaping the results of their sin. Children have been ignored in abusive circumstances, and even been abused by clergy. The church stood by while Nazis slaughtered Jews; and today often ignores poverty that is right in front of it. The church often deals with other faiths in hatred or at least with contempt.

Egregious abuses of individuals in traumatic circumstances are exceptions. The church generally does respond to people who seek it out. The church is generally filled with people who want to do a good job and to serve God. Unfortunately, they often aren't very good at it. The church is out of touch with the realities of everyday life. One of its persistent problems is the inability to recognize or deal with healthy people. Once someone comes in with a problem, they are forever labeled as having that issue. The church talks about God's healing, it just doesn't seem to believe it ever happens.

The church is very willing to respond to negatives. Christians are willing to cry with you, but they throw lousy parties. The church is so wrapped up in pain that it almost demands that one be in pain. Churches are one of the few places where people will insist that you just don't realize you are unhappy, and will insist that you focus on the negatives in your life. Then they want to lead you into healing. Every time I go to a new church they want to save me.

I find this annoying. I'm a reasonably healthy, happy, competent person. My life is not perfect, or trouble free. As I write this my mother has recently died after a 20 year descent into dementia; my financial security has been undermined by an historic recession; my oldest niece, whom I love, is only now showing signs of pulling out of a fifteen-year long pattern of substance abuse and unwise choices. I know the world is a troubled place. I've seen starvation in the third world and the decay of our cities. After nearly thirty-five years as an attorney, I have no illusions about the lengths people will go to as a result of greed or indifference, much less actual malice. But I have a great family, some good friends, and a sense of balance.

6

I have balance in the middle of a life marked by normal, and occasionally larger than normal, ups and downs, primarily because I know God is good. With King David, "I would have despaired unless I had believed that would see the goodness of the Lord in the land of the living." Psalm 27:13. God will make a way through hard times, and will be there whether things are going great or not so great. The troubles still come, and things frequently don't turn out the way I would have wished, but I feel a sense of inner peace most of the time.

In part this is because I don't expect my life to be perfect. God never promised that it would be. Ecclesiastes 9:11 says: …The race is not to the swift or the battle to the strong, nor does food come to the wise or wealth to the brilliant, or favor to the learned; but time and chance happen to them all." The expectation that life should turn out the way we want it to is one of the dangerous heresies promulgated by the modern church. It makes people wonder whether God exists or whether he is actually good. Life is intended to be a roller coaster. We shouldn't be surprised by the ups and downs.

What God does promise, and what he delivers, is comfort during the storm, strength to do what you have to do, and a weird underlying sense of calm that it will all work out somehow. Philippians 4:7 calls it the "peace that passes understanding." The weird calm is actually supposed to be normal. God's love and God's power are real; our preoccupation with the immediate crisis is the fantasy. I know exactly how odd that sounds, but it is true.

Churches are holding out on people. By acting like a private club or focusing only on the negatives, churches create an impression that God is whiny, ineffective or only for the weak. Certainly God loves all people and he has great mercy for those in need, but it doesn't stop there. There is an upside of Christianity that most churches never talk about. In business, the *"upside"* is the positive benefit one anticipates by taking a risk. If there is no potential benefit, no upside—to an action, there is no reason to take a risk. All risks have down sides too—the things that can go wrong. In business you choose whether to do something by whether the upside potential outweighs the down-side risk. Somehow we have lost that concept in the church. We have forgotten there is an upside.

Many Christians, and even Christian leaders, spend year after year focused either on the next church social, or on the negatives. The focus is on pain and suffering, and "don'ts". By focusing on the negatives we miss out on all the good stuff God intends for us to have.

7

Galatians 5:22 describes the fruit of the Spirit—the results of living with God--as love, joy, peace, patience, kindness, gentleness, faithfulness, goodness and self-control. Those are all great things. Who wouldn't want to live a life like that? But most of us miss out on a life like that. We miss out on the lives of contentment waiting for us. The all-out full throttle life where the stars sparkle and the birds sing and the work we do engages our emotions. John 10:10 says that Jesus came to give us life, and "life more abundantly." Some churches talk about an abundant life, but you seldom see it in action. That the church can talk about a life like that, week after week, without anyone in the congregation, including the leadership, showing any evidence that that kind of life is actually real, truly annoys me. I can only imagine how it affects someone who didn't grow up as a church brat. It makes people think that God has nothing to offer, when, in reality, the church has failed, not God.

The church environment I grew up in was supportive in many ways, but very confusing in others. As "insiders" we were privy to *way* too much information about the imperfections of the church, or at least of the people running it. The most difficult thing for me was trying to reconcile the church I knew, with all the squabbling people, the egos and the insistence that the world was a horrid place; with the God I read about in the Bible, who was not like that at all. Evangelical Christians in the 50's, 60's and 70's, did not dance—maybe they still don't. But King David danced in worship of God and cut off his wife when she criticized him for it, 2 Samuel 6:14-22[2]. People in my church did not drink—ever--not a toast at a wedding or a beer at a baseball game, some of them wouldn't eat in a restaurant that had a liquor license. Jesus made wine for a wedding as his first public miracle, John 2. Church was boring. Jesus, and Peter (for a few steps anyway), walked on water, John 6. We spent long hours discussing the color of choir robes. Jesus healed the sick, John 5 and fed thousands, John 6. We held pot luck suppers and gossiped about the people who weren't there.

The disconnect was very troubling to me. I couldn't decide which was an accurate picture of God: the church or the Bible. I couldn't decide what to believe about God's character. To be honest, I did not question his existence. I could look around creation and believe in a god, I just wasn't sure he was the same being I heard about in

---

[2] I've thought that perhaps Michal, David's first wife, who married for love, 1 Samuel 18:20, probably felt that David was more than a little hypocritical when he professed full devotion to God, but had eight wives and an undocumented number of concubines. He married the second wife only a few weeks after Michal saved David's life by helping him escape her father, King Saul. I'm pretty sure there was more to that argument than just the dancing. See 1 Samuel 19; 1 Samuel 25:39-44; 2 Samuel 3:14-16.

church on Sunday. So, after I graduated from high school and left home for college, then law school and beyond, I pretty much stopped going to church for about 10 years. I showed up for major holidays and on visits home, but did not otherwise attend.

My life at that time was pretty typical of other students and young professionals in the 70's and early 80's. It was not the life expected of a carefully raised evangelical Christian; but my friends considered me the straight arrow of the group. I began to notice, more and more, differences between my friends and me. When I smoked pot or drank in college, it was just an experiment, just for fun. When I participated in discussions about the meaning of life; it was an intellectual exercise. I was fundamentally happy and fundamentally grounded. My friends were actually searching for meaning in their lives. I had questions, they had voids. When law school was overwhelming, I could take a break and balance out; others dropped out or became alcoholics or deeply depressed. When I entered the marketplace and had to learn how to deliver unwelcome news to executives who were years older than me and not particularly interested in my opinion; that was stressful, but not insurmountable. Others were paralyzed with fear. And more than thirty years later, I find that fear is still a primary motivator for many in the marketplace. For a long time I thought it was just a difference in personality.

Eventually I came to realize it was more than that. It was really two events, or sets of events, that convinced me. First was a work situation. I was working at the Federal Reserve Bank in Chicago and one of my roles was to provide legal support to the check clearing operation. All the checks that people write (this was before debit cards had been invented so there were lots of checks, over a million a day in the Chicago office alone) have to get from the people who receive the check back to the writer's bank for posting to the writer's account. The Fed moved most of those checks between banks and facilitated the exchange of money for the checks. There are very short deadlines for banks to meet when they handle checks, and interest rates were very high at the time, so even short delays meant big financial costs for banks. It was a high pressure situation. When any organization handles millions of pieces of paper in a day, there is bound to be the occasional hiccup. When I first started handling check questions, I would frequently get calls from one of the bank customers complaining that the Fed had made a mistake and telling me that one of the Chicago Fed offices in another city had told them that the Chicago office had not processed the check properly, or that the Chicago office had said one of the other offices had messed up. The Fed ran an extremely efficient operation.

Most of the time it turned out that none of the offices were at fault and the glitch was completely outside the Fed system, but it was very difficult to convince the customers of that once one of the offices started pointing fingers at another office. It took me over a year to convince the five Chicago Fed offices that they were really one entity and should stop pointing fingers at one another and find out the facts before they told customers we had messed up. They worked together really well for nearly 2 years, and then I left the Fed. In less than 6 months they were back to pointing fingers at one another. My former co-workers who relayed the regression to me were upset about it, but they didn't feel as if they could do anything to encourage cooperation. I never had any magic powers, so I'm certain someone else could have changed the situation by speaking out, but they were afraid to (I was just too young and inexperienced to know better.) When they were pressured, they ducked.

I saw similar patterns and results at my next job. People were fine if I was right there, but didn't have the nerve to carry on by themselves. Many people have no inner balance or sense of security to rely on when faced with a difficult choice. They feel they have no real choice because fear of the consequences is paralyzing to them. (By this time, having seen it work at the Fed, I had developed a habit of just speaking up. Usually it works, sometimes it gets me into trouble; occasionally it gets me into *big* trouble. I have developed more tact and more sensitivity to when to just let something ride as I have gained experience, but I still speak up much more often than is typical. I seldom feel fear and I have always survived. Speaking out isn't as dangerous as it seems.)

I spent a lot of time thinking about what the difference was. I spent a lot of time thinking about what change would allow people to be more comfortable taking the risk to say things they already know. Good managers help, but they aren't enough. People are afraid of good managers too. I came to the conclusion that only God could give them an inner core of peace that things would be ok, so that the fear inherent in a high stress environment wouldn't be overwhelming. I still think that. I have never seen anything else work.

The second influence was a man I dated seriously for several years. We were very much alike in many ways, except one, I'm a happy person and he was consumed by the negative. He saw the ills in the world and what people do to one another and it deeply affected him. His family relationships weren't negative, but they weren't strong either, and he did not have an internal sense of peace. He wasn't sure who he

10

really was and was always looking for something. He was successful, well-respected, healthy, very intelligent, well-educated, came from an affluent background, had some close friends, worked hard and had great self-discipline—far more than me. He had no reason to feel unhappy. We spent a little bit of time talking about it, and I spent a lot more time thinking about it. I concluded that the primary difference in our outlook was God. He wasn't convinced there was a god in the Biblical sense, did not believe in the resurrection, or salvation. He felt the world was spinning hopelessly out of control and it created a negative center in his life. That perception of the world spinning helplessly out of control is very common among others of my acquaintance who don't have a sense that God is real and concerned about them.

The difference in our perspective on that one issue was so marked, and the pervasiveness of the effect of that one difference was so profound, that it convinced me, finally and for all, that our relationship with God has to be a central part of our life in order for us to function properly. I think the lack of a sense of connection to a real God is what causes that hopeless, spinning out of control feeling. No one can change the environment we live in; in fact, a normal American middle class lifestyle is low stress in world terms, it could be a lot worse. Our hope for a centered life has to include an ability to deal with the stressors. Our strength and happiness have to flow from within. External circumstances won't give you a sense of peace. External circumstances are too transient. In the words of Rosanne Roseannadanna[3], "it's always something".

I was feeling some of that same discontent in my own life, something missing, disconnected from the God I believed in, and all at loose ends. So I got a new Bible and went back to church; and it was still really annoying. My boyfriend went with me a few times to be polite and then demurred; and I couldn't blame him. I'd been away 10 years and nothing had changed. Very nice people. Very little connection to current reality. The pastor taught in the books of Corinthians, all about the need for the church to adhere to God's plan—every Sunday for over a year. I don't know how long he had been preaching in that book before I got there. No sign of any change in the congregation or function of the church from all those sermons. I got involved helping

---

[3] Gilda Radner's famous Saturday Night Live character. Check out the you-tube videos, she's very funny. Gilda Radner wrote a book of the same title late in her life as she was battling cancer.

out in the junior high ministry, made some friends, and more or less made a place there, but I still felt odd.

During that time I read the entire Bible through as a book for the first time (it took nearly two years the first time; I thought I would *never* finish Leviticus.) I became more convinced that God is real, it's his world and we are inevitably entwined in his plans. Church was still stultifying. I took a couple of friends to that church who had questions about God. One refused to darken the door of a church again for nearly 7 years after the experience. After that, I kept a careful line between church and the rest of my world. I needed the connection with God, it keeps that spinning out of control feeling in check, but I still didn't like church.

Then I moved as a result of a job move and went to a new church, a very small, very friendly church with decent sermons, and that was the worst yet, in a way. Very nice people again. Very interested in reaching out to others, but even more traditional than other churches I had attended. They really had no idea what to make of a single woman. They kept introducing me to "fine Christian men" with whom I had absolutely nothing in common. They wondered aloud why a lawyer would be teaching Bible School. There were no ministries except children's Sunday School and Bible School programs, and the programming was pretty much mired in the 50's. They insisted on hugging me even after I told them point blank to just shake my hand. It was a very insular group centered around just 4 or 5 families. Despite their best intentions, the church was really a private club. Mind you, this church was the best of the 7 or 8 I had visited prior to deciding to attend there. A couple of those churches had people who scowled at you if you actually sang (not loudly) during congregational singing. I'm not sure what the sermons were like, I nodded off pretty quickly.

After awhile, I just couldn't take the little church anymore. It just didn't seem relevant to my life. So I left, and I was pretty much fed up with church. I decided that I was not going to be involved in a church again. But in the meantime, I had read the Bible through a couple more times and become more convinced that God is the central force of the universe and I thought that church was a necessary evil as part of the connection process. So I started attending Willow Creek Community Church[4], it was close to home and work, and large enough

---

[4] I have no official association with Willow; I'm just an ordinary member. No one from Willow has reviewed or authorized this book, and the opinions I've expressed are only my own personal opinions. Don't arrange a boycott or a picket line—people do from time to time for no apparent reason. Don't accuse Willow of being liberal or teaching

that I thought I could blend in, sit in the back and be left alone. They don't hug strangers at Willow.

A few weeks later they had a food drive to provision their food pantry, one of the largest in Chicago, distributing tons of food every year. I couldn't resist helping to load up food from the parking lot and deliver it to pantry site. They made a party out of it. Then Willow got involved with the Northwest Suburban PADS ministry that provides shelter and food for homeless people in the winter months, opening the church to 30 or 40 homeless people every Thursday night. I had been involved with the local homeless ministry for several years, and I couldn't resist that either. (Homeless people are far more normal that you imagine.)

I actually liked going to services at Willow most of the time. I liked the music in the weekend services. The teaching was varied and relevant. They didn't talk funny, and they actually seemed to like for normal people to show up. It was ok to ask questions. Willow even has regular programs established for people to discuss their questions; any question—even things like "If Christianity is for real, why are Christians so un-Christian?" Willow is far from perfect. It's a big organization; there are still huggers around and people saying "Bless you" when nobody sneezed. There is some preoccupation with the negative, a few co-dependents on staff or in volunteer leadership, and a lot of Republicans. But Willow is an open, accessible, environment and it's real. It's proof that it is possible to have a good church.

Bill Hybels, in particular, has been a great pastor for me. He's very normal; or at least normal in a type A, high energy, positive, fully devoted to the mission, kind of way. He likes to say "the local church is the hope of the world"—sometimes he adds "when it is working right". My take on what he means is that God is the hope of the world and he believes the local church can be, should be and has to be, an effective, positive means of introducing people to God. Bill Hybels has dedicated his life to trying to make that happen and I have a lot of respect for that. Willow has become a home for me and I participate in several ministries. I've made peace with the church, or at least with my corner of the church, but I still think the church has some major problems. I agree that God is the hope of the world, but I still think a whole lot of the local church is impossibly lame and makes it more, rather than less, difficult for people to understand and accept God's interest in them and

---

Christianity-lite. Willow isn't liberal; just rational, and convinced enough of the grace of God to accept miscreants into the fold.

13

love for them. This is a problem because I believe, more than ever, that we all need a real God to be part of our lives in order to truly experience life as it is meant to be lived.

So, the following pages are for people who think God is out there, or wonder if God is out there. This book is for people who wonder what God is like and if he cares. It's for the people who are bored by liturgy and dry sermons, dislike being hugged, are confused by being called "brother" by strangers. It's for people who are tired of hypocrisy, judgment, non-stop gloom, and archaic music. I'm convinced that God isn't impressed by the local church either, but he is impressed with you and he'd like to be better acquainted. We just have to learn to distinguish between the church, whether it is prevailing or failing; and God. Churches are made of up people and all of them are highly flawed. If we focus on the church too much, we will miss God.

This book assumes that God exists and that the Bible presents an essentially accurate picture of God. These may be controversial assumptions to some. However, most people in the US don't seem to doubt these basic assumptions. Depending on the source of the statistics, somewhere between 70 and 88% of people worldwide believe in a god of some sort, and between 80 and 95% of the population of the United States believes in God. According to a 2006 Gallup poll, 72% of Americans are absolutely certain God exists, 14% believe God exists, but have some doubts and only 3% are certain God does not exist. Atheist web sites claim between 5 and 20% of the population is atheist or agnostic. According to the average of three Gallup polls, taken in 2005, 2006 and 2007, about one-third of population in the United States believes the Bible is literally true in all instances, about half believe the Bible is the inspired word of God, but not to be taken as literally true in all instances, and about 20% think it is an ancient book of fables, history and myth[5]. A 2000 Gallup poll showed that 59% of Americans read the Bible at least occasionally. (Interestingly, among people who agreed that the Bible "answers all or most of the basic questions of life", 28% never actually read the Bible at all[6].)

For those not familiar with the Bible, the Bible is comprised of 66 books, written by a number of authors over several centuries. Some of it, for instance the first five books, the Jewish Torah, have been recognized as holy writings for a very long time by both Jews and

---

[5] gallup.com/poll/27682, May 25, 2007 and gallup.com/poll/23470 June 23, 2006; see also freethoughtKamala.wordpress.com; .northstatescience.blogspot.com; atheism.about.com
[6] gallup.com/poll/2416, October 20, 2000.

Christians. The content of the New Testament was the subject of more controversy. Our current format was adopted in the third century. The church councils that adopted the present format of the Bible relied primarily on tests of whether the authors personally witnessed the recorded events, were committed leaders of the first century church, and whether there was a sufficient basis to accurately verify the authorship of the work. For those who are concerned about what texts were left out of the Bible, all of that material is still currently available, and you can read it for yourself[7]. I have only quoted the official Protestant Bible in this book. I have not encountered any compelling writings that were excluded from the official text. I have not read them all, but the ones I have read were written several centuries after Christ walked the earth, and were written as myths, or possibly religious plays. Some of them are simply so unclear or poorly written that I couldn't tell what they meant. There are some incredible things in the Bible, but I don't think there is a compelling case for believing that essential truths or valid counterpoint have been excluded.

For those who want to explore basic questions of belief; such as whether Christ is really the Son of God, or whether God exists, or whether the official Bible is complete and accurate; I'd suggest reading The Case for Christ, by Lee Strobel, Zondervan Press 1998. It is a very readable summary of the arguments, although obviously, concludes in favor of God and the accuracy of the Bible. Joseph Campbell's Transformation of Myth Over Time[8], is one of the more interesting examinations of the opposite view. Joseph Campbell's view is that all religions, including Christianity, are basically a collection of myths around which peoples center their culture—useful for organizing a system of laws, but not actually real. Realistically, no one can prove conclusively that God exists. There is no video clip of God creating the earth, no hidden cameras showing him healing the sick as a result of prayer, no photographs of Jesus walking on water. We don't hear God's voice, at least sane people don't, and we don't see him at Walmart or on talk shows. At some point, one simply has to choose whether to take the

---

[7] One easily accessible source is The Other Bible, edited by Willis Barnstone, HarperSanFrancisco, 1984.
[8] Joseph Campbell, Transformation of Myth Over Time, 1990, Mythology Limited, re-published by Harper Perennial, 1999. Karen Armstrong has also written extensively on the subject. A History of God, Ballantine Books 1993 is an interesting comparison of Islam, Judaism and Christianity (primarily Catholic) theologies from a non-Christian perspective.

basic first step of conceding the existence of God, in some form. As most people have reached that conclusion, we'll start there.

The case for the accuracy of the Bible, at least the part that can be verified, such as the accuracy of descriptions of historical events and places, and the accuracy of transcriptions and translations over time, is much less esoteric. Although questions remain about a number of the stories or facts, the case for the accuracy of the Bible stacks up very well against other early writings that are accepted by scholars as genuine and useful as reliable historical descriptions. For those who are interested, The Case for Christ gives an excellent summary of the research, along with a bibliography of the supporting research and the rebuttal evidence.

I have started from the majority view that the Bible is true and quoted the Bible liberally. When citing to a Biblical reference, I've cited to the appropriate book of the Bible, for example "John", followed by the appropriate chapter and verses, for example, "John 3:16". In some cases, I have just cited to the chapter when the story I am referring to takes up most of the chapter, for example, "John 5". Most quotations are from the New International Version, a few from the New American Standard translation[9]. There are some subtle differences in the translations, but nothing in this book involves those kinds of esoteric discussions. I don't find the discussions personally beneficial and feel the questions are often too nit-picky to be useful. The Bible is not as complicated as some would have you believe. Much of it is a series of biographies that illustrate how God related to people over the course of time. Some of it is poetry or song lyrics, some of it is an historical record of facts and figures. Much of the New Testament is made up of letters from church planters of the time to new churches. The Bible contains no, or virtually no, theology, and very few rules (other than recording the ancient Jewish law.) People have invented most of those behavioral conventions as a part of creating church communities.

This book makes no claims to be a scientific treatise. Much of it is opinion, although I have made an effort to be accurate with respect to any factual references. Some facts, or both sides of a controversy, are footnoted with references, but I have made no effort to conclusively prove any point of view espoused here. I have not footnoted commonly known, geographic or very general information. If something sounds odd to you, try a brief internet search. This book is not intended

---

[9] I have also referred to God in the masculine as "he" because the Bible uses that terminology. God is not a human, so reference to a gender is primarily one of convention.

to be a "how-to" book; no such thing is possible when discussing God. This book is a discussion and exploration of some questions about God and the church; and some thoughts about how to get better acquainted with a real God. It is just the beginning steps of a journey. The journey has to be your own.

Once we are able to figure out who God is, what he is really like, and what he wants. We can get a better acquainted with God, actually know him and have a relationship with him. We still won't hear his voice or see him at Walmart, but we can have an assurance of his presence and that he actually cares about us. That sense of presence of a real God who is interested in you, as an individual, is life-changing—in a very positive way. That is where *the Upside of Christianity* begins.

Chapter One
Who is God and What is He Like?

God's name is Yahweh. It means "I am". Or at least that is the closest we can get. The Jews regarded the name of God as so holy that it could not be spoken. It was always recorded as YHWH, they didn't use vowels at the time, and using the name was strictly forbidden to avoid blaspheming the holy name. God told Moses his name, recorded in Exodus 3:13-14, after God asked Moses to return to Egypt. Moses had run away to escape prosecution for murder and the public condemnation that was certain to follow the discovery that he was born of slaves rather than royalty. He was not anxious to return. God wanted Moses to convince Pharaoh to let more than a million slaves walk away, to the enormous detriment of the Egyptian economy, so that they could cross a desert and go to an unknown land inhabited by warrior tribes to worship at a mountain.

Moses was not enthused. Moses was trying to be polite to God. Moses carefully explained that this was a fool's errand: people were going to say he was nuts, he had no particular skills that would be useful, and on top of everything else, he wasn't a good public speaker. Moses said, "Behold I am going to the sons of Israel, and I shall say to them, 'The God of your fathers has sent me to you.' Now they may say to me, 'What is his name?' What shall I say to them?" And God responded, "I AM WHO I AM'. [YHWH] "Thus you shall say to the sons of Israel, 'YHWH has sent me to you'."

Moses was not immediately convinced, but according to the Bible, Moses went back to Egypt, talked to Pharaoh multiple times, stutter and all and persevered though ten plagues, including the death of all the first born in Egypt. And a few months after God said: "Tell them YHWH sent you", a million slaves walked out of Egypt, while the Egyptians showered them with wealth as they left. Exodus 12:33-36. The timing and historical accuracy of the exodus is hotly debated.[10] Moses' conversation with God is only recorded in the Bible.

---

[10] William Kelly Simpson in *The Ancient Near East: A History*, Harcourt Brace Jovanovich 1971. Records that the collapse of the Egyptian state is recorded in Egyptian historical records at the end of 6th Dynasty, shortly after the reign of Pepi II. The records don't disclose the reason for the collapse, except to indicate it was an internal collapse and economically devastating. Some records record formerly wealthy people working in the fields while their former servants have their wealth. Pepi II had a reign of up to 94 years. There is some confusion as to who succeeded Pepi II, likely either one or two of his sons. Available records confirm that Pepin II's successor died after a very short

reign, about a year; and the second successor fared little better. It is thought that Pepi II was largely ineffective during the later years of his reign and that the resulting malaise was probably responsible for the crumbling of the Egyptian ruling structure. The several hundred year period before Pepi II's death also marks the high point of Egyptian funeral buildings—the great pyramids and the Sphinx, although The Oxford History of Ancient Egypt, edited by Ian Shaw, Oxford University Press, 2000 contends that the pyramids were not build with slave labor. After this era, during the Middle Kingdom and 18th Dynasties and beyond, the taste for grand pyramids had subsided, whether because of the cost or other reasons is unknown. The Pharaohs still built pyramids and other funeral buildings, but on a much smaller scale. See, The Cambridge Ancient History I Part 2 Early History of the Middle East Third Edition, Cambridge Press 1971 and The Oxford History of Ancient Egypt.

Egyptian records also note an historic seven year famine around 450 years prior to this collapse during the reign of King (Pharaoh) Djoser in the Third Dynasty. The Cambridge Ancient History I, Part 2. This interval timing correlates to the Biblical story of Joseph. Joseph was sold into slavery in Egypt by his jealous brothers, then rose to the chief administrative position in Egypt after successfully predicting and planning for a 7-year famine. He was able to save his father and brothers from starvation, and the Bible records this as the original reason the Israelites came to Egypt. After Joseph died, later kings enslaved the Israelites. Genesis 37-50. Their slavery continued for 400 years until Moses led them out of Egypt.

Many people—ok not many, but some people who are interested in the subject--debate which Pharaoh is the Pharaoh of the exodus. Generally accepted historical dating for the Biblical stories of Joseph and the Exodus would place Joseph entering Egypt early in the Middle Kingdom period (around the 12th Dynasty) and the Exodus occurring in the early 18th Dynasty, roughly 700-1000 years later, respectively, than the reigns of King Djoser and Pepi II. Generally accepted historical dating of the exodus is based on internal cross references in the Bible to later dates for which there are better historical records. For example, 1 Kings 6:1 that states the exodus occurred 480 years before Solomon began to rebuild the temple. Ryrie Study Bible, Moody Bible Institute, 1994 edition, p. 86. There is uncertainty in those later dates as well, due to a lack of records, translation difficulties and the differences in calendar and dating systems used among ancient peoples, but 700-1000 years is a big discrepancy; and the information we have about Solomon's temple is generally considered to be reliable.

Both the Middle Kingdom and Eighteenth Dynasties are known for their prosperity, good administration and ordered growth. If one assumes the accuracy of conventional Biblical dating, all of the Pharaohs most likely reigning during the Exodus--Thutmose III, Queen Hatshepsut, and Raamses II [featured in the Hollywood version of "The Ten Commandments"]--were highly successful with no evidence of any devastating calamity affecting their reign. See, The Cambridge Ancient History II, Part 1,The Middle East and the Aegean Region c.1800-1380 B.C. Third Edition, Cambridge Press, 1973 and The Oxford History of Ancient Egypt. We simply don't have complete and congruent records from that far back in history, but Egyptian records are markedly better than those of others of the same time period. Many scholars interested in the topic believe

A purported Egyptian eyewitness account of plagues of Biblical proportions written in the 18th Dynasty, but appearing to relate to the end of the 6th Dynasty period just after the death of Pepi II, was unearthed early in the 20th Century, but largely discounted as too fantastic to be real[11]. Critics point to the lack of any Egyptian records recording what would seem to have been a very significant event, even though Egypt had very complete records for an ancient culture. Critics also point to conventional dating of Biblical events, which would place the Exodus between 700 and 1000 years later than the reign of Pepi II.

---

that the Biblical stories of Joseph and the Exodus can't be sufficiently substantiated to be accepted as fact.

A suggestion made by the Cambridge Ancient History, Early History of the Middle East I, Part 2 ,p. 352 cited above, is that a number of tribal peoples would from time to time locate to the border areas of Egypt in search of greater prosperity, and the Israelites were simply one of those peoples. Egypt would force those tribes to relocate if they became too numerous or otherwise interfered with Egyptian trade and society. The book suggests that Moses and the Israelites were just one more of such tribal groups and not significant from an Egyptian perspective. On the other side of the debate, Starways.net has posted a 1995 article from Jewish Action published by the Union of Orthodox Rabbis, titled, "The Exodus and Ancient Egyptian Records" that is an easy to read summary of the Old Kingdom Egyptian records of the above events.

I won't attempt to reach a conclusion about the dating and historical accuracy of the exodus when others with far more knowledge than I have not resolved the questions.

[11] Admonitions of an Egyptian Sage from a hieratic papyrus in Leiden, A.H. Gardiner (1909.) Historians are almost unanimous in dating this papyrus to the Middle Kingdom around the time of the early 18th dynasty, but relying on and interpreting some more ancient manuscripts dating from the end of the Old Kingdom. The events it describes are believed to deal with the end of the Old Kingdom, the time of Pepi II's successor(s.) Its author, an Egyptian named Ipuwer, writes: "Plague is throughout the land. Blood is everywhere. Death is not lacking…. The river is blood. And yet men drink of it. They thirst for water. Forsooth, gates, columns and walls are consumed by fire. "Forsooth, gold and lapis lazuli, silver and malachite carnelian and bronze, stone of Yebhet and {blank} are fastened on the necks of female slaves. Good things are in the lands (Yet) the mistresses of the house say "Would that we had something to eat".

These passages are part of an extended description of upheaval, civil unrest and the destruction of the previous society. It is followed by a call for a return to religious practices and the prediction of a coming redeemer, unclear whether that is a human ruler or a Messiah figure. While the whole work is somewhat obscure, it definitely records a time of great upheaval and economic collapse.

The Pharaohs reigning during the possible Exodus timeframes using conventional dating were very successful with no sign of any economic or social disruption. But what if the story of Moses *is* real. And what if YHWH *is* real after all and can do what he says he is going to do? That would be important.

So, who is this YHWH? First and foremost, God is a person—a real person. He is not human, but he is a defined personality, with predictable, firmly held opinions and attitudes. God behaves in a consistent manner. Malachi 3:6 says: "For I, the Lord, do not change; therefore, you, O sons of Jacob, are not consumed." Hebrews 13:8 says the same of Jesus, "Jesus Christ is the same, yesterday and today, yes and forever." Just like any other person, we can look at God's behavior throughout the Bible, see its consistency and make conclusions about his character by looking at his actions.

The assumption that God is a definite person is going to offend some people. Most people are comfortable with the idea that there is a god; they believe that. But many people who believe in the existence of god are uncomfortable with the idea that God is a definite, defined person. We prefer to think of God as a life-force that is subject to multiple definitions. There are many opinions of who God is, what he is like, and how he should be worshipped. There is the Jewish view of God, Islam's view, the many Gods of Hinduism, the pervasive force of Buddhism; the Great Spirit of Native American religions. Even Christians disagree among themselves on what God is like and how to worship him. How can we know we have the right, finite description of God? That seems wildly presumptuous.

Ask someone to tell you what God looks like. Many people are offended at the idea that God has a physical appearance. Yet both Daniel and Ezekiel, two Old Testament prophets, describe a being having the appearance of a man, yet glowing like burning metal, (Ezekiel 8:2) and Daniel adds a description of glowing white robes and hair (Daniel 7:9 and 10:6.) Matthew 17:2 and Luke 9:29 describe a similar experience with Jesus. He was transfigured in front of Peter, James and John, his face becoming very bright and his garments shining with white light. The descriptions are very consistent yet Daniel and Ezekiel had no contact with one another. Both were exiled Jews, but Ezekiel was a number of years older than Daniel and lived a private life. Their descriptions were written separately, decades apart. Matthew and Luke both recorded the same event, witnessed by four of the original apostles, centuries after Daniel and Ezekiel lived. The consistency over time and among witnesses gives credence to the idea that God actually looks like that—because eyewitnesses are notoriously inaccurate in their descriptions. Four people would never accidentally provide the same vivid, rather outlandish, description. I have to think that God is physically real and has a recognizable physical appearance, just as you or I, or anyone or anything we see around us, has a consistent, defined appearance.

God also has a defined personality, just like you and I, and everyone else we know, have definite personalities. Even the animals we are acquainted with have definite, distinct personalities. It shouldn't be a surprise that God also has a defined character; even if it is initially uncomfortable.

One of the major criticisms of Christianity is that it asserts its correctness to the exclusion of other disciplines—that is deemed to be presumptuous and impolite. We expect one another to accept our definition of God and to accept our worship of God in the manner we believe is most correct. The current thought is that all beliefs about God are entitled to respect and acceptance. No one has any right to say that one way is more correct than another. It would be presumptuous to define God if we were defining God ourselves. But if the Bible just reveals how God described himself so that we would know what he is like, rather than manufacturing an image of God; that is no longer presumptuous. It's actually very nice of God to let us know what he is like; people have been wondering forever.

Every culture on earth throughout history has had gods. Gods take on every possible form and permutation of character, although most gods created by human beings are pretty nasty characters. Versions of gods range from Greek, Roman and Norse gods, to the Druids tree spirits, the idols of the Incas and Aztecs; and Moloch, the Asherah and the Baals of the Bible. We want god, we just all want to be free to create our own version of a god who suits our particular tastes. We've given up carving gods out of wood and infant sacrifice, but we haven't stopped creating our own gods. I believe strongly that from a political perspective we need to preserve our basic human right to create any god we want. As long as the discussion is just among different people, everyone is on an equal footing and has a right to their opinion.

Agreeing that everyone is entitled to the respect of other people, to the freedom to determine their own belief system and to be free of political and personal harassment and religious persecution is a critical and fundamental hallmark of our society. Frankly, I can't think of any idea that is more ridiculous than the notion that we should shout at, ridicule, belittle, discriminate against, persecute, or kill someone because we disagree with them about the way God has chosen to express his love to mankind. That concept is certainly not anywhere to be found in the Bible. The provision in our Constitution for separation of church and state is foundational to this freedom and should never be compromised. No one has a right to legislate the belief system of another person as long as their religious practices do not cause physical harm to others.

The problem only arises when God enters the equation. If God is real, and if he has an opinion, we aren't free to change it. We can't define God. God is. His name is "I AM WHO I AM". "God" is not an elective office. We shouldn't confuse our constitutional and political right to freedom of religion with an actual ability to determine who God is. We can choose what to believe about God, but that won't actually change who God is. Agreeing that everyone is entitled to their own view of God is like agreeing that everyone is entitled to their own view of what the temperature will be the next day. It's fine to have a preference, it's fine to voice an opinion, but that won't change the temperature. Our opinions of God won't change God. God just is. We can become acquainted with who God is, but not define who God is.

God is immutable. This is difficult for us to accept. Everything else we know had a beginning, it ages, it changes, and it dies. Sometimes quickly, sometimes so slowly we can barely see a difference in a lifetime, but everything else around us changes and eventually dies. What's more, we have some ability to control or at least affect, virtually everything. We've been to the moon, routinely fly around the world, have radically improved health care and life expectancy, moved mountains, built cities in the middle of deserts, and live in climate controlled houses, even in Antarctica and space. From the beginning of time, this lack of control over who and what God is, has been mankind's central problem with God. We are used to controlling our environment. We expect to control our environment. Having a God we don't control bugs us. Adam and Eve rebelled against God because they wanted god-like knowledge, and with it, power. Genesis 3:4-6. We do the same thing every day.

Nothing just is. But God is. Nothing is beyond our ability to affect. But God is. God is not limited by time or by space or by physics. That doesn't make much sense to us either. God created those things as part of the structure of our world—more about that debate in a minute. Since he created them, he can mess with them. Time, space and physics define us, not God. The Bible begins with the statement, "In the beginning, God created Heaven and Earth." In Job 38:4 God asks,

23

"Where were you when I laid the foundation of the earth?" In John 8:58, Jesus said, "Truly, truly, I say to you, before Abraham was born, I am." God was always here, and always who he is now. I don't pretend to understand how that works, but it is one of God's defining characteristics. God isn't going to disappear or flake out on you. That is a good thing. Man wants God to exist.

Generally speaking, we agree that God is responsible for our creation in some way and that we are tied to him in some way. Creation myths abound in every culture; each unique to that culture's god. The Hindus' describe the world riding on the back of a turtle and Native American religions have stories of gods descending from the sky. Atheists and some philosophers hold the view that man's desire to create gods is simply a holdover from a more primitive time. They conclude that the Biblical God is a myth just as the Romans gods were myths, and that there is no god.

The post-modern, mainstream version of the "god is myth" theory is tolerance. We must all accept any version of God our colleagues create as equally valuable. This doesn't make sense from a logical perspective. It actually means that God isn't real at all. If God can be defined by anyone, then God would have no real characteristics at all—he would be a character in a novel. The Bible may not be an accurate picture of God, but whoever God is, he has a defined character. Whatever view of God is accurate, we can't all be right. We can learn who God is, but not define God. We can, and should, respect one another, but we can't change God. It is really a question of which view of God is accurate.

God is. And God has opinions. The Biblical God is very sure he is the one true God. He does not need us to survive, does not need us for food, or money, or air to breathe, or a place to live, or to maintain his self-respect, or to meet his approval needs, or for anything else for that matter. Psalm 50: 7-15 describes it this way:

"Hear, O My people, and I will speak; O Israel, I will testify against you; I am God, your God. I do not reprove you for your sacrifices, and your burnt offerings are continually before Me. I shall take no young bull out of your house, nor male goats out of your folds. For every beast of the forest is Mine, the cattle on a thousand hills. I know every bird of the mountains, and everything that moves in the field is Mine. If I were hungry, I would not tell you; for the world is Mine, and all it contains. Shall I eat the flesh of bulls, or drink the blood of male goats? Offer to God a sacrifice of thanksgiving, and pay your vows to the Most High;

and call upon Me in the day of trouble; I shall rescue you, and you will honor Me."

I can't even imagine what God thinks about all our attempts to define him, but God remains who he is. This is amply illustrated throughout the Bible. One of the most succinct statements was made by Balaam, an Old Testament prophet who been called in by King Balak from Aram to curse the approaching Israelites. Although Balaam was perfectly willing to curse the Israelites for a fee, he received word from God and was unable to curse them (we don't know how that worked exactly.) He blessed them instead, greatly angering the king. In a second attempt to obtain a proper curse, Balak asked Balaam again to look on the Israelites and curse them. Balaam again received word from God and said this: "God is not a man, that He should lie, Nor a son of man, that He should repent; Has He not said it, and will he not do it? Or has He spoken, and will He not make it good?" Numbers 23:19. King Balak was totally annoyed at that point; and Balaam had a really bad day as well, but the Israelites prevailed[12].

Since God doesn't change, we are the ones who have to adjust to the reality of God. In Job 9:32-33, Job, trying to explain to his friends that he still had faith in God after experiencing a truly epic series of unfortunate events, said, "For He is not a man as I am that I may answer Him, that we may go to court together, for there is no umpire between us, who may lay his hand upon us both." Job had to adjust, not God. In the same way that you can get to know another human being, but not change who they are; you can become acquainted with God, but you can't change who he is. That is a good thing. We invent very poor gods. But we still find it annoying.

So, what exactly is God? Volumes have been written on the subject. The real answer is that we don't know exactly. God is a spirit, but not ephemeral. He is just a completely different sort of being than we are. He created physics and the physical laws that govern our existence. He created space, time, gravity, mass and matter. He isn't bound by them, and we don't know how that works.

---

[12] According to Jewish historical accounts, Balaam then worked with King Balak to undermine the Jewish culture from within by encouraging intermarriage with the local culture. That worked better than the curse and Balaam is one of the pariahs of Jewish history.

Both the Bible and science leave us with a lot of unanswered questions about God. The first question is: Does he exist and was he involved in creation at all? There is a huge debate about how the world got here: was it creation or some form of evolution? How did it all happen?

Most people would concede there was some sort of force that got it all started. The first law of physics is that we live in a closed system: matter cannot be created or destroyed, it just changes phase. Since a lot of stuff is here, it must have come from somewhere. There is solid evidence in physics for the Big Bang theory of creation. The Big Bang theory basically says that before the beginning all matter, time and energy was a singularity—a point---and then the point exploded and matter, time and energy began. But something set off the Big Bang, and something came up with all that matter and energy that exploded. God is the most obvious choice of where things started; however naïve people want to make that conclusion sound. Science has a lot of ideas about what happened next, but doesn't have another explanation of how it all started in the first place.

The general pattern of what we know of the development of the earth follows the general pattern of the creation story in the Bible, although carbon records indicate the world was formed over eons rather than a week. The fossils record indicate plants came first, then fish and birds around the same time, and finally mammals arrived essentially all at once, or in rapid succession, in what has been dubbed the Cambrian Explosion. In the Biblical version, plants appear on day 3 of creation, fish and birds on day 5 and mammals on day 6. Genesis 1. I'm not sure how to reconcile all that, the first few chapters of Genesis are pretty wild. I don't pretend to have all the answers to the creation issue.

It is clear, however, that *we* didn't create the world and that we aren't the ones in control here. If you doubt that, sit on your porch and watch a thunderstorm. Stand on the beach while the tide comes in. Watch the moon and stars travel across the sky. Talk to any sixteen year old. We don't control the world we live in; but it isn't random—except maybe for teenagers. The natural world is governed by very reliable systems. The sun rises and sets at a predictable time, the stars revolve in a predictable order, and genetics dictate consistency across all manner of living things, both plants and animals. Plants and animals adapt very readily to short term changes in environments. They don't demonstrate wholesale basic change, but they are quite flexible—very well suited for survival. The natural world is extremely complex and sophisticated. It is always degrading, but will adapt to change and re-format to a stable condition. The idea that it all sprang up by chance in good order defies chaos theory. The idea that it all evolved from spontaneously appearing bits of matter defies all the rules of physics.

If everything evolved, we should have increasing numbers of species over time. It is clear we have declining numbers of species over the span of eons rather than more. We don't have any fossil record of the "link" species showing transformation from one basic type of organism to another that Darwin predicted we would discover to support his theory. Yet, there are still too many varieties of plants and animals around today to have developed at so slow a rate that we don't see the changes happen[13]. The idea that creation points to the existence of God is actually quite rational. Romans 1:20 puts it this way, " For since the creation of the world, God's invisible qualities-- his eternal power and divine nature--have been clearly seen, being understood from what has been made, so that men are without excuse."

Really though, quarreling about creation is a red herring. Whatever happened at the beginning of time, it was a long time ago. The creation debate doesn't change the present debate. The question really is: What is God like and why should I care?

For many people, the question just doesn't seem that important. So what if a god started the whole thing, what does that have to do with me? We will get to a more thorough answer later, but if you think it is a small thing to be God, something that is ignorable or inconsequential to your life, try it some time. It is easy to go around acting like we believe we are the center of the universe, but actually controlling the universe is beyond us. If there is a God with that kind of power, what else can he do? It is an important question.

---

[13] I'm not sure about there being an actual tree in the Garden of Eden either. I've wondered what happened to the fruit. Wouldn't deer and raccoons and birds eat the fruit? We know that bacteria, insects and worms must have eaten it, or the fruit would still be piled up somewhere. They didn't seem to be affected by the fruit. The Bible does say that Eve saw "that the fruit of the tree was good for food" Genesis 3:6, so maybe the whole knowledge of good and evil thing only worked on people. Who knows? Josh McDowell, Evidence that Demands a Verdict (1992), published by Thomas Nelson Inc., and updated and revised in 1999, and the remaining books in that series, provides a much more thorough review of the creation controversy and other debates about the accuracy of the Bible. As I said, I don't believe there is clear answer to the details about how the world came to be the way it is. But I think that, whatever the details, the premise that God began creation, man rejected God and then took over the role of god in his own life with various permutations of created gods, resulting in a royal mess; is sound. We all still do that today.

So, how do we learn about God? We can't know God directly. We aren't going to meet him walking down the street, or go to one of his lectures at the local university. We aren't going to hear his voice. God didn't personally pen the Bible and isn't going to appear for a book-signing or guest on late night talk shows. But we can know God from the effect he has. We can also learn his character from the Biblical record of his interactions with other people.

The first characteristic we learn about God is that he is very sure he is God. God loves us, he wants to be acquainted with us, and to have a relationship with us; but he is not confused about who is God. The First Commandment states, "I am the Lord, your God. You shall love no other god before me." Deuteronomy 5:6-7. This theme is repeated throughout scripture. God said it to Abraham, to Moses, to Gideon, to David, to Isaiah, to Peter, to John, to Paul. To paraphrase an old Saturday Night Live gag, God is God, and you're not. Actually that much should be obvious. We are well aware that everyone else we meet is not God, and grateful that they aren't. It is just less apparent that we ourselves fall into the same category as the rest of the world.

The second thing we learn is that God has a physical presence, but that is also difficult to get grip on. His physical appearance is described several times in the Bible, but the description of his physical presence goes beyond the description of his appearance. God rarely physically appeared to people, but the Bible describes many people sensing his physical presence or perceiving a personal communication from God. When the Bible talks about the presence of God, or one of the prophets hearing from him, like Balaam above, it isn't clear what that means.

Anyone who claims to hear God's audible voice today is definitely crazy; but the prophets were not crazy. The Bible records some instances of very direct actions by God, but no one, not even Moses or Elijah, actually saw the face of God. Despite the lack of detail on how such encounters work, the Bible clearly records that people like Moses, Elijah, King David, and many, many more, encountered a physical presence of God. They were comforted by the presence, they communicated with it. They craved the presence of God. Even today, and this will sound very odd, we can have a sense that we are not alone and that God is actually with us. And his presence is comforting. It's like watching a thunderstorm roll in with lighting and crashing thunder when you are small. If you are by yourself, it's intimidating, even frightening; but surrounded by your mom and dad, sitting snugly on the back porch, it's beautiful. The storm didn't change, but your perspective changed. God's presence changes our perspective in the same way, and is just as comforting. Lightening becomes beautiful.

Descriptions of God give us an impression of God, but no details about God's character. We can only see God's character from his actions. We can see God's actions over a long period of time as he interacts with various people in the Bible. However, the easiest way to identify God's character is to look at the example Jesus gave us. Jesus was also very sure he was God, the second person of the Trinity.

Jesus called himself the Son of God and the Son of Man, a reference to the prophet Daniel's description of his vision of God recorded in Daniel 7:13. Jesus declared himself the Jew's Messiah, predicted for centuries. Jesus began his ministry by reading from the book of Isaiah in the synagogue in Galilee one Sabbath. [Jesus was a real rabbi, it wasn't just a title his followers used] He read a passage describing the Messiah to come and then began his message by stating "Today this scripture is fulfilled in your hearing." Luke 4:21. People were really angry. They tried to throw Jesus off of a cliff, but he "walked right through the crowd and went on his way." Luke 4:28. No idea how he did that.

Messiah claims were not unusual for his day. Men came forward periodically claiming to be the Messiah. Several messiah figures were even endorsed by Jewish leadership, both before and after Jesus. But the belief at the time was that the Messiah was to be a political leader, like the heroes of the Old Testament who led Israel to victory over various enemies. The Messiah would free the Jewish state from the oppression of Rome and restore the glory days of King David and King Solomon when the Jewish state was powerful and respected. Claiming to be a political Messiah was dangerous if the Roman hierarchy felt threatened, but no Jew would kill anyone over it. Claiming to be God was blasphemy and punishable by death. That is why the crowd got mad.

Jesus was different than the other Messiahs. Jesus was not a political activist; he had other priorities. He told Pilate, recorded in John 18:36-37 that "my kingdom is not of this world..." and continued his explanation, "you say correctly that I am a king. For this I have been born, and for this I have come into the world, to bear witness to the truth. Everyone who is in the truth hears my Voice". In John 8:42 Jesus said, "If God were your father, you would love me; for I proceeded forth and have come from God, for I have not even come of my own initiative, but he sent me." In John 5:36 Jesus said, "But the witness which I have is greater than that of John [the Baptist]; for the works which the Father has given me to accomplish, the very works that I do, bear witness of me, that the Father has sent me."

As part of the Trinity of God[14], Jesus' character and actions are very consistent with those of God in the Old and New Testament. The Holy Spirit is never explained at all, except to be described as very holy and not to be minimized or debased, Matthew 12:31. The Holy Spirit seems to be the primary way in which God makes his presence felt by people.

Taking all the descriptions of God together, we get a picture of God's character. It's very important to get that understanding of who God really is. You can't actually have a relationship with someone without a clear picture of who they are—it wouldn't be genuine. Just as important, you need to understand who someone is before you decide you want to have a relationship with them. If God is vindictive, cruel, harsh and demeaning, the kind of god people have created for themselves over history, why should you bother to have a relationship with God? It wouldn't make sense.

God in the Old Testament is often thought of as cruel, harsh and arbitrary. Some things are very difficult to understand and troubling. The great flood, which annihilated most of the earth's population; the plagues of Egypt; the plague on the Israelites who complained of eating manna in the desert and when they worshipped Baa; and the direction to Israel to kill every man, woman and child of the Canaanites living in the Promised Land, just for examples; are very harsh and very difficult to understand. I don't have a complete explanation.

Perhaps God's anger and frustration that led up to the Flood weren't unjustified. We are told that man before the Flood was "full of abomination" Gen.6:5-6 says "Then the Lord saw that the wickedness of man was great on the earth, and that every intent of the thoughts of his heart was only evil continually. And the Lord was sorry that He had made man on the earth and He was grieved in his Heart." We have no explanation of all the details from that far back in time, but we do know some of the accepted practices in less ancient days for which we do have

---

[14] The concept of the Trinity of God is never plainly explained in the Bible. Although volumes have been written about it, the truth is that no one knows how that all works. The Bible describes three persons, God the Father, Jesus the Son and the Holy Spirit, who operate together as "one" -- as Jesus describes the relationship in Mark 12:29, citing the ancient Jewish creed. Perhaps it is some kind of hive mind. I think of the three persons of the Trinity as the mind, body and soul of God. That is undoubtedly some kind of heresy.

historical records were more appalling than the worst things we deal with today. If things before the flood were worse, they were very bad indeed.

God's command to kill all the Canaanites living in the Promised Land is very difficult to reconcile with the idea of a loving God. But perhaps there was a method to the decree. From historical records relating to that time period, we know the ancient Canaanites practiced infant sacrifice to their god, Moloch, and engaged in ritual self-mutilation as part of their religious rites, as well as perverted sexual rituals. We know they treated slaves cruelly and also practiced genocide against their enemies. We know that the Israelites were treated cruelly as slaves by the ancient Egyptians and that the worship of Baal was bloody and included human degradation. We know that when the Israelites disobeyed God and adopted the religious and cultural practices of their neighbors, they suffered for it.

In the ancient world, women and children were property, slavery was accepted, and killing and maiming conquered enemies was seen as an appropriate display of victory. Genocide during war, except for young women and children who could be kept as slaves, was common and accepted. Strict social caste systems governed societies. Social support programs were unheard of. The rich lived lives of excess and anyone who couldn't support themselves simply died. Violent crime was very prevalent and often perpetrated by the power structure itself. There was virtually no means of redress for any crime or affront other than more violence. The world was a mess.

The genocide in the Bible has always bothered me, it seems so over the top, cruel and unnecessary. I don't have a complete explanation of it, except perhaps that it was a means of dealing with some cultures that were engaged in extremely cruel practices even compared to other cultures of the day—and perhaps it was better for the children and young girls to be dead rather than trafficked as slaves. If one looks more closely at some of the practices of the ancient world, I sometimes think God should have killed off more people[15].

---

[15] Just for the record, I don't think anything about the Canaanites in the Old Testament can be read to have any application to the modern state of Israel's relationships with its current neighbors. The Middle East is a very complicated place and it is grossly unrealistic for US Christians to base opinions about the modern day political situation on texts that are 5000 years old and related to different people and a different environment than the ones in the Middle East today.

We always wonder why God isn't more active in preventing and punishing evil, both in the past and now. The world is less violent today than it was 2000 years ago or 5000 years ago, but cruelty and violence aren't hard to find. One of the biggest questions people have about God is why he allows so much suffering in today's world. Is God a cruel being who causes the suffering or just indifferent to it and to us? We don't have a complete answer for that.

We tend to blame God for bad things that happen, but it is hard to say he is to blame for things we do to ourselves—and the things we cause by failing to share resources. We bring a lot of suffering on ourselves by our own choices, and we cause a great deal of pain to other people by our actions. Even many of the ravages of disease and natural disasters could be prevented if the developed world shared resources with the undeveloped world, and the rich shared more resources and opportunities with the poor in their own countries. If you think past the obvious, we are largely living with ills and evils that we create for ourselves, not ones of God's making. He doesn't jump in and correct it all, but then he would be taking over our lives. And we like to be in control of our own destiny.

There is a threshold level of suffering that does just happen to people. We don't cause it, we can't prevent it, and that makes it more painful. It is not easy to see children with painful diseases, the victims of natural disasters; or families torn by deaths from accidents or illness. Everyone eventually dies and that is seldom easy and never happens at the right time. It is painful for those who die and those left behind. The way some people in the world live the short unpleasant lives they have is even more painful to watch than death. We think God should fix these things.

According to the Genesis record, that frictional level of suffering, the suffering that is not directly caused by our actions or inactions, is the result of a blight on the earth resulting from mankind's decision to be their own god and reject God as leader. That is an extremely odd concept in Western culture, that there should be collective guilt and collective consequences that are not the direct result of our own actions. The only explanation I really have is that while none of us rejected God in the Garden of Eden (and whether the Genesis record is historical or allegorical, the same issue remains); all of us have rejected his leadership at some point. Each of us still wants to be the God of our own world. Whatever caused the blight, we all participate on a daily basis. We even contribute to some of the natural disasters by the way we treat our natural resources.

Before we condemn God, we also have to ask what standard we should use to judge what to do about suffering? It is easy to see the extreme cases: the child molesters, the people who torture and maim others for their own gain or pleasure; murderers and thieves. Unfortunately, while most of us avoid those kinds of cruel behavior, we have all done things we are ashamed of in moments of anger or fear or pressure to survive and succeed. We have all inflicted suffering on others, and often on people we love. Even June Cleaver messed up once in awhile. The most efficient way to eliminate the bulk of suffering is to eliminate people. The alternative is to turn people into robots who only do the right thing. God gave us the ability to make choices and he doesn't often intervene in those choices, or the results of our choices. If that is difficult for us to watch; think how frustrating it must be for God.

I don't believe that God actively causes bad things to happen to us, I think he just doesn't micro manage the world. I believe that God is not indifferent to our pain, and I think he tries to make some good come out of it. I know he will lend his presence to help you get through it all. My mother's illness was very difficult to watch. But I learned patience from it and I got to know her in a different way, more like the child she had been, than I would ever have known her as an adult. I don't think of her illness as a horrible tragedy, but just something that happened in our lives. I've lost a lot of people, and I hate death. I didn't go to funerals for years. But I have come to understand that rather than just hating death, we need to value the time we share with people we love and take advantage of the opportunities while we have them. Most of the horrible things we hate in the world we hate because they lead to death, but death isn't necessarily always a bad thing. Perhaps death is the start of something better. If so, then God's failure to prevent all the death we hate isn't such a bad thing either.

Animal sacrifice in ancient Israel is often pointed out as evidence of an inhumane god. But animal sacrifice was a very common religious practice among ancient cultures, even though it seems very odd to us today. The sin of a person, any offense against their god, was symbolically transferred to the animal, and the animal was killed, and frequently burned on some kind of altar. That was considered normal. Most ancient cultures practiced some form of it. There were sacrifices to Baal and to Moloch. It was common among the Egyptians, Chaldeans, Assyrians, Greeks and Romans as well as Aztecs and Mayans. Animal sacrifice was carried over to Islam and Hinduism. The Druids practiced animal sacrifice as late as the Middle Ages. The Israelite practices were tame in comparison to many. The sin of the worshipper was symbolically transferred to a perfect one-year old male lamb or goat, then the animal was quickly and humanely killed and its carcass burned.

There were other sacrifices in addition to a sin sacrifice. There were thanksgiving sacrifices and a normal tithe offering. Like other ancient cultures, the Israelites lived in an agrarian society. Any meat that was eaten had to be slaughtered. Actually, the Israelite sacrifice was most like a community barbecue—the original pot luck supper. Ordinary Sabbath and holiday sacrifices were cooked and eaten. The priest killed the animal. Then a portion of the meat was given to the priest as a tithe, and the remainder was cooked at the temple, and eaten there as a meal in the company of other families who were observing the Sabbath. The meat was either roasted or boiled and was served with other traditional accompaniments, like flat bread and herbs. If the person had to come from too far away to bring the wheat, wine and animals required, they could sell those products, bring the money to the temple and, according to Deuteronomy 14:26, "spend the money for whatever your heart desires, for oxen, or sheep or wine, or strong drink, or whatever your heart desires; and there you shall eat in the presence of the Lord your God and rejoice, you and your household." The God of Israel knew how to throw a party.

The reputation of the Old Testament God as arbitrary and vindictive is not deserved. Even in the Old Testament, a complete reading leaves a different impression of God. The Old Testament doesn't describe a god who is harsh and vindictive. A fair reading of the Bible demonstrates that God is kind, endlessly forgiving, unimaginably patient, and stubborn, and these are all primary characteristics of God. He forgave mankind in general and the Israelites in particular, repeatedly over thousands of years for failing to follow his teachings, and for engaging in the very cruel, depraved practices of the time. God just has a limit and he takes action to correct our errors when we reach that limit—or lets us learn from the consequences of our own poor choices.

People, rather than God, are arbitrary and inconsistent. The first of the famous Ten Commandments is: "I am the Lord your God, who brought you out of the land of Egypt, out of the house of slavery. You shall have no other gods before me." Deuteronomy 5:6-7. Remember, God is very sure that he is God. But Israel *never* followed that commandment. Israel followed other gods from the time Lot split from Abraham until the nation was destroyed by Babylon, and again after it was re-established by Persia, continuing up through the Roman times recorded in the New Testament and the complete dissolution of the Israeli state. The books of Judges, Kings I and II, Chronicles I and

II, as well as Jeremiah, Isaiah, Daniel, Ezekiel, and the rest of the prophets, relate story after story of Israel's failure to worship God.

Israel was always a secular nation that followed after the religious habits of its neighbors. They were over-run by enemies time after time, cried out to God for deliverance, repented for awhile when a champion arose, and then repeated the pattern. This went on for thousands of years. And Israel was the group that was *most* responsive to God and most closely followed his commands. Pagan practices through history were incomprehensively brutal. We aren't that great now. If God were really harsh, he would have killed Israel and the rest of the inhabitants of the earth long ago and been done with it. We have all been ignoring God, at best, and defying him outright, at worst, since history began. God is *very* patient, and *very* forgiving.

Another characteristic of God is that he is protective. God looks out for us, even when we don't see it. For example, the Jewish dietary laws seem arbitrary; but if you look at them carefully, it is very much the Mediterranean diet that nutritionists recommend today. It's based on whole grains, fish, and unsaturated fats. Meat was eaten on special occasions, and all the food was organic. The rules about not mixing meat and milk at the same meal had hidden benefits. There was no refrigeration at the time, and isolating food groups was a good way of detecting when food was bad. The forbidden foods, like shellfish and pork, are foods that spoil easily, are common allergens, or are susceptible to bacterial or parasite contamination. Ancient Israelites didn't have the information we do about the effect of diet on health, and it was presented as a discipline of obedience, but the diet would have been very beneficial if followed. A careful review of some of the other rules shows a similar benefit. The rules requiring certain basic levels of support for married women was a completely new concept in an age when women were property. Isolating women during menses would have protected them against endometriosis and helped cement social bonds between women in the community. The rules on treatment of slaves were extremely progressive for that period of history, protecting them against physical abuse and creating at least some avenue to freedom. The rules requiring that grain be left in the fields for the poor to glean were also groundbreaking. This is one of the first recorded programs of organized assistance for the poor. God's rules provided a benefit designed to preserve and protect those who followed his path[16]

---

[16] The books of Leviticus and Numbers contain a lengthy description of the various laws governing daily life, including the sacrifices, as well as a description of the Tent of the Tabernacle that was constructed as a travelling Temple. They are very dense books, but

even though people didn't have the knowledge base at the time to understand. We still don't completely understand the ways God may be helping or protecting us.

Another primary characteristic of God is that God is really smart. God knows a lot of stuff that we don't know. We've discovered that some fish use tools, elephants cooperate and honeybees have emotions. We've discovered that the DNA ladder is far more variable than has been assumed, and that receptors in individual cells carry electrical "messages" to direct the function of each individual cell. We've discovered that light has mass; and carbon nanotubes can be used to direct cancer drugs directly to, and only to, cancer cells. All that information was there for eons waiting to be discovered. Who knows what else is out there to learn.

The more we learn, the smarter God looks. Isaiah 43:15-16 says, "I am the Lord, your Holy One, the Creator of Israel, your King." Thus says the Lord, who makes a way in the sea, and a path through the mighty water…" Centuries later, men discovered the trade currents that create a consistent route through the oceans. We haven't begun to fully understand the earth, much less the rest of the universe. God created all that stuff—he thought it up, we have yet to even discover it fully.

Read through Proverbs some time; it contains a great deal of wisdom. "A soft answer turns away wrath, but a harsh word stirs up anger," Prov. 15:1. That one is very useful if you negotiate contracts for a living, not to mention dealing with a two year old. "In all labor there is profit, but mere talk leads only to poverty," Prov. 14:23. "Better is a dry morsel and quietness with it than a house full of feasting with strife," Prov. 17:1. One only has to think of the last holiday dinner with extended family to see the sense in that proverb. God is wise, and very practical. Much of the wisdom in the Bible has become ingrained in our culture and one can trace its influence in our legal system in the US and Western Europe.

God is more than practical, God loves beauty. Scientists have commented that the world is much more beautiful than is necessary for its function—and beauty sometimes acts against function. Think how beautiful a cardinal is, singing at the top of tree in bright red feathers. Gorgeous, but also a great target for hawks. Bumblebees are great fun to

---

no one who has read them will ever credit the notion that the books are fiction or myth, or even that the rules are advisory. The books are a list of administrative procedures presented without embellishment. Some parts sound fantastic to us today, but they are written with all the imagination of the Tax Code.

watch, but so non-aerodynamic it is amazing they can fly, much less maneuver in the way they do. Beauty is everywhere. Look at a sunset, the flowers, even the snow against gray bark in the winter. The enormous variety of birds, animals and even insects that are beautifully colored and patterned, whether in bright colors or subtle tones of taupe. Look at the waves crashing against the shore or smoothly rolling in the open sea. The landscape may be stark and harsh like the desert or lush like the rolling hills of Pennsylvania, but it is all beautiful.

Look at the faces of people, the different skin tones and hair color and shapes and sizes of people. Even things that shouldn't be pretty, like dead trees and dry bones, have interesting shapes and textures. Any time you are feeling stressed out, take a walk outside. The symmetry, colors, textures and sounds will creep into your soul and re-order your thoughts. If you think that sounds silly, take a walk with a child. They see the beauty through new eyes and remind us how pretty things are around us. When my great-niece was small she found tiny flowers in the grass that I'd never noticed; tiny blue daisy shaped flowers with white and yellow centers. They are perfect and more beautiful than any hot house flower. She points out how pretty a bluegill is when I have forgotten to notice. The world is truly beautiful, we have just become inured.

I once went on a whale watching boat just off the coast from Boston. It was a fabulous trip. The weather was perfect. A whale swam under the boat and broached—nearly his entire body out of the water--just twenty or so feet away. A number of whales were bubble-feeding in the immediate vicinity oblivious to the boat. There was a mother with a new calf just a few weeks old, guarded anxiously by the father. When the whales first surrounded the boat, people were glued to the rails, fascinated by the huge creatures. After 15 or so minutes, they started to drift away and after half an hour only a handful of us remained on deck watching. The rest had drifted off into the snack bar or were looking for other amusements. It was a once in a lifetime opportunity, and the vast majority of the boat was bored in a few minutes. God has given us beauty, we are simply ignoring it in favor of television and cell phones.

Another major characteristic of God is that he is loving and, inexplicably, he cares for us--individually. This is God's most defining characteristic and it runs as a connecting thread throughout the Bible. In Matthew 6:24-34, Jesus describes this characteristic of God in one of the most moving passages in the Bible.

"No one can serve two masters; for either he will hate the one and love the other, or he will hold to one and despise the other. You cannot serve God and mammon (money.) For this reason, I say to you, do not be anxious for your life, as to what you shall eat, or what you shall drink, nor for your body as to what you shall put on. Is not life more than food, and the body than clothing? Look at the birds of the air, that they do not sow, neither do they reap, nor gather into barns, and yet your heavenly Father feeds them. Are you not worth much more than they? And which of you by being anxious can add a single cubit to his life's span? And why are you anxious about clothing? Observe how the lilies of the field grow, they do not toil nor do they spin, yet I say to you that even Solomon in all his glory did not clothe himself like one of these. But if God so arrays the grass of the field, which is alive today and tomorrow is thrown into the furnace, will he not much more do so for you, O men of little faith? Do not be anxious then, saying, 'What shall we eat?' or 'What shall be drink?' or 'With what shall be clothe ourselves?' For all these things the Gentiles eagerly seek; for your heavenly Father knows that you need all these things. But seek first His Kingdom and His righteousness; an all these things shall be added to you. Therefore, do not be anxious for tomorrow; for tomorrow will care for itself. Each day enough trouble of its own."

The message is very clear. God wants to be in relationship to us, he cares for us and will take care of us, but not if we ignore him and choose to go our own way without considering him. That isn't because God is egotistical and wants attention. I John 1:5 says, "And this is the message we have heard from Him and announce to you, that God is light, and in Him there is no darkness at all." And Hebrews 11:35 points out, "Who has first given to Him [God] that it might be paid back to him again?" God simply won't require us to be in a relationship with him if we don't want to.

Jesus described God's dilemma when talking about Israel, he said, "O Jerusalem, Jerusalem, who kills the prophets and stones those who are sent to her! How often I wanted to gather your children together as a hen gathers her chicks under her wings, but you were unwilling. Behold your house is being left to you desolate! For I say to you, from now on you shall not see Me until you say 'Blessed is He who comes in the name of the Lord'", Matthew 23:37-39. We have the power to choose whether or not to associate with God. God *wants* us to make the choice to relate to him, but we don't have to.

We have to look at the passage in Matthew 6, part of the Sermon on the Mount, quoted above, in context. Jesus speaks these words to a crowd near the beginning of his ministry in an attempt to explain reality to a group of people who are just as focused on their everyday lives as we are. But this is very late in the relationship between God and mankind. That started eons ago at creation. At some point after Adam and Eve had spent time in the Garden, walking and talking with God on a regular basis, they made the choice to disobey the one prohibition that God had established. They bailed on the relationship and decided they wanted to become like God, Gen. 3:5-6 describes the events. The Serpent told Eve that the fruit would not make her die, but would cause her to "be like God, knowing good and evil" and seeing "that the tree was desirable to make one wise", she ate the fruit and shared it with Adam. From then until the present man has persisted in trying to be God. Again, while the Genesis story may seem too far-fetched to many to be taken literally, the problem remains. We prefer to be our own god.

But God is God and he finds it annoying that we keep pretending to be God, while making a royal mess of things and blaming the mess on him. So, after centuries of bailing people out of the messes they created, only to have them repeatedly return to their old ways as soon as he did, God established an idiot-proof method of re-establishing the relationship. He made it personal this time. The relationship is on an individual level; it doesn't matter who your family is or what group you belong to. Every person has the ability to choose whether or not they want to be in a relationship with God. All you have to do is want a relationship with God, as he truly is, and take steps in that direction. Jesus died to make that possible and tells us, in John 14:6, "I am the way, the truth and the Life. No man comes to the Father, but through me." Acts 2:22 says "And it shall be that everyone who calls on the name of the Lord shall be saved". God will find you if you honestly want to experience a relationship with God. This is not some kind of magic incantation. It means that you are starting a relationship; inviting God into your life, on his terms, and making an honest effort to do things his way.

Unfortunately, while this is simple, it isn't easy. All of us experience a great deal of difficulty in our attempts to let God be God. All of us want to define God in our image, instead of the other way around. We insist that he accept us as we are, rather than accepting God as he is and adapting our lives. For years I had to divide my day into 10 minute long segments to try and keep God in the picture. Otherwise I could easily completely ignore God and anything connected with God for days on end. I'm a little better now, but it takes a conscious effort not to scatter my attention in every direction except God's presence.

Also, while God's plan of unearned grace is idiot-proof, it isn't genius-proof. From St. Augustine to Dallas Willard, Christians who have established real, rewarding relationships with God try to explain to the rest of us how to do that. Inevitably their explanations of their own paths sound like behavioral rituals to be followed. In reality, there is a certain level of discipline involved. One has to leave some blank space and time in one's life to actively seek the presence of God. One has to pray and seek God as one would a "real" person; and realistically, we can't know God if we don't take the time to read the Bible. People who want to find God, or at least to feel like they have done the right thing, follow religious rituals they have been taught. Frequently they find that following the rituals didn't have the results they were seeking. They are very disappointed and often feel that they have been gypped, or lied to, or that God is not reachable, or not real.

Sometimes this is because they followed a ritual without actually engaging with God as a real person. You can't fake this. God can see right through you. Hebrews 4:12-13 describes it this way: "For the word of God is living and active and sharper than any two-edged sword, and piercing as far as the division of soul and spirit, of both joints and marrow and able to judge the thoughts and intentions of the heart. And there is no creature hidden from His sight, but all things are open and laid bare to the eyes of Him with whom we must give account."

Sometimes people feel disappointed in trying to have God in their life because they have been misled or misinformed about what a relationship with God looks like. God is always present, we just don't always recognize him. You won't hear voices. You won't start talking like the people at church. You won't get everything you ever dreamed of in a magical stream of good fortune. You won't feel compelled to vote for Pat Buchanan. It is unlikely you will feel driven to quit your job and leave everything you know to move to Africa and open a leper colony. A few people make those kinds of changes, but mostly, the presence of God is a quiet sense of peace. It reminds you not to sweat the small stuff. It reminds you that your family and friends and the people in front of you in line at the grocery store are just as important as you are, and that everyone is important, interesting and lovable. It reminds you that storms will pass and encourages you to enjoy the ride and smell the roses. It nags when you over-react and blow up, when you think a small lie is ok, or when arrogance gets the best of you. It's inexplicably, annoyingly, calm when you are afraid; and it points out how beautiful the day is when you are stuck in traffic and rushing to work. It demands that you spend time you don't have being nicer than you feel like being to people you don't care that much about, and then makes that time fun and rewarding.

It's a little weird and completely addictive. When Moses was leading the Israelites in the desert after the escape from Egypt, he asked God, "Now therefore, I pray Thee, if I have found favor in Thy sight, let me know Thy ways, that I may know Thee, so that I may find favor in They sight." Exodus 33:13, 15. And then he said, "If Thy presence does not go with us, do not lead us up from here." After David sinned by committing adultery with Bathsheba and having her husband killed, he pleaded with God "Do not cast me away from Thy presence. And do not take Thy Holy Spirit from me." Psalm 51: 11. Once you have become acquainted with the presence of God in your life, it becomes increasingly important. You start arranging your life around the experience of it.

The recognition of the presence of God usually comes just a little bit at a time at first. Then as you reach out more to God, slowing down to feel the peace, having respect for yourself and others, acting out what you say you believe— generally just putting your money where your mouth is—literally and figuratively; the relationship grows and deepens. You start to recognize God's presence more readily, and you change. Those people in the grocery store line are less annoying. You hold your temper longer because you just aren't angry over as many things. You tell the truth more because you aren't afraid like you used to be, and it just seems more practical to tell the truth. You aren't saying you love people because that is what you are supposed to do—you actually like them. You aren't gritting your teeth and grumbling because you are missing the latest rave, or because you can't go out and get drunk or get high with your friends, or sleep around with that cute someone across the room—those things just seem like boring or unpleasant ways to spend time. You start to enjoy giving away money to help people, and time spent volunteering is actually fun. Your neighbors are interesting and your family is just the most fun of anybody. The time you spend with your family and friends is more enjoyable and the differences of opinions get resolved more easily. Your tastes change, and over time you feel more and more healthy, happy and calm.

The change is gradual, you probably won't even notice it most of the time. But if you backtrack and don't seek God's presence, you'll slip back into old habits and old feelings of discontent or anger. Then God will nag you to come back because he misses you—not in an overbearing way, but persistently—like your mom calling you to come inside before it gets dark. And it's never too late to come back.

God's motivation for all this is pretty simple. God just likes having you around. It is important to him and he will go to great lengths to make a relationship possible. Again simple, but not easy. Jesus thought it was important enough to descend to Earth, live in poverty, humiliation and confinement for 33 years, ending with an ignominious and excruciatingly painful death on the cross. In John 10: 17-18, Jesus explains, "For this reason, the Father loves Me, because I lay down my life that I might take it again. No one has taken it away from me, but I lay it down on my own initiative. I have authority to lay it down, and I have authority to take it up again. This commandment I received from my Father." "Everyone who calls on the name of the Lord shall be saved." Acts 2:21. "But as many as received Him, to them He gave the right to become children of God, even to those who believe in His name." John 1:12. John explains it with great clarity in the famous John 3:16, "For God so loved the world that he gave his only begotten Son, that whosoever believes in Him should not perish, but have eternal life.

We find these verses particularly annoying. They seem naïve, maudlin, maybe even overbearing. After all why do we need to be saved? Saved from what? Isn't Christianity really about treating others with respect and living a positive life? Most of us live respectable lives, well within normal parameters of behavior. We donate to worthwhile causes. We take care of our families, work, and pay taxes. We are nice, normal people. What is all this raving about sin and salvation? Really, isn't that talk just for those nutty right-wing televangelists with the funny accents? Well, no. As nice and normal as we are, we aren't perfect. We lose our tempers, we snipe at the neighbors, we fib a bit, gossip a bit, shave our taxes, carry home office supplies and while away the afternoon at work on Facebook. Besides that, everyone can think of a time when they went overboard and did something recognizably, definitely wrong. Like experimenting with shoplifting, sleeping with the wrong person, hitting your child in a fit of frustration, undermining someone at work or taking credit for their ideas to look better to the boss. Or that time you went behind your spouse's back, did something you promised you wouldn't do and then looked them in the eye and told a bald-faced lie to cover it up. No one is perfect, and lack of perfection is sin. Sinning doesn't make us bad people, but it does separate us from God.

Because one of God's defining characteristics is his perfection. God doesn't shave the truth, God doesn't gossip, God doesn't take home pencils or pad his expense account. Deuteronomy 32:3-4 says, "For I proclaim the name of the Lord; Ascribe greatness to our God! The Rock! His work is perfect, For all his Ways are just; a God of faithfulness and without injustice, righteous and upright is He."

God is perfect and in order to relate to him, without taking advantage of the salvation offer, we would need to be perfect. "Therefore, you are to be perfect, as your heavenly Father is perfect." Matthew 5:48. We can't do that, but Jesus did it for us. Romans 6:23 lays it out: "For the wages of sin is death, but the gift of God is eternal life in Jesus Christ our Lord." Hebrews 5:8-9 further explains, "Although He was a Son, He learned obedience from the things which He suffered. And having been made perfect, He became to all those who obey Him the source of eternal salvation."

Jesus did this willingly. He understands our imperfections, loves us anyway, and is always willing to hold the door open. Hebrews 4: 14-16 says, "Since then we have a great high priest who has passed through the heavens, Jesus the Son of God, let us hold fast our confession. For we do not have a high priest who cannot sympathize with our weaknesses, but one who has been tempted in all things as we are, yet without sin. Let us, therefore, draw near with confidence to the throne of grace, that we may receive mercy and may find grace to help in time of need." All you have to do to have a relationship with God, is say you want one, accept God on his terms and try to do things his way.

That sounds too simple, and too good to be true. We always want to know what God wants in return. Is this some kind of trap? God doesn't want much, mostly he just wants us to hang out with him and be nice. God wants us to love him, to recognize him as our God, then once we get that clear in our minds, to apply that belief in our behavior by being nice to ourselves and to other people. John 15:12 states God's intentions clearly. "This is my commandment, that you love one another, just as I have loved you." In Mark 12:30-31, Jesus sums up the requirements: "And you shall love the Lord your God with all our heart, and with all your soul and with all your mind, and with all your strength. The second is this: You shall love your neighbor as yourself. There is no other commandment greater than these."

We don't need to be perfect, just committed to the effort. Matthew 18:21-22 has the story of Peter's attempt to understand this concept. "Then Peter came and said to Him, 'Lord, how often shall my brother sin against me and I forgive him, Up to seven times? Jesus said to him, 'I do not say to you up to seven times, but up to seventy times seven". That wasn't intended as a number of chances, it means we need to always forgive others and get the wrong they've done to us out of our head.

Forgiveness does not mean or require that we continue to have an on-going relationship with people who wrong us repeatedly. It does require that we stop holding a grudge, stop holding onto fear, and get on with our lives. For many of us, the wrongs we complain of are relatively petty—our family doesn't understand us or the neighbor insists on mowing over the line. For some people, the pain is much deeper, resulting from physical and mental abuse or betrayal. That kind of pain can leave deep scars. Forgiveness isn't something you can fake. If you just stuff the pain and ignore it without dealing with it, it will continue to cause damage. "Just forgive" is a simple concept, but it isn't easy and may require both time and counseling to achieve when the pain is serious. But if you are still dwelling on not getting something you wanted for Christmas when you were ten, or being unfairly grounded for a week when you were 16, or something your spouse did 15 years ago when you were first married; really, just get over it. It's not that important. Free up some space in your head and heart for more positive things. What difference does it really make if the neighbor wants to mow part of your lawn for you?

It is also difficult to change our own patterns of behavior that hurt other people. We tend to think of forgiveness in terms of forgiving others, but we all need to be forgiven for something. King David is my favorite model. He messed up in very serious ways for his entire life. He was arrogant, abrasive, violent, self-absorbed and ignored problems if they were uncomfortable to deal with. He was an unfaithful husband and neglectful father. He was a murderer and a liar. He slogged his way through life and made lots of mistakes. But David always had in mind to do the right thing and when he got off track, he stopped, apologized and started off again. David was called a "man after God's own heart" (1 Samuel 13:14), not because he was perfect, but because he was willing to admit his failures. That is all it takes. Simple, not easy. Our first reaction when someone complains about something we've done is that they are unreasonable, unrealistic, overly sensitive or just stupid—we didn't do anything wrong! Few people intentionally hurt other people, but we all mess up and we need to recognize that and keep an open mind about correcting our errors. We aren't going to get that right all the time either, we just need to commit to the effort.

God is perfect, we are not. God lets us create our own, very faulted world. He won't rearrange the world, or us, to a perfect state. At least not now. The result is a very flawed place with pain and ugliness, mostly of our own creation. God lets us learn from our own mistakes. God treats us with respect, more than we probably deserve, by letting us choose how to behave. God loves us in spite of it all.

Another characteristic of God, one few people discuss, is that God is unimaginably stubborn, and he has high expectations. Romans 11:29 says, "For the gifts and calling of God are irrevocable". That verse is in a passage talking about the difficult relationship between early Christians, most of them originally Jewish, and the mainstream Jewish population and leadership. Christianity was far from popular in its early days, and converts suffered ostracism, persecution and even death. But the application of the verse isn't limited to its immediate context.

Almost the only volunteer among the heroes of the Bible, Old and New Testament, is Jesus. The human beings we point to as exemplars in the Bible were drafted, and none of the assignments were easy. Sometimes God will draft you into his world plan. Some of the Biblical "heroes" went kicking and screaming down the path chosen for them, others cooperated with more grace. Abraham and Moses both tried to talk God out of their assignment. God didn't budge. Joshua was intimidated at taking over for Moses, but he lead the Israelites in a march around Jericho and the walls fell down. Joseph was sold as a slave so he could save Israel from starvation. Esther won a beauty contest, ended up married to an extremely erratic king, and saved the captive Jews from annihilation. Gideon tried to talk God out of his assignment, God didn't budge and 300 men defeated a force "as numerous as locusts", Judges 7:12. Most of the prophets complained bitterly about their careers, Elisha is the only one on record who asked for a promotion, 2 Kings 2:9-13. Jonah went the other way when God sent him to Nineveh, was escorted back by a great fish. He sulked when the people listened to him and repented and God didn't destroy Nineveh, Jonah 4:1-11. I've always liked Jonah.

Mary, Jesus' mother, was among the few who accepted their assignment with grace, even with joy. Mary said "My soul exalts the Lord, and my spirit has rejoiced in God my Savior, for he has had regard for the humble state of his bondslave; for behold from this time on all generations will count me blessed." Of course, she was probably 14 or 15 when she said those words and it probably seemed like an adventure. The Bible doesn't record her words when she watched Jesus die on the cross. Her job wasn't easy.

The disciples were drafted out of fishing boats, tax offices and political parties. Paul was struck blind in the middle of a rampage against the new Christian movement. God sent a reluctant Ananias to heal Paul and introduce him to his new lifestyle. And God explained that the mission was necessary despite Ananias' belief it was a fool's errand, saying, "Go, for he is a chosen instrument of Mine, to bear my name before the Gentiles and kings and the sons of Israel; for I will show him how much he must suffer for My name's sake."

God doesn't change his mind. But he does stick with people he chooses for a task and helps them complete it, most often in a way that demonstrates that there is no possible way they did it on their own. Every single one of the heroes in the Bible, no matter how reluctant, or how resentful they were in the middle of the mission, came to rely fully on God and to crave his presence. They developed an uncanny peace, and faced uncertain futures and even death with an intrepid spirit that was completely absent when they were first drafted. Peter crashed and burned a number of times, the most famous example is his denial of Jesus on the eve of the crucifixion, Luke 22:55-62. Yet, after the resurrection, Peter preached to 3000 people in one day, Acts 2:14-41. He was beaten, imprisoned, and continued to preach the gospel until he was crucified in Rome about 30 years after the death of Christ. He encouraged others who experienced persecution in the early church, saying, "And after you have suffered for a little while, the God of all grace, who called you to his eternal glory in Christ, will Himself, perfect, confirm, strengthen and establish you. To Him be dominion forever and ever. Amen."1 Peter 5:10-11. Peter founded the church at Rome and truly became the "rock" that Jesus declared he would be in Matthew 16:18.

Paul followed a similar path, writing a large part of the New Testament in the form of letters to churches he had planted. He was shipwrecked, beaten, attacked by wild beasts, imprisoned and ultimately beheaded for his faith. God never wavered in his support of the Biblical heroes and even as they saw their deaths approaching, they praised God for being a part of the adventure and relied on his presence for comfort, support and even joy. God's dependability is truly amazing.

Finally, God is very humble; remarkably humble. I think of all his characteristics, God's humility is the most stunning. We all talk about people who "act like they think they are God", meaning they are arrogant and demand obeisance. God himself never acts like that. If anyone has a right to lord it over everyone, it would be God, but he doesn't do that. Every job God assigns is for the good of people. God never assigned anyone a job with the end of God's own self-aggrandizement—not once in the entire Bible. On the contrary, Jesus came in all humility to serve the good of mankind. Matthew 20:28 says, "just as the Son of Man did not come to be served, but to serve, and to give His life as a ransom for many."

The overall metaphor the Bible uses to describe God is that of a father, and that is the most apt description of God. God is our father---a really good, "Father Knows Best" kind of father. He created us, he loves us unconditionally. He knows all our junk. He thinks we are terrific. He roots for us to make the most of our time and our abilities. He's disappointed when we screw up. He gets angry when we fail to respect each other. He expects us to behave well: to tell the truth, to be nice to our brothers and sisters, to show up, to work, to share. He wants us to enjoy the nice things he's given us, and not to waste time and money on stupid stuff that isn't good for us. He will discipline us when we get off track. And he has high standards that he believes we are perfectly capable of meeting. He's smart. He's fun to be around, always starting a new adventure. He will let us learn from our mistakes and insist we grow up and learn how to take care of ourselves. He will always show up when you need him. He'll die to make sure we have a safe way home; and seeing you always puts a smile on his face.

That is the picture the Bible gives us of God, and it's the best description we have. God is all powerful, all knowing and ever present. He is smart, kind, patient, protective and stubborn. He loves you, and he wants to know each of us as individuals. Above all, he is. Eternal and unchanging, he just is. YHWH.

Chapter Two
Why Does God Matter?

As discussed in the introduction, most people believe a god of some kind exists. In the modern world that doesn't imply any belief that any personal connection with God is possible, necessary or even desirable. We believe it is important to live good lives, to seek our own happiness and that of others, but not necessarily to seek God. Why can't we be emotionally healthy and live ethical, morally upright and socially concerned lives without God? Theoretically, we can. In fact the teachings of the Bible with respect to dealing with other people and ethics will serve you well even if you are an atheist. "A soft answer turns away anger" works really well. "Treat others as you would like to be treated" is a good plan. "Do not lie"; "do not steal" are good ideas to live by.

Dr. Andrew Weil, one of my favorite health and nutrition authors, has written an excellent book <u>Spontaneous Happiness</u>, Little Brown and Company, 2011, exploring how people can improve their personal satisfaction, emotional health, internal peace and well-being through healthy behavior patterns, both mental and physical. He begins by citing both anecdotal and scientific evidence for the fact that many people let their immediate situation dictate their happiness. Many of us go through life believing that just getting that "next thing"—whatever it is, will bring us satisfaction and true happiness, only to be underwhelmed or disappointed when we obtain whatever "it" is and find we still want more. He continues by giving very valuable information about turning our thought process in a positive rather than negative direction through meditation and connection with the outdoors, slowing our pace, taking care of our bodies, and nurturing our spirits through gratitude, forgiveness, helping others and connecting with people you love, all as a means to create an internal peace and strength that gives us a basis for happiness, rather than chasing after more things. It is a wonderful book, and if you followed his suggestions, your well-being would very likely improve.

The only real quarrel I have with the book is that it leaves God out of the equation except as a spiritual 'force" or concept. For myself at least, practicing a positive life does not keep me from wanting more. I still feel that something is out there that I need in order to feel peace internally. I need the additional force of feeling connected to God in order to have a sense of peace. I get bored really quickly without the sense of connection and go back to chasing the next thing—even though I may still make a point of eating properly, exercising, volunteering and trying to deal with others constructively. Sometimes, if I'm not connected enough to God, those constructive things can even take over my life and result in destructive levels of over-commitment.

When I am living a constructive life, but ignoring God, my life goes along well-enough. I am not depressed or unhealthy, but I don't get that full-on joy and I don't have that sense of calm inside. I still look for "it". In the 60's and early 70's self-described "Jesus Freaks" frequently sported T-shirts and bumper stickers that proclaimed "I found IT". Jesus freaks could be really annoying people, but I think they had a point. Beyond the immediate effect on our own personal lives, if God is real, then God matters because he is "IT"

I know that references back to the sixties and seventies date me, but I also have to say that the more modern emphasis on ethical behavior and "spirituality" rather than on a living God with opinions, hasn't improved our ethics or personal relationships, at least at a societal level. Incivility and unhealthy behaviors have certainly increased over the last 40 or 50 years. Personal debt levels are at an all-time high. We have garages and storage lockers full of stuff and the stores are still full of people looking for the next thing. Divorce is rampant. The number of children living in one-parent homes, and showing stress as a result of it, has increased dramatically. The number of people on medication for stress-related conditions has skyrocketed. Even many children are being treated with medication. One elementary school teacher I know had nearly two-thirds of her students on medication for one thing or another. Conditions exist that need medical treatment, but it is statistically impossible for more than half of a group of children to be abnormal. Depression and suicide have increased. Violence has increased. Truly inhuman behaviors like forced prostitution and child abuse have increased. I'm not suggesting a return to the 50's, but ethics alone aren't working. Ethics alone are not producing a peaceful, civil society. We need for more individuals to be acquainted with God, the person, in order to salt society with more positive influencers.

Another concept we have lost as a society is that God is important just because he is God—importance goes with the job. Just like children in their relationships with their parents, we tend to limit our perceptions of God, and our interest in God, to how he relates to us. But, like our parents had a life beyond us that we weren't privy to, there is a lot more to God than we can understand. He does stuff we have absolutely no idea about and wouldn't understand if we did know. God is a real person and he has a life outside of his relationship with us. We have no idea what that life is like, but it should be clear we aren't the center of the universe. We don't know why God bothers with us, why he created us, why he hasn't just destroyed the earth as an experiment gone wrong. It makes no sense, really, to think that he cares enough about us to walk on the earth and die on a cross and continue over the course of centuries to seek out humans to relate to. The fact that he does care that much should be incentive enough to check him out. We would be very flattered and curious if a celebrity showed an interest in us; how much more intrigued should we be by God himself?

But that isn't enough for most people. We have our own lives to consider, God is far away and hard to visualize. God is not immediate enough to hold our attention. So why should we care?

First, because eventually we are going to die and find out whether or not God is real and what happens after we die. Everyone dies: some young, some old, some in accidents, some in war, some from starvation and others safely in their own beds surrounded by loved ones; but everyone dies. Eventually everyone has to face the inevitable and then find out what comes next. Nearly everyone has an opinion on what comes next. Hindus and Buddhists believe in reincarnation, with the possibility of nirvana, which is something like Heaven or at least an exalted state of being. Muslims, traditional Christians and some Jews believe in Heaven and Hell (although they have different opinions about what Heaven and Hell are like.) Jehovah's Witnesses and some Jews believe that some people will go to Heaven and everyone else will just cease to exist. Atheists, many agnostics and many traditional Jews and less traditional Christians believe everyone will simply cease to exist. In fact the "cease to exist" theory is currently the most popular overall theory.

This is another case where we can choose what we believe, but not what will actually occur. There is an ultimate reality—we just have to wait to see what it is. There is an old saying among Christians that if they are wrong about Heaven and Hell and we just cease to exist, no harm done. If those who believe we cease to exist are wrong, that's going to be a problem. That sounds pretty arch, but there is something to it. Obviously one can't, and wouldn't, choose what to believe based on the ultimate risk; you either believe something or you don't. But the idea does underline the importance of the question. The question of what happens after we die is at least something one shouldn't ignore. Eternity is a very long time to be wrong.

The Bible speaks very clearly about Heaven and Hell as real places. Surprisingly the Bible doesn't give a lot of details about Heaven, and mostly the word is used as an adjective. The Bible refers to our "heavenly Father" Matthew 5:48 and "heavenly hosts"--meaning a whole lot of angels, Luke 2:13. The Bible never really says what we do there or much about what it looks or feels like.

Revelation 21 has the most complete description. John, one of the twelve disciples and probably Jesus' closest friend, describes a vision he has of a "new heaven and a new earth" arising after the first heaven and earth, the ones we know, "passed away", Verse 1. When the new earth and heaven come into existence, Revelation 21: 4 says God will "wipe away every tear from their eyes; and there shall no longer be any death; there shall no longer be any mourning, or crying, or pain..." Verses 11 through 23 describe the New Jerusalem, a city 1500 miles square. It has twelve great gates, each made of a single pearl. The streets are paved with gold so pure as to be as transparent as glass, or perhaps to shimmer like glass. The foundation stones are covered with precious stones. The foundation is marked by 12 huge stones, one for each of the twelve tribes of Israel, and each is a boulder made of precious and semi-precious stones. The stones are listed as jasper, sapphire, chalcedony, emerald, sardonyx, sardius, chrysolite, beryl, topaz, chrysoprase, jacinth, amethyst. There is no longer a son or moon "for the glory of God illuminates the City and the gates are never closed". Ezekiel 8:4 also talks about the glory of God illuminating Heaven.

Revelation 5:11 and 12 describes thousands of angels bowing before God and Jesus, all chanting continuous praises; and Isaiah 6:2 describes a similar adoration by chanting angels.

Timothy 2:12 and Revelations 20:6 talk about certain people who will reign with Christ in the new heaven and new earth. (My guess is that the list of people reigning with Christ is a very short list and I'm certainly not on it.) Matthew 11:11 describes John the Baptist as the greatest person to ever live and says the one who is least in Heaven is greater than John the Baptist. That is a pretty high bar. The Bible never says what anyone else will be doing in Heaven or what life looks like there on a day to day basis, although it gives a sense that there is a kind of ordinary aspect to life there. The Bible indicates that people/angels have tasks, they have opinions, they go places and do things I'm hoping to be a gardener. It would be fun with the right amount of rain and no weeds.

We don't know much else about Heaven except that it is a place of reward for those who are granted access after judgment. In John 14:62 Jesus states, "In my Father's house are many dwelling places", indicating that many people will be rewarded with a house in Heaven.

Many of us don't like the idea that we would be judged. Aren't we good enough? But it makes sense if we don't take it personally. It is very easy to think of great evil in the world. Willful abuse, murder, neglected children, children conscripted as soldiers, forced prostitution, forced labor; all brought about by the greed or malice of other people. Shouldn't those people be judged? What about the Mother Theresas and Billy Grahams of the world, shouldn't they be rewarded? Justice demands accountability. Nahum, an Old Testament prophet, states in Nahum 1: 3, "The Lord is slow to anger and great in power, and the Lord will by no means leave the guilty unpunished." Zephaniah, another Old Testament prophet, describes the destruction of the earth in Zephaniah 1:2-3, "I will completely remove all things from the face of the earth, declares the Lord. I will remove man and beast; I will remove the birds of the sky and the fish of the sea, and the ruins along with the wicked." Micah, yet another prophet, says in Micah 7:13 "And the earth will become desolate because of her inhabitants, on account of the fruit of their deeds." (Climate change and the threat of a nuclear winter really are more than the product of the fevered imaginations of aging hippies.)

Revelation 20:11-15 describes John's vision of the final judgment this way:

> "And I saw a great white throne and Him who sat upon it from whose presence earth and heaven fled away, and no place was found for them.
>
> And I saw the dead, the great and the small, standing before the throne, and books were opened; and another book was opened, which is the book of life; and the dead were judged from the things which were written in the books, according to their deeds.
> And the sea gave up the dead which were in it, and death and Hades gave up the dead which were in them; and they were judged every one of them according to their deeds.
> And death and Hades were thrown into the lake of fire. This is the second death, the lake of fire.
> And if anyone's name was not found written in the book of life, he was thrown into the lake of fire."

The whole passage is scary and I don't pretend to understand how death can be thrown into a lake of fire. But the essential message compels attention. The "lake of fire" is hell. Hell is scary. The passage is made scarier because the standard of judgment isn't limited to works. Most people think of ultimate judgment as whether or not we have been good enough, and as decent people we feel we would be good enough; but that isn't what the Bible teaches.

Our deeds are an important part of the equation, but the second part is even more critical. The second part is that one's name is in the Book of Life. Other translations use the phrase the "Lamb's book of life" instead of "Book of Life". The "Lamb" is Jesus, often referred to in the Bible as "the Lamb of God", See John 1:29. The analogy is to the lambs or young goats that were the sacrifices required by the Jewish law to atone for sin. The sacrificial lamb in the Hebrew tradition was required to be perfect, the best of the flock. Sin was symbolically transferred to the perfect animal, and it was sacrificed. None of us are perfect, we need someone else to make the sacrifice. Goats and lambs won't do it. Goats and lambs never really changed anything. The sacrifice was just an act of contrition; a way of demonstrating you were doing your best to live the way God wanted you to.

We don't barbecue goats and lambs anymore, we moved into the simplified era of personal commitment after God walked the earth as Jesus. Our own acts, trying hard to be a good person, isn't enough either. We will never be perfect, we need someone else to make the sacrifice. Jesus did that for us on the cross. He was the lamb of the sacrifice. The early Christians, most of them Jews, perfectly understood the analogy because they lived in the era when the temple sacrifice was an everyday event. In fact, Jesus was crucified at precisely the same time the priests in the temple were butchering the lambs and goats for the Passover Seder.

Jesus could act as the sacrifice only because he was God—and perfect. If he were merely a good man, or even a great man, the sacrifice of his life would not have had any power to open an avenue to God. Millions of good people have died and hundreds of thousands have sacrificed their lives for others, in war or by other acts of protection or provision that required the sacrifice of their own life. Those are grand and glorious acts that we should respect, and they may inspire us to reach for higher goals, but they have no power to connect us to God. None of those people have transformed human history by their death. None of them were God in the flesh.

The Bible teaches that our name's presence in the Book of Life is based on a "who do you know" standard rather than a "what have you done standard". We understand this standard. It is disturbingly reminiscent of corporate America, but far healthier and far more egalitarian in this context—Jesus came for everyone, not just the insiders. But you can't just work your way to the top.

Another metaphor the Bible uses is "redemption" from sin. In ancient times, redemption was a way out of slavery. People who couldn't afford to pay their debts became indentured servants—slaves. When someone paid off their debt—they were "redeemed" and could go free again. Jesus was very clear in his claim that he had been sent to "redeem" the world, at the request of God the Father. Redemption being necessary, as Paul points out in Romans 3:23, "for all have sinned and fall short of the glory of God. Jesus paid our debt to God for the sins we commit. Unfortunately, very often the more fantastic we are as people, the less we see any use for God We don't see ourselves as needing atonement or redemption, or even as sinners. That is a problem. We may be fantastic people, but we aren't perfect and we aren't God.

Jesus described his crucifixion on the cross as being the sacrifice of his life in atonement for the sin of the world—as atonement for each person in the world. Mark 10:45. Then he rose again, on the third day, defeating death and sin, and returned again to Heaven to reign as God. Jesus thought we needed to be redeemed. He went to a lot of trouble based on his belief that we needed to be redeemed.

Those whose "names are written in the Book of Life", are those who accepted Jesus' sacrifice in atonement for their sin and declared that God would be God to them, and who do their best to follow God's teachings. They are listed because of their association with Jesus, not because of their good deeds. They will still be judged on their deeds, good and bad. The Bible describes this as some getting great rewards, some small rewards and some scraping by into Heaven by the skin of their teeth I Corinthians 3:13-15.

All of this may sound complicated, but the Bible frames the entire discussion as a simple matter of God wanting to give people a gift for no good reason except that he loves them. God would like us to be in Heaven and you can't earn Heaven; as Ephesians 2:4-9 says:

"But God, being rich in mercy, because of his great love with which he loved us, even when we were dead in our

54

transgressions, made us alive together with Christ (by grace you have been saved), and raised us up with Him and seated us with Him in the heavenly places, in Christ Jesus, in order that in the ages to come He might show the surpassing riches of his grace in kindness toward us in Christ Jesus. For by grace you have been saved through faith; and that not of yourselves, it is the gift of God; not as a result of works, that no one should boast."

Fortunately, we don't have try to be perfect or try to earn Heaven, we can accept that Jesus did something for us that we can't do for ourselves, acknowledge God as our personal God and join God's team and take advantage of the upside.

On the other hand, one can earn Hell by rejecting God and concluding that he is irrelevant to our lives. As discussed in Chapter One, God is very sure he is God and he thinks he matters. He thinks he is the center of the universe he created and that created beings should be paying attention. In Matthew, Chapters 24 and 25, Jesus describes the end of the world and final judgment. Matthew 25:31-34 and 41, 46 quotes Jesus as saying:

"But when the Son of Man comes in His glory, and all the angels with Him, then He will sit on His glorious throne. And all the nations will be gathered before Him; and he will separate them from one another, as the shepherd separates the sheep from the goats; and He will put the sheep [his followers] on his right, and the goats on the left. Then the King will say to those on His right, 'Come, you who are blessed of My Father, inherit the kingdom prepared for you from the foundation of the world.' " [Then Jesus describes the acts of the righteous in serving the needs of the poor and oppressed as evidence of their acceptance of God as their King, and contrasts the acts of the unrighteous who ignore the poor and disadvantaged, concluding with the following:] "Then he will also say to those on His left, 'Depart from Me, accursed ones, into the eternal fire which has been prepared for the devil and his angels'...And these will go away into eternal punishment, but the righteous into eternal life."

This kind of language offends a lot of people. We tend to make light of the concept of eventual punishment. Blogs by people citing Billy Joel's classic line, "I'd rather laugh with the sinners than cry with the saints" are not hard to find. That line resonates with anyone who has ever been to a church potluck dinner. Hell seems a very extreme concept—some kind of ancient holdover like animal sacrifice. Some modern theorists conclude that Hell is too horrible a concept to be congruent with the idea of a loving God, and reject the existence of Hell completely. Others say the images of Hell in the Bible are meant to be allegorical. Unfortunately, as the passages from Revelation and Matthew quoted above indicate, the idea that the final judgment and punishment are mere allegories is not really supported by reading the plain language of the text.

Even conservative, mainstream modern theology debates whether Hell is an eternal state of torment, as the church has traditionally taught; or whether a more accurate reading of the scriptures is that the wicked are ultimately killed, body and soul by the fires of Hell. They will point to Jesus' references to the eternal fire of "Gehenna" (the word for Hell used in some translations) as evidence that Hell is not permanent. Gehenna was a trash dump outside of Jerusalem where trash and unclaimed bodies were burned. The fire there smoldered continuously, but obviously, the trash and bodies thrown into the fire eventually were completely consumed. This view holds that while the fires of Hell may be eternal, those that are thrown into the fire are consumed.

Frankly, I think the text could be read either way, although the simple language of the text seems to refer to an eternal state of punishment. Jesus' allegorical story in Luke 16:19-31 of a rich man consigned to Hell while a poor beggar Lazarus was comforted by Abraham, describes the rich man in Hades as "in torment from the flames". He begs Abraham to send Lazarus to warn the rich man's five brothers so that they would not "also come to this place of torment." Revelation 14:11 provides another example. It describes the punishment of those who reject God in the last days saying: "And the smoke of their torment goes up forever and ever; and they have no rest day and night, those who worship the beast and his image, and whoever receives the mark of his name."

Whichever alternative is true, hell sounds pretty unpleasant. We don't know completely what hell is like, and no matter how many people put forth theories, we aren't going to know now. I'm not trying to prove one theory over another. I'm just saying that the possibility of eventual accountability is something to consider in determining whether it makes sense to take some time out of our ordinary daily rush of life to consider what lies beyond.

The study of the end of the world is called eschatology and it is popular among theologians. John Ortberg, Senior Pastor at Menlo Park Presbyterian Church near San Francisco, and a former Willow teaching pastor for 9 years, once taught an excellent message series on Revelations and the end times. According to his messages, there are three schools of thought on Revelations. The first, and probably the most widely accepted, is that Revelations is talking about the end of the world, sometime in the future. A second school of thought is that the futuristic portions of Revelations are talking about the fall of Rome and are deliberately written with some obscurity to protect the then-revolutionary new Christian church from efforts to exterminate it. There is a third school of thought which can be summarized as: "I don't understand all the details, but things get really bad, there is a big fight and God wins." John Ortberg suggested this third theory mainly in jest, but I find I am firmly committed to the third school.

As a personal matter, even though I believe in both Heaven and Hell as real eventualities, they are too remote to have much motivational power for me. An eternity spent in Heaven with the weeping saints of my acquaintance is not particularly appealing. The idea of reigning over something with people following me around asking me to make a bunch of decisions for an eternity sounds even worse. The idea that I might one day simply cease to exist doesn't bother me in the least. The idea of an eternal Hell scares me, but, to be completely honest, I can't really keep enough of a grip on the concept to affect my day to day behavior. What's more, I'm not all that concerned about the end of the world. I'm fairly sure I won't live to see it. I have perhaps twenty or thirty years left to live, thirty–five years if I'm very lucky; and I'm more focused on what I can do or be while I'm alive.

What is important to me is that eternity starts now. To me, Christianity isn't about what happens when we die, it is about what happens while we live. I can really only focus on now. One gets up every morning and spends the next 14 or 16 or 18 hours doing stuff. It can be meaningless stuff akin to walking on a treadmill, or it can be something that makes one feel alive, happy and useful. Meaningful stuff is better. Meaningful stuff is energizing. Meaningful stuff brings a feeling of joy and satisfaction. Living a life defined more by meaningful stuff than meaningless stuff is intrinsically important to our own well-being. So what does that have to do with God? Why can't people live meaningful lives apart from God? In theory, one can, and some people do. Clara Barton, for example, founder of the Red Cross, was not strongly identified with Christianity, but made huge contributions to society; and she isn't alone.

However, in practice, the belief in God and feeling of community with God is a primary motivator for adapting our behavior to choose more meaningful acts. And perhaps more importantly, to be able to help out of strength rather than our own need requires a level of maturity that isn't common outside of faith. As much as I criticize the church, and there are many really unhealthy people hanging around churches; the people I know who are the most emotionally mature, reliable, healthy and happy are overwhelmingly committed Christians who make an effort to put their beliefs into practice. A connection with God does change your life for the better.

Many, certainly not all, but many, people who spend significant portions of their lives working in public service capacities in the secular world, serve out of their own need. The literature on counseling talks freely about the high incidence of co-dependence in those entering the field. To practice as a psychotherapist, one has to undergo psychotherapy and maintain a mentor/therapist relationship. I taught a counseling ethics class at a local university a few times, and every single one of my students had a story of personal pain or trauma that had led them to the profession. They each acknowledged that they were still recovering themselves and had significant issues in relating to other people. During that time there were several students who either dropped out or were encouraged to re-consider their choice of field because they were still too damaged to cope with their own lives and were not prepared to help others.

Co-dependence is common among Christians drawn into helping professionals as well. I won't try to deny that; one of the premises of this book is that a lot of Christians are pretty confused and don't represent the faith well. But the ones that come through those situations and heal their own lives through a relationship with God (and often counselling) and go on to help others, make a huge impact. There are even a few bright lights who choose to help others out of their strength without the traumatic start.

I can't document any research that conclusively proves that a relationship with God changes people in a positive way. I don't believe it is possible to test the results of a connection with God in any scientific manner. I don't think we can reliably identify people who integrate their faith into their life well enough to even conduct a study. I can't conclusively *prove* that we need God at all. But committed Christians who spend their lives trying to apply Christ's teaching have made a tremendous difference in the world. We can see the effect of a deep relationship with God in their actions.

Mama Maggie Gobran, Mother Theresa, Albert Schweitzer are/were truly extraordinary, but more normal examples abound. Gary Haugen, founder of International Justice Mission, Rich Stearns, head of World Vision, and the hundreds of workers in those ministries around the world, have made a huge difference in the lives of the people they serve. The Salvation Army is the largest single provider of homeless services in the country. One in six child care centers are provided by churches or other faith-based organizations. There are literally hundreds of faith based organizations in the US that are focused on helping people, and thousands of people working with those organizations to successfully help people improve their lives. Secular and government help exists as well, but the anecdotal evidence suggests that the faith-based initiatives are more successful. A relationship with God will increase one's interest in helping others and one's ability to do so.

President George W. Bush created an initiative to coordinate government services with private faith-based organizations because of the perception that the faith based organizations were more successful at achieving their goals; and that government money would be more efficiently spent by supporting the existing faith based organizations rather than creating or expanding government programs. President Obama continued the initiative with some amendments designed to meet criticism that the version of the Executive Order signed by President Bush walked a very fine Constitutional line.

The initiative encountered difficulties because of complications inherent in attempting to meld government requirements with the operations of faith-based organizations. However, the initiative focused attention and research on what makes people volunteer, what makes people behave in altruistic ways, on trends in altruistic behavior in the US over time and on the success of faith-based organizations compared to secular organizations. While the research community has struggled to quantitatively document how success should be measured and why organizations are successful, there is a consensus that religious people are generally happier and more willing to help others.

On a qualitative level, at least, there is a consensus that faith based organizations are more successful at changing lives and that deliberate, focused introduction of religion into behavior change is successful at changing the way people behave. People choose to stop self-destructive behaviors more frequently and with greater permanence when they adopt religion as a lifestyle. See *"The Sociological Study of Faith Based Communities and Their Activities in Relation to the Spiritual Ideal of Unlimited Love"* Byron Johnson, University of Pennsylvania, Institute for

Research on Unlimited Love, Altruism, Compassion, Service; unlimitedloveinstitute.org, for a great summary of the research. (Yes, the Institute for Research on Unlimited Love is a real institute and boasts Rosalynn Carter and Harvard professors on its board, although it has not been very active since the end of President Bush's tenure in office. Its focus is on behavior and its research includes all major religions and secular motivations for altruistic love.) We need God to change our focus from self-involvement to altruism.

I'll probably never get to altruism—I'm a lawyer after all, but I need God to keep me from being completely focused on my own life. God prompts me to be involved with the world around me and to take some action to help others who are less fortunate, or at least to take a few steps in that direction. I probably benefit more than the people I'm trying to help. When I spend too much time focused on my own life, I can get into negative thought patterns. Helping others takes me out of my little world and helps me see the big picture. When I look at the big picture, I feel much more positive. I'm not alone in this reaction.

Research confirms that helping others contributes to our own sense of well-being, and it helps to keep our own problems in perspective. *The Health Benefits of Volunteering: A Review of Recent Research,"* The Corporation for National and Community Service, Office of Research and Policy Development, Washington DC, 2007 reviews the many benefits of volunteering to the volunteers themselves. It is cited on the HelpGuide.org website. HelpGuide is a non-profit, ad-free site devoted to providing resources to people seeking information on health challenges they are facing. According to the research, volunteering, and particularly discretionary volunteer activities involving significant time commitments, has a number of benefits *to the volunteers.* Volunteers, aside from improving the community for those they serve, become more connected to the community, leading to stronger relationships and better contacts. This can lead to development of job skills, better job contacts, and increased relationship skills. Volunteering can also combat depression, usually because of improved and increased relationships. Volunteering can improve physical health from increased activity, particularly among older adults. Volunteering increases self-confidence when the volunteer learns to deal with new environments and a greater variety of people.

From a personal perspective, although I like people and feel a concern for those less fortunate, my life commitments tend to crowd out people that I don't know. I have work to do, a business to build, a house to clean and friends and family I already know and love to relate to and spend time with. I believe in volunteering, but without a nudge from God, I would probably not engage in it beyond writing a couple of checks at Christmas. I don't have the time. But I make time to volunteer on a regular basis because I've learned how valuable it is to keep my own head on straight, and because it is fun to meet new people and experience new things. I like making a difference for people, but mostly I recognize how my natural tendency to be introverted can lead me into unhealthy isolation. Volunteering invigorates me and gives me a fresh perspective.

The best example I can think of was when I was between jobs a number of years ago. I had severance for several months, and just before my severance ended I landed a part time contract job that looked like it was going to turn into a full time, permanent job and paid decently. But I was depressed about being out of work and anxious about the future. When I decided I had spent enough time indulging in worry and self-pity, I decided I would look for a volunteer opportunity to fill up the extra time and take my focus off of myself. I scouted around and ended up volunteering at a local day-center for the homeless.

I only helped around the office a few hours a week, but I met a number of the clients and the staff. It was a pretty rough environment. The occasional fight broke out and there were any number of alcoholics, drug users, prostitutes, runaways and people off their meds. They turned out to be quite a nice group of people, most of whom had horrific back stories of abuse and abandonment. I had expected it to be a sad environment, but it wasn't. They were a surprisingly upbeat, if completely unrealistic, group of people. Most of us worry about our families, our jobs, and the security of our futures. They didn't have any of those things, and so they really didn't worry all that much. If they had a meal for the day, a safe place to stay out of the heat and a safe place to spend the night, they were pretty happy. They spent a lot of time watching the news or reading at the library and had well-informed opinions on current events. They were even pretty honest in a way. They were open about their various cons to support themselves and about their negative habits, although one obviously couldn't leave anything of value lying around. As a group, they were creative and open, freed up from the "I can'ts" and "we don'ts" that often characterize mainstream suburbia. It was fun, it was invigorating, and the people were instructive for me.

That environment put my situation into a whole new, more positive, light. It helped me to stop moping and focus on what I could do to change my situation. I was the product of a loving home, good schools and to that point, a successful, uneventful career progression. I was unfamiliar with failure, have a natural affinity for order and security, and I was very affected by the job loss. I felt much more at risk, injured, and depressed than was really justified by the circumstances. Volunteering showed me that and helped me out of the slump. It increased my ability to relate to different kinds of people and to communicate to a broader variety of people. I was more ready to meet new people at the new job and to deal with the inevitable politics of the situation. It was great training for dealing with 3000 sales guys who all wanted their contracts reviewed first. Talking to homeless people helped me to be less attached to traditional solutions and more ready to look for a creative solution. It made me a better lawyer and a happier person. That was not my first volunteer experience by any means, but it was the first time I really stepped out of my comfort zone.

Now I make a point of volunteering on a regular basis. I volunteer with the PADS ministry for homeless people, have guests to my house when Willow holds its annual Leadership Summit, often host a discussion group with the budget ministry or evangelism ministry, and usually volunteer to babysit with the two-year olds at an evening Christmas service (once a year is enough of the two year olds)—all of it grand fun. A little chaos is good for me. But the truth is, I would not have reached out to volunteer at the homeless center without a nagging voice from God that my moping was not consistent with my actual state of risk. I highly recommend volunteering to shake up your world. The benefits are very real. There are lots of volunteer opportunities. It's a good idea to check around and find one that fits you before you dive in. Everyone is a little different and you may need to check out a few opportunities before finding one that suits your temperament. Homeless people might make you a little nuts, but you might discover you enjoy volunteering with Meals on Wheels or cleaning up brush at the local forest preserve. There is an opportunity for everyone to contribute.

God is necessary to shake up our myopic view of the world. God is real, and his idea of our lives is that they should be rich in joy and "abounding" in love and mercy; and the bounty comes from some unexpected places if you are willing to go along for the ride. John 10:10 quotes Jesus as saying, "The thief comes only to steal, and kill, and destroy; I come that they might have life and might have it abundantly." When we connect with God and feel his "spirit upon us" as the Bible describes it, we are more alive. Rather than just going through the motions or plodding our way through life, we feel engaged with our lives. We have more energy and we are drawn to more meaningful things. Colossians 3:23 describes this as "working with all your heart". The results are better relationships, more confidence, and more openness to helping those we aren't personally acquainted with. Serving the needs of others in some way becomes a normal part of life; and we reap the benefits as much as the people we serve.

Occasionally living with more abundance means dramatic acts of service, like Gary Haugen's decision to leave a successful law practice to start an organization that frees people from modern slavery and sexual trafficking. Often living with more abundance is a much simpler thing: planting native plants in your yard for the butterflies, volunteering at the local food pantry, looking forward to donating school supplies to the local back-to-school drive, picking up your neighbor's kids at school when they get held up at work, answering your three year old's twentieth "Why?" of the afternoon with a grin instead of a grimace, or finding out you actually enjoy your ten year old's piano recital. When we reach out of our comfort zone to connect with God and with his ideas for how we can spend our time, we benefit by obtaining a new, healthier perspective about our own life situation.

For me God is most important now for the little, everyday things of life. I need God to thank for the blue sky. I need God to thank for the rain, for the birds, for the snow, for my automatic coffee maker that wakes me up when the coffee is finished and keeps it hot without overcooking. I need God to thank for the roof over my head, food to eat that I don't have to grow, clean water that comes out of the tap, nice neighbors and a wonderful family. I thank God when the Cardinals— and stunningly even the Cubs---win the World Series and the Blackhawks win the Stanley Cup. Okay, I don't really believe God fixes baseball games, but James 1:17 says, "Every good thing bestowed and every perfect gift is from above, coming down from the Father of lights, with whom there is no variation, or shifting shadow." I do believe an afternoon at the baseball park with the sun shining and maybe a beer or an ice cream is a good thing. Living in a country where having the means and opportunity to attend an afternoon of baseball once in awhile is normal, is a very good thing. I thank God that I am living that kind of life. A normal middle-class American life is a rare and wonderful privilege from an historical and global perspective.

Gratitude is one of those slippery concepts that research shows is a hallmark of happy people. This isn't limited to Christianity, it is a widely accepted and studied phenomenon. The Japanese refer to an attitude of gratitude as "on". Living with gratitude enhances our sense of well-being. Gregg Krech, is the Executive Director of the ToDo Institute, an education and retreat center near Middlebury, Vermont which is dedicated to the Japanese discipline of Naikan, or living in a state of gratitude to develop greater mental health and happiness. His seven principles for cultivating gratitude are:

1. Gratitude is independent of one's objective life circumstances;

2. Gratitude is a function of attention;

3. Entitlement makes gratitude impossible;

4. When we continue to receive something on a regular basis, we typically begin to take it for granted;

5. Our deepest sense of gratitude comes through grace -- the awareness that we have not earned, nor do we deserve what we have been given;

6. Gratitude can be cultivated through sincere self-reflection; and

7. The expression of gratitude (through words and deeds) has the effect of heightening our personal experience of gratitude.

Roshi John Daido Loori, a Zen Buddhist master, describes the transformative power of gratitude this way:

> "Expressing gratitude is transformative, just as transformative as expressing complaint. Imagine an experiment involving two people. One is asked to spend ten minutes each morning and evening expressing gratitude (there is always something to be grateful for), while the other is asked to spend the same amount of time practicing complaining (there is, after all, always something to complain about.) One of the subjects is saying things like, "I hate my job. I can't stand this apartment. Why can't I make enough money? My spouse doesn't get along with me. That dog next door never stops barking and I just can't stand this neighborhood." The other is saying things like, "I'm really grateful for the opportunity to work; there are so many people these days who can't even find a job. And I'm sure grateful for my health. What a gorgeous day; I really like this fall breeze." They do this experiment for a year. Guaranteed, at the end of that year the person practicing complaining will have deeply reaffirmed all his negative "stuff" rather than having let it go, while the one practicing gratitude will be a very grateful person. . . Expressing gratitude can, indeed, change our way of

seeing ourselves and the world."

Even Liberty Mutual, the insurance company, recommends saying thank you as part of its "Responsibility" project. People who say thanks get better results, higher commitment levels, and they feel more in-tune themselves with their working environment.

Gratitude is different than just an appreciation that what we have is nice. If one is grateful, it means you believe the benefit was granted to you, unearned. We can appreciate our own accomplishments, but there is no need to be grateful to someone else for what we earned. When we are grateful, we recognize an element of chance in the benefit. We may have had a part in earning the benefit, but we were not entitled to it, the benefit might just as well have gone to someone else. Think of all those Oscar acceptance speeches, each of the nominated actors did good work, and sometimes there is an obvious winner, but anyone who troops to the front and grabs the golden statue with nonchalance and a sense of expectation is widely, and properly, regarded as egotistical and unrealistic. It is the Adelle Adkins of the world, radiating joy and surprise at her win for "Skyfall" (when she was the only one in the room who was actually surprised), who experience joy. They are grateful, despite their obvious gifts.

We could just thank the Universe for the good things in our lives. The problem is that the Universe didn't really give us anything. The "Universe" is a vast expanse of nothing punctuated with inanimate masses of gas and rock, and it has no ability to give. Only someone real can give you something. And as Mr. Krech states, "Our deepest sense of gratitude comes through grace -- the awareness that we have not earned, nor do we deserve what we have been given."

That is where God comes in. He gives us life and good things and we really don't even know him. Unearned beneficence. God makes me grateful, and gratefulness gives me a positive attitude, and a positive attitude makes my life run smoother. Without someone real to thank, I would grow inured to the miraculous, or at least start to feel as if everything good in my life is the result of my own work—with no need to thank anyone else. That kind of egotistical attitude would be very bad for my relationships with family, friends and co-workers. That attitude would suck joy from my life, and it would be easy to fall into it. God is important to give us the sense of wonder and renewal that comes with gratitude. We need God to thank for the good things in our lives.

Besides being a source of good things in my life, I need God for companionship, when things are going badly and when things are going well. I live alone and I have for years. I'm single without children. I have a great family, but they live hundreds of miles away so I don't see them very often. I have some very good friends that I see regularly and thoroughly enjoy, but they have families and lives of their own and are spread around the Chicago metropolitan area and beyond. I spend more time alone than many people. I am used to solitude, and I have no qualms about travelling alone or eating out in a restaurant or going to a movie, a concert or a festival alone, although I enjoy doing all those things with friends and family. Truthfully, I enjoy being able to move at my own pace and select the activities I want to do. This next part is going to sound very odd—but I never really feel alone. I always feel that God is with me. I don't see God; I don't hear God; I don't hear voices; I don't see dead people; but I sense a sort of kind presence. The presence of God makes my life better: more secure, more interesting, more joyful.

I actually look forward to long road trips as time to spend with God. I don't mean quiet, monk-like contemplation, kind of time with God. I mean radio blaring, windows open, driving down the road (sometimes 2 lane highways instead of the expressway) looking at the scenery, stopping at the world's largest ball of string, chatting with strangers, trying the pie at local diners, and finding hotels at midnight without a reservation, kind of time with God. Really you should try it; you can pray and eat ice cream at the same time, no problem.

God is good, God is kind, God is fun. God is great company; and that is important. All of us have to go through some periods in our lives alone. Often we feel most alone when things are most difficult, for example after the death of a loved one. Depression is a major issue for many people today and their depression is often linked to a lack of meaningful, positive relationships with other people. Feeling depressed makes it more difficult to get out of the house and develop the kind of meaningful, positive relationships that make life run more smoothly. Having a positive relationship with God as baseline in your life makes a tremendous difference in your mental health and mental attitude. You don't feel alone, you don't get as depressed, and you are more able to form positive relationships with others. Just as being too much alone can start a difficult spiral of loneliness and depression; a relationship with God can start a positive upward spiral of stronger, healthier relationships and a positive mental attitude.

I need God for comfort as well as company. As I write this, I've been to five funerals in the last 7 months and encountered six significant deaths. (I skipped the service for a cousin who was murdered by an ex-boyfriend, I would have been there, but I couldn't get out of town to attend.) Three weeks ago. I was with the daughters of a close friend at her bedside when she died, after a 6 month bout with cancer that was already fully metastasized when it was diagnosed. My mother died 3 days later. I'm sad about their deaths, all of those deaths. I miss all of them, they were each unique, wonderful people that I cared about.

The first death was a kind and funny man who was married to one of my cousins. He had been ill for 20 years, and it never stopped him. The second death was my aunt, my mother's sister who turned 100 two weeks before her death. She was too ill to attend her party—a great disappointment as her family and friends had been very much looking forward to celebrating with her. She was still working part time 7 months before her death and was an engaging, energetic and positive person up to the end.

The third death was the murder of my cousin. I did not know my cousin well, but had met her and liked her, and care a lot about our shared family. That one was a particularly nasty shock. The fourth person was a long-time friend, the warm and wonderful oldest of 9 siblings who treat me like one of their own. The fifth, a close friend, was my "wingman". We helped each other paint our homes and discussed everything from our jobs to our families. She is the one I called to take me to the emergency room when I cracked both bones in my knee in a fall off of a ladder trying to cut a limb off of a tree with an electric saw, and then walked in a parade. She never pointed out that may not have been the best choice. She was a lot of fun, a wonderful mother, and according to her 5 grandchildren, the best grandma in the world!

Finally, my mother died after a 20 year journey into dementia. My mother was the kindest person I have ever known, with a warm, sparkly personality and seemingly endless patience. My nieces would argue that she had the "best grandma" title. She would light up and greet me, and the rest of the family, with a hug and a kiss, ten years after she could no longer reliably identify us by name. She was entirely unique and one of the most impressive people I have ever met.

Each of these people had a firm grip on God's love. Each of them had chosen to accept that they needed God in their life and had centered their choices around God. None of them were remotely perfect. They lived ordinary lives. They had faults and virtues and made some good choices and made some bad choice. God loved all of them and his mark was clear in their lives. They each loved well. They lived good lives.

That is not enough, I miss them and feel that all of their deaths, all deaths in fact, are untimely and painful. I believe that anyone who makes light of the death of someone they love is simply in denial. There is no good time to die. I could be crushed by that much loss in so short a time, but I am not. I'm depressed at a normal level, my life has some gaps in it that will take time to fill, and none of those people can be replaced. But I do not have a counselor on speed dial. My family and friends have been wonderfully supportive, but God gets me through this kind of thing. I feel the warm presence of God telling me I am not alone. God helps me talk to my friend's grieving daughters, to my sister, brother, nieces and cousins about their losses and mine; to the friends who grieve with me over the loss of their sister. God's presence made the wakes and funerals and phone calls bearable, with some enjoyable moments of sharing memories and laughter interspersed with the pain and loss. God helps me find work interesting and enjoy raking the leaves. Without God's comfort, I'd likely be reeling and spinning out of control, but I am still centered.

I'm much less able to deal with the deaths of people whom I know had no use for God in their lives. I don't freak out, but I'm a little haunted by those deaths, even if I disliked the person. I'm particularly bothered by the deaths of people whom I know were treated badly by the church and rejected or ignored God as a result. I find myself wondering, sometimes years later, if there was more I could or should have done to bring up the issue, and whether I helped or hurt their impression of God. Ultimately, I can only rely on God's compassion to deal with those uncertainties. I am certain he doesn't allow our failures to influence his grace. And I resolve once again to not add to a negative perception of God that someone may have---and regret the times I've broken that resolution. As I've said, Christians are imperfect people who frequently do dumb things that make people think God also does the same kind of dumb things. Unfortunately, I can't claim to be an exception to the rule, however much the failures of the church and Christians annoy me.

God's presence helps me deal not just with death, but with all the losses and uncertainties of my life: the leaking roof, ailing car, job losses, betrayals by friends, bad break-ups, and financial uncertainty. Every time I experience loss, I feel God's presence saying, "it's not the end of the world; it will all work out". At the time, that comfort seems unrealistic and impractical. But things do work out. That comfort is a wonderful reference point to have when my world turns upside down.

I also need God as the centering point for my life choices. You've heard the advice never to do anything you can't explain to your spouse, your children or your parents. That is very good advice, it will keep you out of a lot of trouble.

I don't have a spouse or children, my father died years ago, my mother was past embarrassment long before her death, and the rest of my family lives a long way away. I have low approval needs. The list of people whose good opinion is critical to me is very short and none of them really have an opportunity to know what I do on any given day unless I tell them. I could lie, cheat and even steal a bit and pretty much get away with it. I could be lazy, critical, self-centered, back-stabbing and egotistical. I have a well-developed capacity for all of those things. I have some experience in behaving in those ways, and it was never a good experience.

The presence of God calls me back when I head in that direction. The sense that God loves me, that He cares how I behave and is disappointed when I behave badly, keeps me from doing a lot of self-destructive things. It gives me the strength to take responsibility when I am afraid of blame. It gives me the strength to point out to sometimes intimidating people when things are getting off track—necessary in the legal department of a large corporation or as outside counsel to a small one. It gives me the patience to deal with trying people, or at least to restrain the all too frequent impulse to complain aloud of their ignorance. (As I find with annoying frequency that the ignorance has been mine, restraining that impulse is particularly beneficial to my well-being.) God's presence has saved me from inflicting a lot of grief on myself. I wish I listened more carefully and more often.

I need God to motivate me to work hard and to stay focused. I have the attention span of a gnat; and there are endless opportunities to fritter away time, or spread my time so thinly among many activities that I don't accomplish anything. As Proverbs points out, frittering time can be very damaging to one's well-being. Proverbs 15:19 says, "A lazy person has trouble all through life; the path of the upright is easy." Proverbs 6: 6 really lays it out: "Take a lesson from the ants, you lazybones. Learn from their ways and be wise! Even though they have no prince, no governor, or ruler to make them work, they labor hard all summer, gathering food for the winter, But you, lazybones, how long will you sleep? When will you wake up? I want you to learn this lesson:

69

A little extra sleep, a little more slumber, a little folding of the hands to rest---and poverty will pounce on you like a bandit; scarcity will attack you like an armed robber."

Working hard is the single most significant contributor to physical and financial well-being. Accidents of birth and talent contribute. The more basic intelligence and advantages like education one has, the easier it is to succeed. But those advantages would be wasted without hard work. There are numerous studies that demonstrate the value of hard work. Even the studies that point out the intrinsic advantages of talent, come to the conclusion that hard work is a very good approach if you want to be successful. *"The Procrastination Equation"*, Piers Steel, <u>Psychology Today</u>, October 8, 2011, Psychologytoday.com. is an excellent summary of the research.

Second generation business owners are often the death of a small business. As a group they often lack the motivation and/or skills required to make a business successful. A combination of feelings of entitlement, lack of respect for others' contributions, laziness or just a lack of sufficient experience, make second generation owners notoriously unsuccessful. I see that repeatedly in my practice. Transition of a family business to the next generation is always perilous.

By contrast, successful entrepreneurs, according to Jeff Haden's May 14, 2012 article in <u>Inc.</u> magazine, titled, *"9 Qualities of Remarkable Entrepreneurs"* are marked by 9 characteristics:

1. They find happiness in the success of others. They build teams.

2. They relentlessly seek new experiences.

3. They don't think work/life balance, they think life. That means that they don't follow rigid guidelines for organizing their life into buckets. They manage to include family and recreation and hobbies and reading, for enrichment and pleasure, because all of those things are important to them. Successful people are engaged in their lives, they don't just go through the motions.

4. They are incredibly empathetic. They don't pretend to care or mouth polite things, they actually care.

5. They have something to prove—to themselves. They have goals and they are motivated to meet the goals

70

6. They ignore the 40 hour work week hype. They work harder than other people—a lot harder.

7. They see money not just as a reward, but a responsibility. They use money to build up the business, to reward their employees, and to make the world a better place. And they don't do it to see their names in the newspapers. They see money as a tool, not as an end.

8. They don't see themselves are remarkable. They view themselves as hard working, the recipient of a lot of good advice and very lucky. They are quick to share the credit.

9. They recognize that success is fleeting, but dignity and respect last.

Obviously anyone could choose these behaviors, but most of us are more prone to the kind of behavior that characterizes the second generation of business owners. There is a reason that exhibiting the 9 behaviors of a successful entrepreneur is remarkable; those behaviors aren't common. It takes a lot of self-control, patience, and genuine peace and joy to live out those 9 behaviors. Not coincidentally, Galatians 5:22-23 describes those characteristics as things that God instills in us when we choose to live our lives according to his plans. And Paul wasn't the first to think of it. The book of Proverbs, mostly written by Solomon, one of the wisest people in history, has a wealth of advice geared toward obtaining a successful life—some of it seems like common knowledge—yet hard to implement, but much of it counter-intuitive. Much of it echoes the 9 Qualities Jeff Haden cites in his article.

> The generous prosper and are satisfied; those who refresh others will themselves be refreshed. Prov. 11:25

> Kind words are like honey, sweet to the soul and healthy for the body. Prov. 16:24

> Intelligent people are always open to new ideas. In fact, they look for them. Prov. 18:15

> A wise person is hungry for truth, while the fool feeds on trash. Prov. 15:14

> Get all the advice and instruction you can, and be wise the rest of your life. Prov. 19:20

A relaxed attitude lengthens life, jealousy rots it away. Prov. 14:30

People curse those who hold their grain for higher prices, but they bless the one who sells to them in their time of need. Prov. 11:26

Lazy people are soon poor; hard workers get rich. Prov. 10:4

Wealthy from get-rich schemes quickly disappears; wealth from hard work grows. Prov. 13: 11:

Lazy people are a pain to their employer. They are like smoke in the eyes or vinegar that sets the teeth on edge. Prov. 10:26

A wise slave will rule over the master's shameful sons and will share their inheritance. Prov. 17: 2

Develop your business first before building your house. Prov. 24:27

Only a stupid prince will oppress his people, but a kind king will have a long reign if he hates dishonesty and bribes. Prov. 28:16

Workers who tend a fig tree are allowed to eat its fruit. In the same way, workers who protect their employer's interests will be rewarded. Prov. 27:18

The wise are glad to be instructed, but babbling fools fall flat on their faces. Prov. 10:8

We may throw the dice, but the Lord determines how they fall. Prov. 16:33

Plans go wrong for lack of advice; many counselors bring success. Prov. 15:22

Zeal without knowledge is not good; a person who moves too quickly may go the wrong way, Prov. 19: 2

Wise people don't make a show of their knowledge, but fools broadcast their folly. Prov. 12:23

It is better to be patient than powerful; it is better to have self-control than to conquer a city. Prov. 16: 32

Upright citizens bless a city and make it prosper, but the talk of the wicked tears it apart. Prov. 11:11

We all have happy memories of the godly, but the name of a wicked person rots away. Prov. 10:7

Choose a good reputation over great riches for being held in high esteem is better than having silver or gold. Prov. 22:1

This is all good advice, but not easy to implement. I need God and his guidance to remind me to work hard, to ask for help, listen to advice, and remember to say thanks and share. In theory, I could do that without God, but in practice, I know I run madly about, fritter time and money and get so wrapped up in looking for a result that I forget to enjoy the journey and forget that people matter more than results. After more than thirty years as a corporate attorney, I feel pretty confident in saying that a lot of people share my tendencies to be unproductive or unhealthy.

Procrastination, fear, indifference and laziness are rampant in the marketplace and a high percentage of leaders model their behavior more on Machiavelli than Christ. Many large and small companies have a revolving door in their senior management positions, and it is rare that one of the high pressure managers is missed when they leave. In some companies dodging work, credit-grabbing, ego massage and back stabbing are practically Olympic events.

Unfortunately, none of those unhealthy behaviors ensures success, or job security, or contributes to the bottom line. In fact, those behaviors tend to obscure financial realities and can be extremely detrimental to the health of a company over time. The bankruptcy court is littered with businesses brought down by senior management's single minded egotism. On the other hand, "However you want others to treat you, so treat them…" Matthew 7:12, is really good advice for running a business. It leads to high levels of employee retention, stable vendor relationships and customer loyalty. If you allow God to actually influence your behavior in your everyday life, good things happen.

I need God's influence because as much as I would like to think I will make healthy, productive choices on my own, I have too much experience with what happens when I wander off the path to believe that I will actually implement all those healthy, productive plans I make. My track record of healthy choices while ignoring God is probably about average, but I have much higher levels of success and much less mess to clean up when I stay close to God and focus on actually implementing the teachings of the Bible. Following God isn't just about Heaven and Hell, it's about experiencing the upside of life now.

Trying to implement God's teaching doesn't make problems disappear. In some ways, it causes problems. There is a perception in the world I frequent that Christians are unrealistic patsies—that I must have just fallen off the turnip truck to believe such rubbish. The practice of law can be contentious at times anyway, but the added assumption that being a Christian makes me gullible always amazes me. I find myself talking to people on a regular basis who try to convince me of some really silly things or to steamroll me into agreeing to something stupid-- or who use pseudo-Christian guilt to try to take advantage. "You call yourself a Christian, you should [insert any number of lame, overreaching and overbearing demands and assumptions.]" People lie to me with the same kind of smirk used car dealers use—try buying a car as a single woman sometime—they actually say, with a completely straight face, that the list price is the price and they can't change it.

I'm not alone. A friend of mine started following Christ seriously at a time when she was the Vice President of Marketing for a mid-sized, national company. Until that point, she was well-respected in the company and had worked out a stable position within the normal company politics. Almost as soon as she went public with her faith, she started to see negative feedback. People told her silly things, tried to dump bad projects on her and started to target her accounts. It was amazing. Her business acumen had not changed, nor had her performance numbers. It was just the assumption that Christians must be out of touch with reality that caused the change. I've seen that smirk and heard that tone more times than I can remember. It's such an odd assumption. People believe God exists, but then assume it's foolish to behave as if he exists.

Some unscrupulous people use Christian labels deliberately to draw in perceived easy marks. You've seen the ads--little fish or crosses all over, the business is named "Integrity Something", with prices twice the market rate and service half of market standards. (Frankly I never patronize any business that makes a point of advertising itself as Christian. That may be an over-reaction, but I don't see how the label is relevant.) A business that is truly operated in a Christian manner will have good service, fair prices and be responsible about correcting its mistakes. It will develop a good reputation, and that should be advertisement enough. The crosses and little fish always strike me as insincere. It takes some discernment to wade through the false messages about Christianity. Making God a part of your life is not a magic cure all, but it helps.

Following God gives me a stronger spine to stand up to stresses and challenges of life, and the will to shrug off the attempts to take advantage. If you think one has to be weak and miserable to be a Christian, read the Gospels. Jesus was not co-dependent in the least. Jesus was wise, kind, and adventurous. He engaged with strangers and set appropriate limits. He had a magnetic personality and great personal strength. Jesus enjoyed life. You can too. God has a lot to offer that isn't available from any other source. God can change your life and your eternity. He matters.

Chapter Three
Christianity is for the Strong

We have been suckered by the modern church into believing that a relationship with God is only for weak people who are poor or suffering in some way. It is for children in Sunday School, single moms, divorced people, grieving people, sick people, old people, dying people. Real men don't need a relationship with God; real men don't need church; real women don't need church either. Successful business people don't need the psalm-singing whiners who frequent church. Happy people with healthy families benefit from considering spirituality and ethics in their personal relationships, but this "relationship with God stuff is just nonsense." I disagree. Healing through a relationship with Christ is all well and good, but Christianity is for normal, healthy people too and the strong need God the most.

Strong, successful people are the ones taking all the risk. They are the ones speaking up in meetings, starting new programs, coaching soccer, laying it on the line to earn a living to pay their bills, going out on a limb to educate their kids, sticking their necks out to help their parents, extended family members friends, neighbors and strangers. No one calls poor, sick, dysfunctional, whiny people at 3 in the morning to ask for help. It is the "go to" people who get those calls—and the "go to" people get out of bed and go. The "go to" people work when they have a bad cold or the flu. The "go to" people stay up until 1 am finishing Halloween costumes for their kids. The "go to" people keep their head when things blow up at work; the "go to" people defuse the argument at home or in the neighborhood. The "go to" people stick with their exercise program, get the report in on time, bring food to the grieving family next door, stop and help with the flat tire, cut the grass, paint the living room, tell the truth on their expense report, remember the customer's name, and make that one last call. "Go to" people do these things with a smile on their face and think they are normal. Because of this good humor and cheerful attitude, people often think it is easier for the "go to" people to accomplish these things than it is for other people to do these same things. It is not. "Go to" people get very, very tired.

Surprisingly, rather than getting a lot of credit for being a 'go to" person, receiving accolades and raises, many "go to" people are sneered at and are rewarded by having more work dumped on their plate. Airline gate agents are probably the ultimate "go to" people, and who has any respect for them?

Co-dependent people often pass as "go to" people for a time, but they lack the normalcy that characterizes true "go to" people. Co-dependent people are carrying the weight of the world on their shoulders and eventually they crash and burn. "Go to" people carve out some time for themselves. They take a nap, have a beer, watch a game or get a pedicure—and then they go back to work. "Go to" people aren't plaster saints, they are just highly functional. And that is where a relationship with God can be a real benefit. Having a relationship with God makes you a more functional person.

My dad was a "go to" person. He was the first one up in the morning and didn't go to bed until everyone was in. No one reminded him to take out the garbage or cut the grass. He was happy to build things out of Tinkertoys to keep us amused while my mom spent Saturday morning running errands and visiting with friends and family. As a teenager in World War II, he saw duty in every theater of war as armed escort for tanker convoys, and he described that as fun. He was a cement finisher and heavily involved in the union, becoming the foreman of choice for every contractor with a large job in his 5 county territory. He held every office in the union except President, was on the negotiating committee for over 20 years. He conceived the union's vacation, health and retirement programs, and worked tirelessly to convince others to adopt the plans. He organized strikes and enforced the contract against reluctant contractors. He ultimately was elected to the top job of business agent, and declined to run again because it took him away from home too much at a time when my brother was in his early teens and starting to experiment with drugs and beer and some less constructive friends. (My brother wasn't that bad by any objective standard, but my parents were never objective.)

My dad was encouraging, loving, protective almost to a fault, devoted, emotionally mature and demanding. He had ultimate confidence in our ability to succeed, and no tolerance at all for lack of effort or lack of commitment. He was strong, punctual, hard-working, reliable, often blunt, sometimes profane, believed physical force had a place if it was necessary in defense of your family or your country (but never to be used aggressively), and endlessly devious, but mostly in a really constructive way. He could explain why you should do your chores in a way that made it seem like your own idea and only sensible. I've met people who disliked him or feared him, but no one who lacked respect for him.

My dad loved God as much as he loved us. He didn't come across as a devoted Christian; he sat in the back row at church and liked

77

staying home on Sunday mornings and listening to sermons on the radio. He came across like the construction worker he was, and his behavior away from home was more rough-edged than at home. He grew up in a rough and tumble environment and he didn't see a problem with the rough edges—the edginess was well suited to parts of his life and he found it useful to manage his work environment. We didn't see that side of him at home, but we knew it existed. My dad loved God deeply and relied on God to get him through some very long, very trying days.

My dad enjoyed explaining to other men on construction jobs that they needed God in their lives. He made friends with the Jehovah's witnesses who came to the door, gently attempting to draw them to the conclusion that Jesus is not just a good man created by God, but is God. He thanked God when there was work despite a rival business agent's attempts to divert good jobs away from him, he thanked God when the sun went behind the clouds on a 104 degree day in July, he thanked God when my brother survived scarlet fever as an infant, and when I outgrew my college habits. He thanked God before every meal, and I think he prayed for the Cardinals because they used to win a lot.

My dad took full advantage of the upside in the middle of a pretty ordinary life. He exuded joy. He was a devoted husband and father, a trusted friend and a reliable neighbor. But probably his defining characteristic was a lack of fear. He occasionally told stories about World War II, like how the ship in front of him and the one behind hit mines in one trip through the Panama canal; or running aground off the coast of South America in an effort to evade a submarine. His version was that the problem with the ships hitting mines was that it slowed the convoy while they moved to the side, extending his watch and interrupting the card game he had planned. He thought the evasive action to avoid the submarine was probably unnecessary, and running aground was just plain silly, but that it was nice he got an R & R leave out of it. We asked him if he was afraid. He said no, you prayed and did your job and just assumed it wouldn't be you that died. If you did, it wasn't that important, you went to Heaven—no need to stress over it. He lost a brother in World War II, so that wasn't just something he said. He had the same attitude when he died at 76. No big deal; he was old and sick and not having a good time anymore—good timing.

My dad was just an ordinary guy, but he had extraordinary strength; and it was because he relied on God. He didn't waste energy on fear, and that gave him more energy to do what he needed to do. That is the upside. You can have it too.

My mother was a "go-to" person as well, a kinder, gentler version. She was smart and pretty, had a sparkling smile, endless patience, beautiful manners, a kind heart, and a relaxed attitude toward housekeeping—no threat of the health department showing up, but no worries if you left a bit of dust in the corners. She loved people and it showed. She was an elementary school teacher for 16 years. We had pictures of her students on our Christmas tree for more than 20 years after she retired. She kept their notes and gaudy presents tucked away along with our scrawled cards and my dad's love notes. She was the good Baptist in the family, teaching Sunday School for nearly 50 years and patiently putting up with the rest of us. Our house was the place everyone came to play. She was fun and giving and listened. She also had high standards and a stubborn insistence that we do the best that we could at whatever task was at hand. She was just more gracious in her expression of those things. Perfect strangers would stop to tell me my mother was one of the nicest people they knew.

My mother was actually nicer at home than at her job as well, but there was no dichotomy in her behavior. The only really annoying thing about her was that she was practically always right. I never met anyone who didn't like my mother, or anyone who didn't respect her. She helped everyone in the family, and the neighbors, and volunteered at church and at school, and danced through it all with an effervescent smile. And she loved God. She prayed a lot raising three kids who took after their father. She remained cheerful, gentle, peaceful and patient even when, more than 15 years into dementia, she couldn't put together a coherent sentence or find her room without assistance. That is the upside, and you can have it too.

Most people would view my father as a strong person, he fit the profile. Fewer people would have listed strength as one of my mother's defining characteristics. Most of us tend to equate strength with the sort of personality traits frequently displayed by action film characters, pro athletes or, in the business world, a number of executives. We equate strength with aggression. We expect strong people to be argumentative, abrasive, quick tempered and critical. We expect them to be not just Type A, but Type A negative. This is not an accurate view of strength.

Some people with strong, very assertive behavior patterns are strong, like my dad. However, many people with those behavior patterns are not strong. They are very uncomfortable with themselves. They are trying very hard to prove something to someone, or to themselves. It is rare that they ever feel they have achieved enough or have enough. They often quail in the face of adversity, looking for scapegoats when something goes wrong and becoming very depressed in the face of failure. Often they need the comfort of a crowd of cheering fans. They want to be in charge, but not take responsibility. Some Type A negative people are just impatient or heedless of the effect they have on others, or they may believe that behavior is necessary to suit the circumstances. Sometimes they just haven't thought about it much at all—insulated by self-centeredness. You can tell the difference between strong people and Type A negative wannabes by the strength of their spine, and by how they treat people they are not required to be nice to. Strong people are respectful of others, kind, helpful and maintain their sense of humor in a crisis. Wannabes snap at waiters, bark at secretaries, scoff at the idea of making an occasional photocopy by themselves, and point fingers when the numbers are less than expected.

I've worked with a lot of executives that have the Type A strong leader appearance. They are tall, smart, fast moving, quick talking, impatient, demanding, aggressive—universally regarded as strong leaders. Many of them have also been insecure, moody, more impressed with themselves than their performance would merit, unkind, disdainful of others, and fearful. Many of them expect to be waited on hand and foot for even simple tasks and some of them even throw temper tantrums. One rarely finds a high powered executive with the spine to buck the current their peers are swimming in and speak up when a policy or business plan is unethical or just stupid. One rarely finds anyone in corporate America willing to do that. To hear what people really think, you have to go the local coffee shop or after-work watering hole. You frequently hear complaints about being "forced" to do something stupid or unethical; yet not one of them has said a single word against the plan at any time when it might have done some good. That is not strength.

The Bible paints a very different picture of what strength looks like. Type A, certainly, but Type A positive. Strength in the Bible is strength of character. The heroes in the Bible care about people. The heroes in the Bible are honest, and they don't bail when things get tough. They are "go to" people.

The Bible has a lot of examples of strong people who accomplished great things, but almost none of them started out as strong people, at least from a Biblical perspective. Nearly to a person, the heroes of the Bible told God he had made a mistake and had the wrong person. They were very flawed people. Over time, however, as they followed God and developed a relationship with God, they developed great personal strength. God did not choose them because they were strong, go-to people. They became strong, go-to people because they relied on God. They discovered the upside.

Certainly some of the Bible heroes had the kind of Type A personality we associate with strength. They started out as Type A negative people, but over time, grew strong in character as well. King David, for example, was brash even as a teenager. He openly criticized seasoned soldiers, calling them cowards or laggards for failing to fight the giant, Goliath. Then he sauntered out to fight the giant himself, refusing armor and carrying only a slingshot and 5 stones. He won and that did absolutely nothing to develop humility. But, for all his failings and brashness, David had character even as a young man. When two of his men sneaked through enemy lines to bring him water from his hometown well in Bethlehem, he poured it out as an offering to God rather than drink it—refusing to encourage them to put their lives in danger to court his favor. 1 Chronicles 11:17-19. Later, after David survived a long, bloody war to sit on the throne of Israel, he remembered his promise to his best friend Jonathan (son of King Saul and Prince of Israel) that no matter what happened, the two would remain friends and take care of each other's families. Jonathan was killed in battle, as was most of Saul's family. David sought out Mephibosheth, the last surviving male heir of Jonathan. Mephibosheth was crippled, destitute and living in exile. David restored his wealth, set an overseer over his lands to care for them, and took him into the palace to live, giving him a place of honor at the palace table. 2 Samuel 9.

My personal favorite of the Old Testament heroes, Samson, had a lot more brawn than brains. Samson was the son of devout Jews and was dedicated by his parents to God as a Nazarene when he was born. A Nazarene was to be a servant of God, and did not cut their hair or drink liquor as a symbol of the vow. Samson was a big, strong guy. He killed a lion with his bare hands, and carried off a city gate when his enemies thought he was trapped. He didn't pay that much attention to the vow his parents had made. One time he brought home honey from bees living in the carcass of a lion he had killed—unclean food for a Jew, and gave it to his parents to eat without telling the source of the honey.

He was arrogant and insisted on baiting the Philistines who controlled the land. He also insisted on dating and marrying foreign women—based completely on their looks. This created a lot of trouble and he didn't mind at all. He liked getting into fights. He liked showing off his strength. He once killed 1000 men with the jawbone of a donkey and set fire to his enemies' crops by tying 300 foxes into pairs with a torch between their tails and turning them loose to run through the ripe grain as revenge for a slight. Samson did a lot of stupid things, picking fights and repeatedly marrying or dating the wrong women.

You know the story, he kept his long hair, but didn't really respect his vow. Eventually he told his girlfriend Delilah the secret of his strength, knowing that she had already attempted to betray him to the Philistines several times. She called a barber to cut his hair off and his strength was gone. (His strength wasn't really in his hair, it was a special gift from God as a Nazarene. When Samson betrayed his vow to God and backed out of his commitment, the strength went too.)

Samson was not the smartest man in history, but he did have the sense to recognize his errors and change. He did not blame God for his situation, and he trusted God to accept him back. At the end of his life, when his poor choices had made him a slave, blind and ridiculed, he prayed to God for return of his strength. Standing between the support beams of the house where he was paraded as a public spectacle, he pushed away the beams, allowing the roof to fall in and kill him, and more than 3000 of his enemies. Judges 14-16. Samson had no fear—in life or death. He was a go-to person, or at least became one.

Other Biblical heroes had a quieter strength. Joseph and Daniel were quietly confident. Elijah, probably the most powerful man in the history of the world, varied between trash talking the priests of Baal, 1 Kings 18 and hiding out with a widow and her son in a neighboring country, quietly providing food to sustain them during an extended famine 1 Kings 17. Mary Magdalene braved a Roman cohort to visit Jesus' grave. Matthew 28.

God shows a preference for quiet strength. When God chose humans to safeguard his son during his life on Earth, starting out as a vulnerable baby, through his childhood years in a large, very poor family, living in a dangerous time and dangerous place; he did not choose King David. King David was brash, cunning and persistent, but he was a lousy father. One of his sons, Amnon, raped his half-sister, Tamar, then discarded her as if she was at fault. David's reaction was to ignore the whole thing and sweep it under the rug. When her brother, Absalom, killed Amnon two years later to revenge his sister, David did his best to ignore that too, until Absalom led a coup attempt against David. David loved his children, he wept inconsolably when Absalom was killed in battle—against David's express order to keep him alive. But David was an absent, inconsistent, neglectful father. 2 Samuel 13-15.

God didn't choose Moses to raise his son. Moses was a fabulous leader. He prevailed on the Pharaoh of Egypt to free the Israelite slaves and led them through 40 years of wandering in the desert, but that didn't leave much time for family. He sent his wife and two sons away to live with her family for a time. While they rejoined him once Pharaoh released the Israelites, they disappear from the story shortly afterward and are never mentioned again even though Moses' biography is one of the most detailed in the Bible. Exodus 18.

God didn't choose Abraham to raise his son. Abraham was another hero of the faith. He was the founder of Judaism, chosen by God to father the Israelites and all the other Semite peoples. He established a covenant with God to safeguard the means of preserving the relationship between God and men until Christ's sacrifice on the cross made that relationship easily accessible to everyone. God loved Abraham, but Abraham wasn't a great father either. Abraham had a son, Ishmael, with Hagar, his wife's maid—at his wife, Sarah's request. Abraham banished Hagar and Ishmael into the desert to die when Sarah became jealous after Isaac was born 13 years later. Genesis 15-17. Ishmael and Hagar survived and apparently Abraham retained some relationship with Ishmael because he and Isaac were both with Abraham at his death. Genesis 25:9. After Sarah's death, Abraham married again and had six more sons. Before his death, he settled an inheritance on all of his children except Isaac, and sent them away—never seeing them again. Isaac inherited Abraham's principal estate, but there were apparently a number of strained relationships in the family.[17]

God didn't choose any of the heroes of the faith to raise his son. He didn't choose great warriors or great leaders. When it came to the most important mission God has ever entrusted to a human, God chose a starry-eyed, intrepid teen-aged girl, named Mary; and a very kind, very humble, very reliable man named Joseph. Joseph was not loud and brash, he didn't rant or make a big fuss over anything, but Joseph was a "go to" guy. When Mary told Joseph she was pregnant, he knew the baby wasn't his. He didn't believe the angel of God story, and his hurt and humiliation had to be enormous. But his reaction was kind. He intended to quietly break the engagement without embarrassing her—or calling for her to be stoned to death, which he had the right to do. Matthew 1:18-20. When he had a vision that the story about the angel

---

[17] Abraham's aborted offer of Isaac as a sacrifice, substituting a ram at the last minute, Genesis 22, probably contributed to a lack of trust.

from God was true and that Mary was pregnant with the son of God, not the son of a shepherd boy, Joseph believed that. Most people would have written off such a dream as indigestion. Joseph married Mary, and made a home for a child that wasn't his, and six or more children of his own. Joseph found shelter in a very crowded Bethlehem in time for a very inconvenient birth. He refugeed to Egypt and earned a living in a foreign country when King Herod came searching for the baby Jesus. When the threat was passed, Joseph brought Mary and their children back to their home town of Nazareth and lived with the rumors about the length of time between his wedding and his first son's birth. Matthew 1-3.

The Bible doesn't give many details about Joseph after Jesus' birth. He is mentioned in just one more incident, recorded in Luke 2: 41-52. Jesus decided at the age of 12 to stay behind in Jerusalem in the temple, engaged in discourse with the rabbis, after his mother and father departed for home with the rest of their friends and relatives at the end of the Passover celebration. Joseph and Mary travelled an entire day before discovering Jesus had stayed behind. They returned to Jerusalem and spent 3 days looking for Jesus before finding him in the temple. I can't even imagine what my parents' response would have been if I pulled a stunt like that. Mary and Joseph asked, "Why have you treated us this way, we were worried about you and have been looking for you for 3 days." Jesus' reply was not helpful. He said, "Why were you looking for me, didn't you know I had to be in my father's house". Then he got up and went home with them and as Matthew puts it," continued under their authority" until he reached adulthood. Joseph and Mary didn't freak out or get angry. They did not understand their son, but they simply wondered in their hearts and loved him.

Joseph is not mentioned again and scholars assume he died when Jesus was a teenager, not an uncommon occurrence at the time[18]. There isn't much more detail about Mary either, but she is mentioned a number of times in the accounts of Jesus' ministry. Mary was with Jesus throughout his ministry and travelled with him much of the time[19]

---

[18] When Joseph died, Jesus, as the oldest son, would have become responsible for taking care of his mother and siblings. A lot of responsibility for a teenager. Mary is the one who told Jesus to make wine for the wedding at Cana, his first public miracle. John 2. I'm guessing as the head of family with at least 8 people to feed, Jesus "trick" of multiplying food and wine started at home.

[19] Mary probably accompanied Jesus and the disciples to protect his reputation. Jesus frequently spoke and ate with women who weren't his relatives, which was unheard of at the time. A number of women were included among his supporters and were substantial

Trekking around Judea in the first century with an itinerant, very controversial rabbi was far from easy. Mary watched at the foot of the cross when Jesus died. John 19. Mary is rightfully respected by the church. She was amazing; truly a go-to person. Joseph and Mary weren't flashy, or brash, but they were incredibly strong people. They knew Jesus probably better than any other people could have. They did not understand him, but he changed their lives. They believed he was the Messiah.

The true epitome of strength in the Bible is Jesus. Jesus exemplified all the fruits of the Spirit listed in Galatians: love, joy, peace, patience, gentleness, goodness, kindness, faithfulness and self-control. Our view of Jesus is colored by those pictures of the long haired man with a dreamy look on his face. We think of him as gentle, taking time out to talk to small children and women—both of whom were regarded as property in the first century and routinely ignored by anyone with power. Certainly no rabbi would willingly talk to woman who was not a close relative, much less the prostitutes and others of questionable moral character that Jesus encouraged. But the picture of the dreamy-eyed man is somewhat misleading. Jesus was gentle and kind, he did care for the weak and minimized, but he had enormous strength and vitality.

Jesus taunted the religious and political leaders of his time. He challenged powerful people like Nicodemus and Zacchaeus to follow him. He inspired a rag-tag group of 12 fisherman, tax collectors and political zealots, each a strong leader in his own right, into following him for three years on a mission to change the world. The apostles were not a group of quiet nerds. They had nicknames like "Rock" and "Sons of Thunder". Leading that group required a lot of voltage, and Jesus managed it in a walk—on surface of the Sea of Galilee during a huge storm. The disciples were challenged to keep up with Jesus and were continually baffled and amazed at what he did and said. Jesus often taught crowds for several days at a time; healing hundreds of people

---

donors to the movement, even the wife of a prominent member of Herod's household. Luke 8:2-3. Some women even travelled with the group. Matthew 27:55-56. In addition to those relationships, he often focused his efforts on converting the undesirable elements of society, including prostitutes, Luke 7-35-39 and the notorious woman at the well portrayed in John 4. He was criticized by the religious leaders of the day for such associations, but there is no evidence that they ever accused him of inappropriate relationships with women. Having your mother travel with you is a good way to quash rumors.

who swarmed around him wherever he went. All four Gospels repeatedly record Jesus surrounded by crowds. Jesus was a rock star.

Jesus did not act like a rock star. Jesus said it was good to be patient, kind and loving. He had two rules: Love the Lord, your God, with all your heart, mind and strength; and love your neighbor as you love yourself. Treat your neighbor as you would like to be treated—what we now call the "Golden Rule" Matthew 7:12, Luke 10:27. That takes a tremendous amount of strength. It isn't easy to "turn the other cheek"—that phrase, now a cliché, was brand new information in the first century when Jesus first spoke the words, Matthew 5:40. In the first century, "an eye for an eye" was the generally accepted mode of behavior—and meant very literally. If you caused an accident in which someone lost an eye, they were entitled to put out your eye unless you paid recompense. Exodus 21-19-25. Jesus was not a dreamy nerd. It took extraordinary force of character to lead the disciples and the people flocking to hear him. The world hasn't been the same since.

Putting the Golden Rule into practice isn't any easier today than it was then. Our neighborhoods and our families are filled with very flawed people. A number of them are not easy to love. It isn't easy to look for the good in people when it isn't obvious. It isn't easy to show up when you are expected and to hang in when things get tough. Frankly, it's even hard to want to do that, much less achieve it. It is much more natural to want adulation with as little responsibility as possible. Showing up and hanging in are not glamorous, and the rewards are not immediately evident.

The reality is that many of us can pull off Type A negative behavior by ourselves, but Type A positive is hard to pull off without some assistance. Over time, without reinforcement, even the person with the strongest spine will bend or break under stress. There are certainly some people who do manage to live impressive, full on Type A positive lives without God. But how much easier would it be, and how much more could they achieve, if they discovered the upside. Think of the potential. Many of these people have been cheated out of a relationship with God because they don't understand the upside is available to them. They are conditioned to think of a relationship with God as something for weak people with dysfunctional behavior patterns. Type A positive behavior is much easier when you are reminded by God that Type A positive behavior is both normal and expected; and when you know God loves you and is proud of the work you are doing to remain positive.

A relationship with God can give you the strength to not just persevere, but to flourish under stress that sends others to the therapist's office. This part is difficult to explain, because a large part of the explanation just really isn't practical at all. Directing one's thoughts toward a relationship with God, appreciating the world he has made, expecting comfort and sustenance in our daily lives, looking for the good in people, all work together to generate a sense of joy and lack of fear that frees up a lot of energy for more positive things. Everyday life is more fun, and the bumps are much less noticeable. The crises don't seem insurmountable. You really have to try it to see how it works. Try praying for a sense of God's presence, to see the beauty around you and to see the good in people around you. You will be surprised how tangible the results are. God is real and he is interested in relating to us in a specific, personal way.

Even better, God can be a source of strength to the strong. Strong people tend to run out of people to rely on. Everyone relies on them. This is an issue even for non-go-to people. As we get older, lose our parents and others of that generation who love us unconditionally, or when we move away from family to unfamiliar places, or rise through the leadership ranks, we become more and more the person others look to for leadership and support with few close friends or peers to compare notes with. We no longer have the luxury of consulting with others with more experience. People flock around asking questions, asking for direction, asking for assistance. Not too many people offer assistance or fresh ideas. Strength, leadership and even age alone, can be isolating.

This isolation can be worse for strong Type A leaders because they tend to surround themselves with followers, not peers. Type A leaders are frequently so focused on the mission at hand that they develop the habit of discouraging new information at any time they are not absolutely desperate. That habit tends to chill any flow of new or different information that might come their way. As a result, when Type A leaders finally are desperate enough to ask for help—not much help is around.

God, on the other hand, is not intimidated by Type A people. They, like the rest of us, look more like cranky two year olds in need of a nap than an ogre to be appeased. God loves us even when we've been out there doing our Type A thing, ordering people around and ignoring details until the roof starts to cave in. And just like we love the two year olds in our lives and want to hang around with them even when they babble on about nothing and obsessively clutch their plastic toys; God is always there for us. God is there when we need that extra break, or encouragement to take the next hill or just some time in the quiet presence of someone who loves us and doesn't need to be impressed, managed or placated.

Weak people certainly benefit from a relationship with God. They can be healed from traumas they have experienced and find help to scratch and crawl their way through another day. But it is the strong—trying to leap tall buildings in a single bound, who can really use the help.

Usually strong Type A people have greater propensity, and capacity, to engage in self-destructive behaviors than others. Often our greatest strength can be our greatest weakness. Grit can become stubbornness; self-confidence can become arrogance; intelligence can become disdain; independence can become distance; mercy can become enabling of destructive behavior; truth telling can become blunt unkindness; diplomacy can become lying and avoidance. Every personality trait has a positive and negative spectrum. When we get tired, sick, overwhelmed, stressed out or challenged, our behavior tends to swing over into the negative end of the spectrum.

Type A people generally have bigger personalities with stronger personality traits, and that amplifies the risk of destructive things happening from those lapses over to the dark side of the behavior spectrum. Think Bernie Madoff, Bill Clinton, or Lance Armstrong. They all knew better, but they let their egos overcome their common sense. And the list is endless. Anyone who has spent more than 5 years in corporate America has seen at least one executive fired in disgrace from some kind of indiscretion brought on by ego. The syndrome isn't limited to business, sports and political leaders. Religious leaders, educators, investment bankers and contractors are regularly featured in news articles about people who just got carried away. Outsized egos and misplaced enthusiasm can derail anyone. Millions of people crash and burn from self-inflicted destructive behaviors every year. They all know better, but they still can't see it coming.

Taking out some time each day to cultivate a relationship with God by reading the Bible and praying—even just spending 10 or 15 minutes a day centered on seeking a relationship with God, can be life changing. It is much harder to lie at 10 am, when you were reading the Bible at 6. Just taking that time to pray and articulate what you think, what you are thankful for, and what you need, is centering. Feeling a sense of presence from someone who knows who you are, all your thoughts, good and bad, all your wants, needs, failures and successes;

and who still loves you—lends a sense of perspective. Feeling a sense of being loved for no particular reason makes it easier to get through a day with a lot of people pushing and pulling around you. You become less susceptible to being influenced by praise and criticism from those around you (tempering the praise is really the hard part.) You become less likely to lose your temper and more inclined to listen—and so people around you become more inclined to share information that can keep you out of trouble. A relationship with God can be a key part of keeping a crazy, busy, stressful, high-powered life on track. And if messed up, broken people can see great change and healing; think how much benefit is available for people who are already healthy. The potential is endless.

King David was certainly one example of a very strong person who relied on a relationship with God to recreate himself after not just one, but multiple, epic failures. He survived a decade long manhunt from King Saul before becoming king, multiple wars, a sex scandal, 2 coup attempts, and untold plotting and scheming. He survived it all, not just to remain in power, but to remain a respected and, for the most part, emotionally healthy person. Shortly before his death, while instructing Solomon on what to expect when he became king and the first steps to take to solidify his political standing and power, David started his instruction with these words:

> I am going the way of the earth. Be strong therefore, and show yourself a man. And keep the charge of the Lord your God, to walk in His ways, to keep His statutes, His commandments, His ordinances, and His testimonies, according to what is written in the Law of Moses, that you may succeed in all that you do and wherever you turn, so that the Lord may carry out His promise which He spoke concerning me, saying, 'If your sons are careful of their way, to walk before Me in truth with all their heart and with their soul, you shall not lack a man on throne of Israel.' I Kings 2:2-4.[20]

Solomon did well when he followed that advice, but he ultimately failed as king. Late in his life, Solomon stopped worshipping God and started to worship the foreign gods favored by his many wives and concubines. He faltered as a king and his ego-driven building projects nearly bankrupted the kingdom. When he became king, Israel

---

[20] Note that contrary to our modern perceptions, David thought it was wimpy and unmasculine *not* to follow God. In David's mind, following God's direction was the single most important element of being a good king.

was a state with incredible wealth that is still spoken of today. At his death, the state could barely pay the bills on its building projects and the people were near rebellion over high taxes.

Two rebellions arose very shortly after Solomon's death, resulting in the Kingdom of Israel splitting into two part. The rebellions were prompted when Solomon's son, Rehoboam refused advice to back off of his father's destructive spending habits. Solomon was considered extremely wise in his day and is still described as the wisest man who ever lived, but I remember thinking when I was young and first heard the story that it wasn't all that smart to blow up his life the way he did. Contrast that end with Samson. No one ever called Samson wise. Samson's life was messy, he did some really stupid things, but he maintained his allegiance to God, and that made the difference. In the end he was smarter than Solomon. Type A people get into trouble when they don't follow King David's advice to keep God first.

Zacchaeus is a New Testament example of a strong Type A person who found God, Luke 19:1-10. Of all the people in the New Testament, Zacchaeus is probably the best example of someone who grabbed onto King David's advice and went with it. Zacchaeus was a tax collector, a hated profession in ancient Israel. Tax collectors bid for the position with the Roman rulers. Whoever bid the highest number got the job, and set about collecting whatever they could collect as taxes from an unwilling and resentful population. The tax collector turned in the amount they had bid and kept a cut of the take, and any excess they managed to collect, as payment.

Zacchaeus was rich, and like a lot of rich, high-powered executives, he didn't care much for public opinion.[21] Zacchaeus had heard about Jesus and was very curious to see him. But Zacchaeus was short and couldn't see over the crowds. He ran ahead and climbed a tree to get a look at Jesus. First century businessmen wore long robes and sandals, they were very conscious of their social position, and they didn't run anywhere--ever. Servants ran, not the head of the local IRS. Zacchaeus was the ultimate Type A guy who didn't care what anybody thought. Jesus liked intrepid people, and he liked Zacchaeus. Jesus went over under the sycamore tree where Zacchaeus was perched, hidden in the leaves, and said "Zacchaeus, hurry and come down, for today I must

---

[21] Bible commentators like to characterize Zacchaeus as dishonest, but I think he just had the kind of expedient attitude about money that characterizes corporate America. Why not deal with the Romans and make some money? It was a way up in a society that had extremely strict class structures.

stay at your house". And Zacchaeus climbed down the tree and hosted Jesus and the disciples at his house. Luke 19.

That caused a lot of people in the crowd to grumble about Jesus hanging out with a sinner. Jesus didn't care. Zacchaeus signed on, at full throttle, apparently like he did everything else. In response to the crowd, he said "Behold, Lord, half of my possessions I will give to the poor, and if I have defrauded anyone of anything, I will give back four times as much." That is wholesale conviction[22]. The Bible doesn't have any additional information about Zacchaeus. We don't know what he did next or how he lived the rest of his life. My guess is that he continued to live life at full throttle; but centered around a relationship with God. That is what God has in mind for us-- a Type A positive life lived at full throttle. That is the upside.

---

[22] I think it is also a denial of wholesale fraud. After giving away half his possessions he would have been unable to pay a lot of people back four times what he had taken, and this was not an occasion for hyperbole. In addition, the penalty under the Mosaic Law for stealing was to reimburse twice the stolen amount. He is offering to double the penalty. Repeating or doubling a reference in ancient Israel was a form of emphasis. I think he is admitting his accounting isn't perfect, but strongly denying dishonesty. Zacchaeus was tough and indifferent to public opinion, but he wasn't a cheat.

Chapter Four
What Does God Want From Us?

What does God want from us? This question has plagued mankind for millennia. Once someone becomes convinced that God is real, and is committed to, or at least intrigued by, the idea that they want to relate to God, the next question is How? What does God want?

The disciples came at the question from a Jewish perspective, heavily influenced by their history and context. Israel was firmly under Roman rule at the time of Christ, and it wasn't pretty. The first century historian, Josephus, recounts the events in two works, The Histories, and The Jewish War. Josephus was born around 37 AD, about 5 years after the crucifixion of Christ. He was a Jewish leader at the time of the revolt of the Jews during the reign of Nero—the same period in which Peter was crucified and Paul was beheaded by the Romans. Josephus tried to influence the Jews against the revolt, He was widely reviled at the time for consorting with the enemy, and for betraying his own forces to save himself. Josephus survived the revolt, moved to Rome and made a place for himself among the hierarchy there. Among other things, he occupied himself with writing the history of the Jews. While his accounts of events are often criticized as being shaded toward a Roman view in order to be politically correct for the society in which he lived, the works are considered very valuable, largely accurate histories. The Jewish War, Josephus, Penguin, 1981 revised edition. Even Josephus' cleaned up version of the Roman rule of the Jews is horrific.

The Romans were harsh rulers in many ways. Taxes were high and based mostly on a system of extortion. Captive nations paid the cost of the army that occupied them, as well as financing Rome's expansion and the lavish lifestyle of a small elite. The Hunger Games novels[23] are

---

[23] Hunger Games, Suzanne Collins, Scholastic Press (2008); Catching Fire, Suzanne Collins, Scholastic Press (2009); Mockingjay, Suzanne Collins, Scholastic Press (2010.) The novels follow 16 year old Katniss Everdeen in her fight against the forces of the Capital City of Panem, a futuristic empire in which the districts of the empire have been subjugated to the Capital. The people in the districts starve while the Capital indulges in Bacchanalia-like excesses. Children from each of the districts are forced into a televised competition to the death each year in retribution for a past rebellion. Katniss volunteers for the competition after her younger sister is selected by the lottery to compete. She manages to survive and force the Capital to allow both she and the other representative from her district to survive, making the audience believe he is her boyfriend. She isn't sure herself whether he is her boyfriend or it was all just a good way to survive. That small victory over the Capital's total dominance incentivizes a rebellion of which Katniss is the confused and sometimes hapless symbol. She gets caught up in the dangerous and confusing world of the struggle for power and search for democracy in Panem.

patterned on Rome's excesses and the picture they paint isn't too unrealistic a portrayal of the ancient Romans. The vast majority of the population in Judea scraped by at a subsistence level. Roman soldiers could, and often did, confiscate property and conscript labor. Random, and not so random, beatings, rapes and murder were common, and there was virtually no legal recourse. Offending persons could be conscripted for forced combat or as the victim of certain-death "contests" in the arenas for public amusement, as well as for public torture and execution.

Rome also had a practice of displacing local religion and culture by re-assigning its own gods and holidays in place of the native gods and holidays[24]. For polytheistic cultures, usurping the culture was an issue. It was offensive, but not overwhelming. The Romans were good at supplying "bread and circuses" and it was no great stretch to equate Zeus with Jove, Hera with Juno or Mars with Ares. Their roles and personalities overlapped quite a bit anyway. Often the captured country just added Rome's gods to its own. The practice of later Caesars, including Nero, of declaring themselves gods and demanding worship was also annoying, demeaning and expensive to other cultures. But it was not a large departure from their own culture. The Babylonians and Persians had similar practices. Roman rule was very harsh everywhere and most captured nations eventually accepted the "Romanization" of their world. For ordinary citizens, life tended to resolve itself into a new pattern that was not too dissimilar from their old life as long as they didn't engage in any form of political rebellion and stayed out of the way of soldiers and other authorities.

For the Jews, on the other hand, cultural usurpation was a big problem. Many Jews worshipped multiple gods and followed the culture around them, but devout Jews and the Jewish leadership had an entirely different attitude. Jews worshipped one God, Yahweh, the God of Abraham, Isaac and Jacob. This is the God who brought them out of slavery in Egypt, made them the preeminent power of the Middle East under David and Solomon and sustained them during hundreds of years of occupation and dispersion after the defeat by Babylon-- beginning in about 609 BC and recorded in the Old Testament in the books of 2

---

[24] This is why we celebrate Easter according to the calendar for an ancient fertility holiday instead of at Passover. It is also why we celebrate Christmas at the winter solstice. Scholars agree that Jesus was probably born in spring, most likely sometime in April. When Constantine converted the Roman world to Christianity by decree in the third century, he continued Rome's tradition and used or invented Christian holidays to usurp native ceremonies.

Chronicles, Daniel, Nehemiah and Jeremiah. The Jews regarded themselves as a theocracy. They believed they were directly ruled by God himself, through the intervention of the priests. The priests also served as political leaders of the captive state and interceded with the governors appointed by Rome.

Jewish leadership often tried to cooperate with the Romans to an extent, but the Jews did not accept the Roman gods and reassignment of their holidays. They did not accept the worship of Roman Caesars. They did not acknowledge the right of Rome to tax them. The Jews stubbornly insisted on maintaining their allegiance to the one true God and on maintaining their cultural identity. The Jews were a constant thorn in the side of Rome, and they paid a steep price for it. Lashings, often to death, were common, as was crucifixion—and not just for leading rebellions. Theft, murder, and lesser crimes were punished by death. If someone in power wanted to take over your property, trumped up charges were a perfectly acceptable mode of accomplishing that end. Josephus describes a scene, from the time of the revolt, where crosses filled with victims lined both sides of the road into Jerusalem for several miles. It is difficult to imagine what Josephus left out of his accounts to whitewash the events.

The Jews were looking for a Messiah who would lead them out from under Roman persecution in the same way as the Judges like Samson had been warrior kings before David and Solomon. The Jews were looking for new David to take over the throne, throw Rome out, and reassert Israel's rightful place a world power. The result was a long series of would-be Messiah's seeking to lead a revolt against Rome, and they were harshly punished. There was a particularly persistent revolt that occurred around the time of Jesus birth that had resulted in a particularly brutal reaction from Rome. Hundreds of people were crucified, property confiscated and harsh constraints imposed on everyday life. Many of the religious leaders at the time of Jesus' ministry were personally acquainted with those events. Things had eased a bit by the time Jesus began his ministry and the ruling priests were very focused on preserving the status quo. They placated Rome and carved out a small niche to be able to worship God at the temple   and conduct every day activities with a small measure of autonomy. The priests did not like Messiah wannabes rocking the boat.

That was the world that Jesus entered. From the beginning of his ministry, he did his best to rock the boat. Andrew and Peter were the first to join Jesus. They had been followers of John the Baptist. Andrew met Jesus at his baptism, and heard John proclaim that Jesus was the

Messiah. After Andrew heard this, he went and collected Peter and told him, "We have found the Messiah", John 1:41. John 1:49 records another disciple, Nathanael's, reaction to meeting Jesus. He said, "Rabbi, You are the Son of God; You are the King of Israel". One of the disciples was known as Simon the Zealot. Zealots were a factional political party advocating the overthrow of Rome.

Jesus went out of his way to upset Jewish leadership, calling them "hypocrites" and "white washed tombs" and worse. He publicly twitted Herod about his leadership foibles. He kept performing unexplainable miracles. He ignored the leaders' criticism about honoring the Sabbath rules and associating with undesirables. He drew crowds everywhere he went, and everywhere he went he talked about change. Jewish leadership feared change. They disliked Jesus for the marked lack of homage in his treatment of them; they feared the crowds would incite the Romans to quell the movement—and their comfortable niche; and they decided to find a way to kill Jesus off. John 11.

Despite following Jesus for three years, and Jesus own denial that he had political ambitions, the disciples continued to believe that Jesus was going to establish a kingdom on earth. They had a number of discussions about who would be greatest when that time came. James' and John's mother even got into the fray, asking that her sons be given the seats of honor, at Jesus right and left, when he came into his kingdom. Matthew 20:20-21.

Jesus himself always spoke about his kingdom in non-political terms. Standing on trial in front of Pilate, when questioned whether he claimed to be King of the Jews, Jesus responded: "My kingdom is not of this world. If my kingdom were of this world, then My servants would be fighting that I might not be delivered up to the Jews; but as it is, My kingdom is not of this realm." Pilate responded by asking Jesus if he was indeed a king, and Jesus responded, "Yes you say correctly that I am a king. For this I have been born, and for this I have come into the world, to bear witness to the truth. Everyone who is of the truth hears my voice." To which Pilate famously responded, "What is truth?" and publicly washed his hands of the matter. Pilate turned Jesus over to be crucified to pacify the Jewish leadership and the mob that had formed. They were incensed that Jesus had claimed to be God. Pilate, to the great annoyance of the Jewish leadership, wrote the words "King of the Jews" in three languages on the plaque over Jesus head where the criminal charge was ordinarily inscribed.

The disciples were dazed and confused after Jesus death. The prospect of rescue from Roman rule was over; and they did not understand the idea of a spiritual kingdom. They were not expecting the resurrection. They did not believe the resurrection until Jesus appeared to them after his death. Even after that, they weren't certain what to do with the information. Peter's initial reaction, as the leader of the group, was just to write off the whole experience and go back to fishing. John 21 records the story of Jesus last appearance to a group of 7 of the disciples, including Peter, James and John. Peter had decided to give it up and go back to fishing, and the rest decided to go with him. They fished all night and didn't catch a fish. The next morning, as they were headed back to the beach, Jesus, whom they didn't recognize at the distance, called to them from the beach to let their nets down on the other side of the boat. In a reprise of the first time Jesus called them to ministry, recorded in Luke 5:3-11, they let down their nets and made a huge catch. Finally recognizing Jesus, Peter ditched the catch and the boat and swam to shore to greet Jesus. Jesus repeated, three times, his earlier call on Peter's life to spread the word about Jesus, and Peter never looked back.

Peter spent the rest of his life spreading the news that God had walked the earth. Peter founded the church that has survived to this day, and was crucified himself in Rome some 35 years after Jesus. In fact, all of the remaining 11 original disciples, and Paul, followed that path. Each of them travelling long distances, enduring great persecution, sometimes exile and imprisonment, and, ultimately, death, to convince people that God had walked the earth and wanted to be acknowledged as king of their lives.

God still wants us to acknowledge that he is king of our lives. The question we have is: "what does that look like?" The major issue we have in sorting through this question is that we think of God in human terms—the ultimate Type A person. Usually, through association with human leaders, we think of God as the ultimate Type A negative person: someone to be carefully placated and managed. Our first reaction is that God must want something from us that will detract from our own well-being and self-interest.

When Type A leaders we know want homage, they are seldom nice about it. They are often inconsiderate, demanding, unrealistic and self-absorbed. They expect you to die for them, either figuratively or literally. When people invent their own gods, they usually give the gods similar negative characteristics. In primitive societies, self-mutilation and human sacrifice were common forms of worship. While those practices are long gone, most people still see God as either a demanding figure to be appeased or a distant spiritual force with no real connection to people and little interest in them except to drain whatever they have of value for God's own self-aggrandizement.

Even mainstream Christians tend to view God as weighing whether we have been good enough and done enough good deeds to be accepted. We believe we have to earn God's love and good graces. We tend to believe that our physical rewards in life are a direct consequence of whether we are good enough. If something bad happens we believe we have done something to annoy God, or at least that if we are good enough that God will reward our good behavior and change our situation to suit us. We believe that we will go to Heaven if we are good enough and not otherwise.

We have widely varying views of what "good enough" is. Pretty much everyone believes that Mother Theresa, Billy Graham, and their own mother or grandmother, is good enough to get to Heaven. After that, the system breaks down. Some people believe that pretty much everyone goes to Heaven. Some people believe that only the saintly few go to Heaven. And what about all that time spent here on Earth? What are we supposed to be doing? Do we have to go to Africa and preach to the masses? Do we have to take a vow of poverty and work for the church? Is that witch at the local PTA meeting really going to Heaven? Isn't enduring yet another soccer game or Boy Scout camping trip enough? What does God want from nice, normal people today?

What God wants is really much simpler, and much more positive than all that stuff. God wants your attention. Most of us don't pay much attention to God until something goes wrong. God actually expects to hear from us on a daily basis. The ancient Jewish law was a very detailed behavioral code that governed every aspect of life. Read Leviticus and Deuteronomy sometime; they are mind-numbing. The Jewish leadership had added to the law, breaking up the basic commandments into a very detailed series of requirements, presumably in a misguided attempt to clear up any confusion about the requirements. Attempting to follow the law kept God in the forefront of one's mind and life. The law ran through every aspect of daily Jewish life in the first century. It covered everything from what one ate and wore to the way daily activities were conducted. It was impossible to fully conform to all aspects of the law and violations required repentance and atonement. The law wasn't intended as something to shame people because they couldn't fully comply—or at least God's version wasn't. It was intended to keep order in society and keep God as part of the focus.

For the most part, violating the law was not cause for severe punishment, nor was it a long term blight on one's "permanent record." When you violated one of the tenants of the Jewish law, you either washed or sacrificed an animal at the temple. If you had wronged another person, you apologized and reimbursed the loss. After doing that, you were square with God and moved on. A few things that were destructive to society, like violent crimes and adultery, had much more stringent penalties, including being stoned to death. Blasphemy also carried the death penalty (hence the reaction of the mob to Jesus' claim to be God.)

While we aren't concerned today about mixing linen and wool in our fabrics (Leviticus 19:19—no clue what that rule was about), a review of the Law does illustrate the depth of commitment God expects. God really expects that our thought processes and behavior will be centered around his opinions about what we should be doing. Fortunately, although God does expect our attention, he isn't the Type A negative personality we are used to. God is more like a concerned parent. He wants us to behave in positive ways that are conducive to our own well-being and that of our neighbors on the planet. The Ten Commandments, given to the Israelites thousands of years ago, are still the best summary of what God wants. Recorded in Deuteronomy 5:6-21, they can be summarized this way:

1. Honor God and make him first in your life.

2. Don't worship other gods or other things in place of God.

3. Don't misuse God's name as a swear word. God is not someone to be taken lightly or demeaned.

4. Remember to take out one day every week to rest and remember your connection to God.

5. Respect your parents. Take care of them when they get old.

6. Don't murder.

7. Don't sleep with anyone you aren't married to.

8. Don't steal.

9. Don't lie.

10. Don't be envious and resentful of what other people have. Seek contentment in your attitude.

In Mark 12: 29-31, Jesus condensed the list even further—to two basic rules. He said, "Love the Lord your God with all your heart, and with all our soul and with all your mind, and with all your strength. The second is this, you shall love your neighbor as yourself" –what we refer to as the "Golden Rule". The first four of the Ten Commandments can be folded into Jesus' first command, and the last six of the Ten Commandments can be folded into the second command.

Note that Jesus never suggests we ask the question, "What would Jesus do?" We don't think like Jesus and there is no real point in trying to figure that out. Instead the question is the same question your mother asked when you were young, "How would you feel if your friend treated you that way?" If we continue to manage our behavior by applying the Golden Rule, we will be much more considerate and understanding of those around us.

The six Commandments that deal with other people have obvious value in improving our interpersonal relationships. None of us like to be on the receiving end of the proscribed behaviors. Those behaviors reduce trust, increase stress and increase conflict. The "don't sleep around" rule is somewhat in disrepute in our society, but with AIDS and the high incidence of casual sex, divorce and infidelity—and all the emotional damage those practices carry with them--you might want to consider it. Whenever any of the Big 10 seem like a bad plan and not conducive to your best interest, think about what it would be like to be on the receiving end of that behavior—and what would happen if you got caught. If you wouldn't want someone to treat you that way, stop and reconsider. You are likely to make much healthier choices.

Many of us, really most of us, have reduced religion to the second of Jesus' commands—to treat ourselves and our neighbors well. Treating ourselves and others with respect and consideration is good. We should do that. But, in Jesus' teaching, that rule is second. The first rule is to love God. Christianity is not, at its core, a system of ethics for personal interrelationships. It is about having a relationship with God.

The primary focus is first to love God, just as God has committed to love us. When we have the relationship with God, our lives change and we start to implement the second rule of loving others out of a desire to help them rather than an obligation to help them. As our own relationship with God makes us healthier and more open to new adventures, we naturally improve our treatment of others. Jumping ahead to the second command before you have engaged with God, trying to behave as if we love others when we are really bored and frustrated dealing with them; will just make you tired and cranky. You will turn into one of those zombie Christians running around churches making everyone a little nuts.

2 Corinthians 3:17-18 puts it this way: "Now the Lord is the Spirit, and where the Spirit of the Lord is, there is freedom. And we, who with unveiled faces all reflect the Lord's glory, are being transformed into his likeness with ever-increasing glory, which comes from the Lord, who is the Spirit". Okay that is a little circular, but what it says is that when we determine to include God in our life, he enters into a relationship with us, and that changes us to be more like him— loving and patient and kind—and we find freedom and health. Most of us have it backwards, we try to reach God by being nice to other people. That doesn't work. Other people aren't all that loveable. You can't love others if you don't first love God.

So, let's say we have decided to give this a whirl and "love God". Our question again is: "What does loving God look like?" We don't see God; we don't hear God; God does not come over for dinner and a movie or join the group for a drink after work. How do you "love" a spirit?

Loving and respecting God is simpler than it seems. The first three commandments actually get met just by trying to keep in mind that you want to keep the commandments. Loving God and making him a center of our lives does not require some weird or extraordinary behavior. We don't need to pick up and move to Africa. We just need to keep in mind that we'd like God to be part of our lives on an everyday basis. Really, there is nothing weird about any of this. For example, that rule about resting one day a week is very helpful to maintain the physical and mental reserves it takes to actually care about other people and handle our lives in a constructive way.

Since God is real, if we make a choice to want to relate to him, he is there. He has already made the decision that he wants to relate to us—he is just waiting for us to show up. That is the essence of what God wants from us—some face time when we acknowledge his existence and relevance.

A lot of us get bogged down at this point, because we were taught that one relates to God by following church rituals, and we have never connected to God through a church ritual. The church rituals we are acquainted with were meaningless, boring or seemed faintly—or very—ridiculous. So we conclude that God isn't real, or that God isn't interested in us or that this whole Christianity thing doesn't work except for a few "religious nuts". Actually the problem is not with God. The problem is with the premise that religious rituals are the only way to relate to God; and the corollary that the religious rituals we have experienced are the appropriate way to approach God. For example, I know a number of people who believe that being baptized, either as an infant or adult, regardless of whether one actually has any faith or interest in God—is somehow binding on God. Many people believe that reading "prayers" which are nothing more than lovely poems to which the reciter has no emotional connection, is a necessary form of worship that God demands[25]. Many people believe that standing in church mouthing the words to an ancient hymn that makes no sense, played poorly on an out of tune organ, is worship.

This is just not the case. These things are not connections to God and they are not worship. God is not remotely co-terminous with, or controlled by, church rituals. I am not discounting church as a means of connection with God. A community of believers can be an excellent source of encouragement and affirmation. Hebrews 10:24-25 recommends church strongly as a means of encouraging one another and learning from well informed leaders. I think good churches are an important part of developing in a relationship with God—churches just don't *define* God. (I am also suggesting that many churches could do a MUCH better job of presenting Christian beliefs in a way that makes it clear those beliefs are relevant and valuable.)

---

[25] For example, when Pope Francis greeted the faithful on St. Peter's Square the day his papacy was announced, he reached out to pray a blessing on Pope Emeritus Benedict. Pope Francis seems like a really wonderful person, and he's turning out to be a great Pope. Blessing Pope Emeritus Benedict was a kind, honorable and appropriate choice. But then Pope Francis, along with the crowd, recited the Lord's Prayer (the "Our Father") and the "Hail Mary", neither of which mention Pope Emeritus Benedict, nor say anything about commending his service or blessing his life. When you talk to a real person, you use words that convey what you intend to say, you don't recite a beautiful poem and walk away thinking you have communicated with them. If your six year old wanted lunch and came up to you and recited the Our Father; and you, wanting to express how much you loved your child, responded with a Hail Mary; what would that accomplish? While God knows our thoughts, he still expects the courtesy of actually communicating what we think.

I prefer large churches with contemporary services, but people have different, equally valuable, approaches to genuine worship in a church setting. For some people, liturgy and ritual hold deep meaning and are an extremely valuable way for them to feel connected with God in a deeply personal way. Some people even find deep meaning in reciting form prayers—I don't know how, but they do. The differences in connection styles has attracted a lot of discussion in church circles. People have different "love languages". Our love languages reflect our communication styles and personality make ups. Those methods of communication are wired into our personalities and permeate our relationship styles. Gary 'Chapman's books, Five Love Languages, Moody Publishing, reprint (2009) and God Speaks Your Love Language Northfield Publishing, (2009) are classic discussions of the subject. We each connect with other people and with God in our own relationship "language".

God is multi-lingual. He connects in all the love languages and communication styles—after all he invented them all and declared them "good". He understands that we have different ways of relating, and is open to that. Some things are still essential, however, or we would be creating our own god in our own image. God is real and definite, and we can't change him. It is necessary to pray and to read the Bible to get a sense of what God is really like. But there is a lot of flexibility in other ways we relate. One book on the subject is Sacred Pathways by Gary Thomas, Zondervan, 2000. He describes several types of people and how they are likely to best relate to God. Naturalists feel connected to God when they are in nature, Ascetics feel close to God through contemplation, Activists through social change, etc. Thomas lists nine different personality types. Other books on the subject focus on activities. For example, some people feel very connected to God through music and participating in private or congregational singing. For some people being alone and spending time reading or journaling their thoughts is very valuable. Others go totally nuts if left alone with a blank piece of paper and prefer to engage in group discussions and study. The point is: all of these things are just fine. Just try some means of directly connecting with God that sounds like it would be interesting and see how it goes.

Any method of connecting with God has to be consistent with who and what God is. You can't get better acquainted with God when you are out carousing--looking for a hook-up or a fight--because God isn't going to join in with an activity that is unhealthy for you. Getting better acquainted with God as a person has to be the first step to developing a real connection.

Start with the Bible. It isn't enough to let other people tell you what it says. See for yourself, it isn't as complicated as you have been told it is. In fact, you should be a little wary of anyone who tells you not to bother reading the Bible, or that you need someone to interpret it for you. Most of the people Jesus dealt with directly had a very basic education. They were literate, but they didn't have advanced degrees in theology. If they could understand Jesus, so can you.

For anyone new to reading the Bible, pick a translation that uses modern language, like the New International version or the New American Standard version. Start with one of the Gospels: Matthew, Mark, Luke or John. Those four books are each the story of Jesus' life and ministry and were written by four of the people who accompanied him at the time. They are short and easy to understand. You can read through one of the Gospels in about a week reading just 15 minutes a day. Reading the Gospels gives you a very clear picture of who Jesus is and what he is like. After that, try the rest of the New Testament—and just see how it goes. Don't get discouraged if some of it doesn't seem to make that much sense (a lot of Revelations, for example, is hotly debated by Biblical scholars and I still don't understand most of it.) The details aren't all that important the first time around, just try to get a sense of who God is.

Remember that the letters (books like Romans and Corinthians) were written by the disciples to early church congregations spread around the Middle East. Those books were written mostly by Paul and Peter to real people starting little church congregations in their homes. The letters are not dissertations in theology. The letters respond to things that were going on at the time in those particular congregations. Sometimes the context is given and sometimes the context is too cryptic to tell exactly what concerns those congregations had. The letters are not intended to say anything different than Jesus said—so if you get confused by something, refer back to the Gospels to see what Jesus said on the subject.

Then pray. For anyone new to prayer, there just aren't any rules. Just talk to God like you would anyone else. Really, you aren't going to shock or offend him; he has heard it all before. Hebrews 4:13 says" And there is no creature hidden from his sight, but all things are open and laid bare to the eyes of Him with whom we have to do". And just a few verses later, in Hebrews 4:16, it says "Let us therefore draw near with confidence to the throne of grace, that we may receive mercy and may find grace to help in time of need." God just likes to hear from you. On the other hand, reciting poems that have no meaning for you and calling it "prayer" is discouraged. Matthew 6: 5 says, "and when you pray, you are not to be hypocrites; for they love to stand and pray in the synagogues and on the street corners, in order to be heard by men. Truly, I say to you, they have their reward in full." And Matthew 6:7-8 says, "And when you are praying, do not use meaningless repetitions, as the Gentiles do, for they suppose that they will be heard for their many words. Therefore, do not be like them, for your Father knows what you need before you ask Him."

Jesus goes on to give the model prayer—we call it the "Lord's Prayer" or the "Our Father". The model prayer was not intended as a poem to be recited endlessly, but as a format to explain how to pray. We acknowledge God is there and listening and is God. We express that we want God to be our personal God and be part of our lives. We ask for the things we need and want, for ourselves, our family, our friends and the larger world. We ask forgiveness for the less than desirable things we have done, and we offer it to those of our acquaintance who didn't follow the Golden Rule that day where we were concerned. God is a real person, just talk to him.

Prayer isn't meant to be limited to formal situations or one time during the day. 1 Thessalonians 5:17 says, "Pray without ceasing." That means just check in with God as you go through the day. Notice how beautiful the sky is. Thank God for your food. I'm not ashamed to say I pray for parking places when I'm in a hurry—and I end up with some really good parking places way too often to be accounted for by coincidence. You can pray silently with your eyes wide open as well as you can pray on your knees in church. I pray for patience when I'm in meetings with other lawyers or stuck in traffic. I thank God for Van's Frozen Custard---a one-of-a-kind little place in East Dundee Illinois. Bill Hybels' book "Too Busy Not to Pray", Inter-Varsity Press originally published in 1988 with a 20th anniversary edition released in 2008, is a concise, practical explanation of the power of prayer and how to incorporate prayer into your life. But, really, just pray—it isn't complicated.

Those two activities, reading the Bible and praying, are the most important things you can do to bring God into your life in a real way. The remaining thing you need to do is to make an honest effort to incorporate your beliefs into your activities. This does *not* mean that you make up a list of a bunch of things you have to do to impress God or to clean up your act. It just means that you try to keep in mind that God wants you to be nice to people and put that into action. After all, you can say you believe in exercise, but unless you actually go out and walk or run, or do yoga, or whatever, you aren't actually someone who exercises. You won't see any of the benefits of exercise just by saying you believe in exercise. A relationship with God is the same. Saying you believe it is fine, but you won't be in a relationship with God, and won't see any benefits, until you put your beliefs into action.

Jesus told a story in Mathew 21:28-31, when he was talking to the religious leaders, to illustrate the concept. Jesus asked the religious leaders:

> "But what do you think? A man had two sons, and he came to the first and said, 'Son, go work today in the vineyard.' And he answered and said, "I will, sir' and he did not go. And he came to the second and said the same thing. But he answered and said, "I will not'; yet afterward he regretted it and went. Which of the two did the will of his father? They [the religious leaders] said, 'The latter son'. Jesus said to them, "Truly I say to you that the tax gatherers and harlots will get into the kingdom of God before you. For John [the Baptist] came to you in the way of righteousness and you did not believe him; but the tax gatherers and harlots did believe him; and you, seeing this, did not even feel remorse afterward so as to believe him."

You can see why the religious leaders were not big fans of Jesus. They were VERY annoyed by this story, but the point is simple. Talk all you want, but unless you actually attempt to implement patience and kindness, you haven't really committed to making God your personal God.

God keeps the bar low. This is not complicated or difficult. Just as you don't have to do Iron Man competitions to benefit from exercise, you don't have to do a bunch of bizarre things to experience a relationship with God. Start small. Check out the Big Ten above and keep those in mind. When you feel like telling a lie or blaming someone else to cover up some mistake you made. Stop and think. Take responsibility for your actions, apologize if it was personal, and correct the error. Call your mom, and help her out if she needs help. Try to consider how your spouse, children, extended family, friends and co-workers like to be treated. Be considerate of people you love. Communicate in a civil manner and say "I love you" out loud when that is what you mean. Let the small stuff slide. If you are holding a grudge about something, try to forgive and move on. Pray about these things as you do them. Being patient with a stubborn 2 year old or a stubborn Vice President is not easy. You won't do it perfectly—just keep in mind that you actually want to act in a kind manner. Make an effort, and you will get better at it over time.

What happens is amazing. You start to experience two things. One is the natural result of treating people around you like they matter. People respond positively to positive treatment and a positive attitude. It's contagious—they start treating you more kindly and with more honesty. This works particularly well with people who love you already. It can freak out people who don't like you and think of you as an enemy, so proceed with caution and don't expect reciprocity from your enemies. But a positive attitude toward your enemies will still have a positive effect in your life. The overall result is more honest, more open, more civil relationships. You will experience less strife and more peace (except for the freaked out enemies. They take a long time to come around. Some of them just keep getting more and more freaked out the nicer you are—that's kind of fun too.) You will experience joy and peace and love, and you will want to be kinder, more honest and more loving. The effect snowballs in your life—the results aren't the result of hard work, they just flow.

The second thing you experience is an increased awareness of the presence and love of God. This is hard to explain. You will feel loved and a sense of companionship with a presence that you know is somehow real. You will be much less likely to feel lonely, or even to feel alone. You will be less afraid. The presence, and this is God, is warm and very positive. There is an energy flow that is life-giving. Again this is not something weird. You will not hear voices, you will not see God, you will not see angels and you will not turn into someone strange or unpleasant. You will feel like yourself, only calmer and kinder and more fulfilled than you had anticipated feeling. You will want to have a greater association with the positive life force of God.

This is where the pathways or love languages come in. Once you start feeling like you would like to have a more in-depth experience with God, start setting aside some time, maybe just 15 or 20 minutes a day, to more actively seek out God's presence. That may be a walk outside, some time spent journaling, hand weeding the yard instead of using herbicides, or volunteering at a local food pantry. Just take a little bit of time and set it aside and say to God that you would like to feel more connection to him during that time.

As you become more connected with God, your increased health and reduced stress will increase your capacity to connect with other people beyond those you already know and love. As your personal

106

relationships improve and become more functional, you will find that you start to be more concerned about people beyond your immediate sphere. The problems facing under-resourced people start to matter more. People with a poverty attitude aren't quite so annoying. It occurs to you that reducing waste of our natural resources is a good idea and not as much trouble as you thought it would be. Go with those impulses. Volunteer somewhere in a way that suits your temperament. You can volunteer at your local Salvation Army, Boys and Girls Club, food pantry or open space support group. You can serve on the board of a community development organization or help the single mom down the street rake the leaves and shovel the snow off her front steps. Your concern and heart for others will grow, and you will enjoy doing these things. If you don't enjoy doing what you are doing, do something else. If you aren't developing actual relationships with the people you are serving, do something else. Serving others is not a penance, and it is not a top-down activity between a superior and a subordinate. Serving others is intended to be an exercise in community.

There is one more thing that will make a major difference in your ability to connect with God. God wants to have a primary place in our consciousness and in our behavior. The biggest single indicator of our priorities is how we spend money. Everything we do costs money, and none of us—or very few of us—have an unlimited supply of money. We have limited funds (and limited time) and we have no choice except to prioritize what is important to us and spend our money and our time on those things. Whatever we think our priorities are, our real priorities are reflected in how we spend money. Besides spending time with God, God wants you to spend a tenth of your income—a tithe— on his priorities and he wants you to do that before you do anything else with the money.

The Bible is clear on this point. Tithing was an important element of the law. Deuteronomy 13:22 says, "You shall surely tithe all the produce from what you sow, which comes from the field every year." In an agrarian society, produce of the land was income. Malachi 3:8-10 is blindingly clear.

> "How will a man rob God? Yet you are robbing Me!
> But you say, 'How have we robbed you?' In tithes
> and offerings. You are cursed with a curse, for you
> are robbing Me, the whole nation of you. Bring the
> whole tithe into the storehouse, so that there may be
> food in My house, and test Me now in this," says the
> Lord of hosts. 'if I will not open for you the windows

of Heaven, and pour out for you a blessing until it overflows."

Tithing is not just an Old Testament thing, but again, it isn't some rule or hoop to jump through. God is looking for commitment on our part. Jesus spoke about tithing several times. Once was to the religious leaders, and he criticized them for turning tithing into an empty ritual. In Matthew 23:23 he states, "Woe to you, scribes and Pharisees, hypocrites! For you tithe mint and dill and cummin, and have neglected the weightier provisions of the law, justice and mercy and faithfulness; but this you should have done without neglecting the others." Another time, talking to a rich young man who wanted to know what good things he needed to do in order to be justified before God, Jesus made the point that God's place in our life has to be above our money's place in our life. Matthew 19:16-26 recounts the episode. Jesus tells the man to obey the commandments, the man says he has obeyed all the commandments from his youth (this is a bit of self-delusion, no one actually keeps all the commandments). Jesus looked at him, and Mark 10:21 says "felt a love for him" and told him in order to be complete, he should sell his possessions and give the money to the poor. The man left, disappointed, because giving up his wealth was too high a price to pay for redemption.

The last of Jesus' comments is recorded in Mark 12:43. Jesus was watching people put their tithes and offerings into the offering box at the temple. Some people put in a lot, others less, but one poor widow, put in two very small coins, worth about a penny in total. Jesus commended her saying," Truly I say to you, this poor widow put in more than all the contributors to the treasury. For they all put in out of their surplus, but she, out of her poverty, put in all she owned, all she had to live on."

Jesus is not directing us in the stories of the rich young man and the poor widow to donate all of our money all of the time. If we did that, we wouldn't be able to support ourselves and our families. The Bible has a lot of very practical advice about working hard to earn money, to save money, to pay our bills, and to take care of our families. The book of Proverbs is the original budget manual. 1 Timothy 5:8 says that failing (willfully) to provide for your family is a "denial of the faith". 2 Thessalonians 3:10 says that whoever won't work (willfully) shouldn't be provided with food. God expects us to work, manage our money and take care of ourselves and our family. God is very practical.

God does want our attachment to him to rank above our attachment to money. He does want us to tithe, and what's more, he wants us to do it cheerfully. In 2 Corinthians 9, Paul is encouraging the church at Corinth to send a gift and to help the poor. Verse 7 says, "Let each one do just as he has purposed in his heart; not grudgingly or under compulsion; for God loves a cheerful giver." When Jesus talked about the religious leaders making a big show of their donations, he said they already had their reward, but that the appropriate attitude was to give quietly, not for show, but as a way to worship God.

Giving away money has an almost immediate effect on our internal attitudes. We tend to hold on tightly to money, to think there isn't enough and that we can't possibly give any away, or at least not a tenth. That seems outrageous. For people with higher incomes, the amount seems even more outrageous. Research indicates that charitable giving actually decreases as a percentage of income as income increases, until income reaches upper class levels. The more money we have, the tighter its hold on us becomes. In addition, many of us don't trust churches with our money. Most of us believe the church is just teaching this stuff to get into our pockets and that the church isn't living in the real world or just wastes the money anyway.

When we tithe, we have to let go of something we really want to keep. When we let go of money, it loses that hold on us. We are less afraid and surprisingly, we are more inclined to feel like we have enough. Our sense of peace and security increases rather than decreases. When we put God first, and click the tithe button before we click the mortgage button, we also increase our connection with God. The flow of contact and sense of relationship with God increases. Tithing will require some adjustments in your spending habits, and you might need to work up to it. If you can't cut a tithe check (or sign up for a debit card payment) cheerfully, then send in whatever amount of money you can cheerfully give. After nearly 30 years of tithing, I can say the discipline you learn by tithing is invaluable in learning to handle money constructively.

It is also gratifying to see the effect money can have to improve the lives of others. Even small gifts can make a huge difference to people who are struggling. For about $1.75 a day you can help feed a family in the third world *and* send their children to school so that they have a chance at a future. Things cost more in this country, but a single mom would really appreciate a $50 gas card. It is amazing how even a small amount of money can make a big difference to someone in a very practical way.

Try tithing—if it doesn't work for you, you can always stop. You will be amazed at the positive effect giving away money has on your life. If you aren't associated with a church, or if you don't like your church or don't like what they do with money, then give the money to someone else. Just give away some money. Don't send it to me. Don't send it to an evangelist on late night TV. Pick out a cause that touches your heart and serves others: human trafficking intervention, relief for disadvantaged children in the US or abroad, community development, disaster relief, ELS classes for immigrants, environmental conservation or your unemployed neighbor's mortgage or grocery bill. If you aren't personally connected with the organization, check it out on GuideStar.org—an organization that investigates and rates charities on their economic effectiveness. Send a donation and don't ask for a T-shirt or a plaque. Watch what happens. Your heart will grow and your life will change.

All God really wants is to be treated like a real person, someone who exists and who matters to you on a personal level. God knows who we are, what we are really like, and what we really think. Saying he matters is not going to do it; he has to actually matter. This is real, so we need to act on our intent to have a relationship with God by how we use our time to make an effort to find out about God, by how we treat others, and by how we spend our money. Nothing weird, just pay some attention to God in your daily life.

The result of a relationship with God is the upside. We gain increased joy, peace and strength. More than that, the result is a sense of connection with the enormously positive life force of God.

Chapter Five
How Does the Upside Work?

How will that connection with God actually change our lives? It should be obvious that Christianity is not some magic panacea. Christians have all the usual ups and downs of life. Christians die, get into car accidents, suffer from illness, get caught in floods and fires, and have bad hair days just like anyone else. Sometimes being a Christian can be an active disadvantage. In some parts of the world Christians are persecuted for their faith. For two centuries Christians were persecuted as blasphemers and rebels by both the Jewish culture from which they rose and the Roman Empire. In a number of countries today, Christianity is still a capital offense. In 2001, David B. Barrett and his colleague Todd M. Johnson started collecting statistics on martyrs. In their seminal work *World Christian Trends AD 30 – AD 2200* (Pasadena: William Carey Library, 2001), they concluded that up to the year 2000 there had been some 70 million Christian martyrs, of which 45 million were concentrated in the 20th century. Current estimates, as of 2011, are that approximately 105,000 Christians are killed each year for their faith.

It is highly unlikely that anyone in America is going to be martyred for their faith. The worst thing that will happen is that someone will sneer at you for being naive. But the absence of any "magic genie effect" from Christianity raises a question for many of us. How can anyone say that Christianity is better than some other religion or that it provides real benefits, in the face of the realities of life? That is an excellent question because the circumstances of your life will not change when you decide to cultivate a relationship with God. A relationship with God will not prevent the normal ups and downs of life. In some cases, the circumstances of your life will get worse. People you know and like are very apt to question your decision. People whose respect you want are likely to decide you have gone off the deep end. Some people will think you are naïve or less intelligent than they had thought you were. In some social, political or religious circles, the consequences will be more serious. You may even be ostracized from certain relationships. What benefit is there in a relationship with God that outweighs those risks?

The chief benefit of developing a relationship with God is that, since God is real, you aren't alone when you have to face your life. Those people you are worried about don't stop you from feeling alone. Often the demands from those people that we follow the social conventions of our circle, and their criticism when we fail to follow the rules, is the thing that makes us feel alone. Not being alone is a huge thing. It changes your risk evaluation. More than 20 years of research studies have consistently shown that human beings are less afraid and less stressed when they face challenges with other people. The closer the relationship they have with their partner, the more comfort they gain from the companionship. The military recognizes the value of community. It uses the buddy system, pairing up soldiers to look after one another. The military will even make an effort to keep friends together who enlist together and ask for the buddy system. It isn't guaranteed, but friends can typically stay together at least through their initial training and first assignments. That companionship increases the recruits' success rate.

Anyone who has been to a family funeral or travelled to a strange place knows the value of having someone you know along. Having God as part of your life has that same effect. When you feel God with you, you have more confidence and less stress facing life's challenges. You aren't alone and you are with someone who is strong and encouraging. The unknown becomes less of a threat and more of an adventure.

A relationship with God doesn't have the same concreteness as going on a road trip with your sister; but over time, the sense of the presence of God can become more real and very comforting. It changes your attitude, and attitude is everything. To survive any challenge, there is always some action required. If you are sick, you need to manage the medical treatments. If you are out of work, it's all those resumes and interviews. Dealing with a teenager or a bad boss requires keeping your temper and maintaining an even tone in your conversations. The more stressed out and afraid you are, the less likely it is that you will take the actions necessary to improve your situation. It is also less likely that you will be effective when you do take action. I've seen stressed out candidates for local political office virtually order people to vote for them—that doesn't work. Going into a job interview and talking about needing a job because you are behind in your mortgage is a bad idea. You get the picture. The more stressful the situation, the more effective your actions have to be to survive the crisis. Positive mental attitude is key.

A relationship with God can give you a positive mental attitude. In Philippians 4:6-7, Paul advises, "Be anxious for nothing, but in everything by prayer and supplication with thanksgiving let your requests be made known to God. And the peace of God which surpasses all comprehension, shall guard your hearts and your minds in

Christ Jesus." Paul was in prison when he wrote those words, or at least under house arrest. It was a year or so after Nero became emperor of Rome, and a few years before Paul was killed by Nero for his faith. Philippians is a short book, it is a letter to the church at Philippi, and only a few pages long. It is one of the most positive books in the Bible. Paul shows no stress whatsoever at his situation. We say that isn't normal, but the point is, such peace can be normal in your life. And peace like that makes you more effective at coping with both normal and abnormal stresses in life. Paul was an enormously effective leader, even in prison. Not only did he convert a number of his guards; but he wrote letters to many of the churches he had started that helped them and form much of our current New Testament. Positive mental attitude made the difference.

Many people have demonstrated this kind of peace, both Christian and non-Christian. It is actually more common than people imagine to choose positive behaviors in the face of stress—or at least in the face of disasters. A 2012 article in Time magazine chronicled research showing that people tend to pull together and be more positive in the face of disasters than one might imagine. We think disasters are an opportunity to observe people behaving in selfish modes out of an instinct for self-preservation—looting and rioting for example, but the opposite is often the case. *How Disasters Bring out Our Kindness,* Maia Szalavitz, Time, Oct. 31, 2012. This is true whether or not the people involved are Christians, but religious affiliation is a significant factor in those choices. Dr. Harold Koenig, Director of the Duke University Center for Spirituality, Theology and Heath, has written extensively on the positive correlation between mental health, peace, kindness and religious commitment (although not specifically Christian religious commitment.)

Peace, and joy, and the other fruits of the spirit, are the result of choices that you make. When a Tanzanian priest was shot in the head in February 2013 by two men on a motorcycle who objected to his Christian affiliation, the bishops of the local church called for peace rather than retaliation. catholicnewsagency.com/news Feb. 22, 2013. The local Muslim and political leadership joined in that call to peace. Tanzania has traditionally had peaceful relationships between its minority Christian population and the majority Muslim culture, but recent developments emanating from the Arab Spring of 2011 have caused tensions to develop. It would be easy to call for retribution; but the bishops chose peace.

It would be tempting to attempt to draw a distinction between Christians as a whole and other religions as a whole. One could cite, for example, the recent string of riots and cries for government action when a citizen of the Netherlands posted a derogatory cartoon about Mohammad on the internet, or the fatwa calling for the death of author Salmon Rushdie, or conflicts between Buddhists, Hindus and Muslims in India. The truth, however, would require that one acknowledge the Crusades, the Christian church's too-long silence in the face of Nazi genocide, claims that AIDS is God's retribution for sin, jingoistic internet calls for violence against mosques and Muslims, rants against homosexuals, and any number of other not very peaceful and not very kind positions that the church and church leaders have espoused.

I don't believe we can fairly draw the conclusion that religion alone—any religion, including Christianity, can reliably produce joy, peace and satisfaction in one's life. Any church that mixes religion and politics has a great deal of difficulty separating the two and will tend to equate its own political will with God's will.[26] That is never going to produce peace, on either an individual or societal level. Historically, the track record of combined church/state structures is dismal at producing love, joy or peace at any level.

Even churches without political overtones suffer from a glut of rituals and conventions that often replace real interaction with God, or even between people. One of the premises of this book is that the Christian church is messed up. Frankly other religions are messed up too. "Groupthink"—the tendency of people acting in groups to go along with the crowd even when they are convinced the crowd action is entirely wrong—is alive and well in any organized religion. Groupthink, bad enough in a corporate or social setting, is frequently reinforced by calls by leadership to adhere to "God's will"—as interpreted by leadership. Failures to adhere to the social norms are described as affronts to God. Social rituals, political or religious, have nothing to do with God. No set of rituals will give you peace. No religion can give you peace. Ethics, while a very good thing, will not give you peace.

---

[26] That is the basis for terrorist acts committed in the name of religion—really terrorism is about political power and money—it has nothing to do with anyone's god or religion. The pawns who sacrifice themselves in terrorist activities may be true believers—but the "religious" leaders who send them are too familiar with climbing the rungs of the institutional leadership ladder not to understand the centrality of the acquisition of personal power as a prime motive. They may be committed to the goals they want to achieve with that power, but they are also committed to personal, political power.

The truth is that peace and joy are very personal choices. They are the result of a very personal relationship between you and God. Only God can give you the "fruits of the spirit"—love, joy, peace, patience, kindness, goodness, faithfulness, gentleness and self-control. Those things are the upside, and they can change the quality of your life. You don't need to be Christian to behave well, be a nice person or even obtain some measure of peace and joy, but you won't ever get to the upside without a relationship with God. This is difficult to explain, but a relationship with God multiples your opportunities for positive benefit, and, more importantly, multiples the availability of those positive benefits. God is real and he has a real effect. You need to engage in a relationship with God to experience the effect of a relationship with God. That relationship depends on the access to God made available by Jesus and the freedom that accompanies the presence of the "Spirit of the Lord." Everything else is just ethics and religion—and those won't change your life.

There is a difference between making moral choices based on a developing relationship with God and making moral choices based on conscience or culture or sheer will. Those reasons are good, but choices based on culture will not give you freedom. In fact, making choices for the sake of culture or ethics can be exhausting. Choosing positive behaviors because a relationship with God has increased your capacity to love others is entirely different and not at all exhausting. Those choices are the *result* of changes in our attitude, and those choices are easy and invigorating. Those choices don't seem like choices at all—you just kind of wander around doing things you want to do, and positive results flow out of positive actions and positive attitude.

Peace and joy, and the other fruits of the spirit—all the benefits of a relationship with God, grow out of what my dad used to refer to as "going with the flow". Things happen. Things always happen. You "put one foot in front of the other" and keep moving forward until you get to the goal. You don't waste time lamenting unfortunate and unpleasant things that happen. You don't say "why me?" You don't permit your personal sense of worth to be derailed by circumstance or others' nastiness or insecurities. You notice that lightning is beautiful when you get stuck in a thunderstorm. You look at your awful, backstabbing boss and your primary reaction is that he must be very afraid of something. This is the "peace that passes understanding'. It only comes from God. Peace is normal, or it can be—and it's very pleasant.

The fruits of the spirit are independent of our personal circumstances, not the result of our circumstances. Joy is not happiness.

Happiness is situational and can be difficult to hang onto. Joy is a God-given spark within that lights up long, dark nights. The fruits of the spirit lead our circumstances and can change not only us, but others around us. There aren't other words that illustrate the effect of the other fruits of the spirit as well as the difference between happiness and joy, but that illustration gives you an idea of the concept.

Fruits of the spirit are not just fleeting emotional reactions—they are gradual, permanent attitude adjustments. It is difficult to explain the difference between mere emotional reactions and the connection to the life force of God that results in emotional growth unless you have an experience of association with a real, living God. Emotions come and go, but God is a constant, dependable source of confidence. God is a life force that changes how we react to our circumstances.

When our emotional growth causes us to react positively to our circumstances we push to positively change the environment in which we find ourselves. As a result, we will often experience a positive change in circumstances as well. But even if the circumstances don't change, our experience of those circumstances will. My friend who died of cancer a few months ago died without fear. She was ready to be free of pain, but more curious than anything else about what the next life would hold. She had been going through life with God for a very long time. She had a "whatever" attitude about a lot of things. She looked forward to life, and finally to death, with a sense of adventure. She actually had more concern about how her illness and impending death were affecting her fiercely devoted daughters and young grandchildren than on how they were affecting her. She made light of the pain, tiredness and frustration to spare her family and friends grief. Her death was still very painful for the rest of us, but at least we had the comfort of knowing that fear of death wasn't adding to the pain she was in.

I am not advocating unrealistic optimism. My friend had no illusions that she was going to beat her cancer and she took her pain meds. I hear Christians talk on and on about their belief that God will grant their desires—however unrealistic. They regard God almost like a genie. They may put their house up for sale, overpriced, in a down market and expect that God will send them a buyer so that they can upgrade to a nicer house. They may run up credit card debt buying consumer goods they don't use and expect that God will keep raising their income to pay for it. They eat junk food and don't exercise and wonder why God lets them have heart disease. God is not a genie and life happens. We change when we walk with God, life doesn't. We often get better results during all those life emergencies, but that only happens if you focus on the process of growing with God and not the results you want.

Cultivate a "whatever", go with the flow, attitude and see what happens—your results will improve. To gain that "whatever" perspective it is necessary to keep the focus on staying connected with God, rather than seeking to change the circumstances directly. If we focus on changing the circumstances, our stress levels will rise, and we will use negative techniques that tend to make matters worse—for example, demanding votes or demanding a job because there are bills to pay. If we focus on God and the fact that he is with us and we will be fine no matter what happens—even if we die—the fruits of the spirit result, our attitude and behavior are more positive; and that brings a lot of positive, concrete changes in our results as well.

We can have the "peace that passes understanding" referred to in Philippians, if we go with the flow. This is a process and both very simple and very difficult. It involves trust and positive mental attitude, but not self-delusion or unrealistic expectations. To trust means to believe that God has plans for us, as he did for Israel when it had been taken over by Babylon. Waiting for deportation, the prophet Jeremiah sent a letter to the surviving elders laying out his prophecy of promise, in it he says, "For I know the plans I have for you,' declares the Lord. 'plans to prosper you and not to harm you, plans to give you hope and a future.'" Jeremiah 29:11. Trust means to believe that the words of Paul's letter to the Romans are still true:

> "And we know that in all things God works for the good of those who love him, who have been called according to his purpose."…."What then can we say in response to this? If God is for us, who can be against us? He who did not spare his own Son, but gave him up for us all---how will he not also, along with him, graciously give us all things?...For I am convinced that neither death, nor life, nor angels nor demons, neither the present nor the future, nor any powers, neither height nor depth, nor anything else in all creation, will be able to separate us from the love of God that is in Christ Jesus, our Lord. "
> Romans 8:28-29, 31, 38.

To trust means to believe that even though things might not turn out the way we wish, they will turn out all right—and to move into the new reality—whatever it is.

We tend to focus on our circumstances and to let our circumstances dictate our emotions. Emotions and circumstances are related, but circumstances don't have to dictate our emotions. For example, as a college student, I was pretty broke. I once lost a quarter in a Coke machine and it ruined my budget for the week. I was a bit anxious and I looked forward to when I would have a job and more money, but I had a base level of joy and enjoyed college. My first apartment during law school was a very small efficiency on the edge of a very rough neighborhood. There was a large collection of roaches and a few prostitutes among the neighbors. I was not fond of the teenagers cruising past in cars shouting out the window to ask if I was a prostitute. I was a bit anxious riding the bus late at night and still looking forward to having a real job and money, but I still had a base level of joy and I enjoyed that time. I enjoyed my friends and the little Vietnamese restaurants in the neighborhood. I even enjoyed the stray souls offering freshly stolen car radios—still trailing wires—as they walked by on the street, saying "it's not hot, really".

Now I live in a comfortable house in the suburbs with a big yard and lovely neighbors. I'm still a bit anxious about money, and I'm still wondering what the future holds, and I still have joy. I am happy and enjoy my circumstances now —but I am not happier than I was counting every quarter. In fact, if I let myself focus on life's tasks, like maintaining the house or paying the bills; I run the risk of being less satisfied and more stressed than I was during times of far greater risk and uncertainty. It is all about attitude.

Joy and peace are not situational. You can be short of physical resources, and either happy or depressed, your choice. You can be rich and either happy or sad, your choice. You can be sick or well, young or old, fat or thin, pretty or ugly, single or married, smart or slow, athletic or klutzy, alone or surrounded by friends and family—and either happy or depressed, your choice.

Gentleness, goodness and patience are not situational. You can be respected, ignored, or scorned—and either happy or depressed, your choice. You can choose to treat others with tolerance and dignity even though they mistreat you—and regardless of whether the offender is deliberately offensive or just ignorant.

Self–control is not situational. You can speak kindly to people or rant at them, or hit them, your choice. And that choice doesn't depend on their behavior or how reasonable they are. Really, how you treat other people is entirely up to you. Think of all the teachers trying to convince 9th graders that algebra has a point, or the moms of toddlers who just learned the word "no". Self-control is a choice.

Faithfulness is a choice. No matter how much time you spend with a co-worker, or the neighbor down the street, and no matter how unappreciated you are by your family or your spouse, faithfulness is a choice. When your parents get old and need care, faithfulness is a choice. When a friend goes through a bad spell, faithfulness is a choice. When you have a chance to take advantage of your employer for a bit more money, or to take confidential information and use it to your advantage, faithfulness is a choice.

Finally love is a choice—and love is a verb. We tend to think of love as warm fuzzy feeling. It can be, but really it is about how you treat people. I've talked to fathers who claim to love their children, but don't pay child support, don't visit and don't call. That isn't love. I've seen adult children who claim to love their parents, but don't visit and don't call, don't help with maintenance around the house, don't drive them to their doctor's visits and shout when their parents can't remember things or move too slowly. That isn't love. And those are the easy people to love.

God actually wants us to treat *everyone* with love, including our enemies. That doesn't mean we are supposed to send them flowers. It means we treat all people with respect and honesty. It means we stand up to mean people when they pick on weaker people. It means when we become aware of someone in need and have the means to help, we share what we have.

1 Corinthians 13:4-7 has the ultimate description of love and every attribute requires action. "Love is patient, love is kind. It does not envy, it does not boast, it is not proud. It is not rude, it is not self-seeking, it is not easily angered, it keeps no record of wrongs. Love does not delight in evil, but rejoices with the truth. It always protects, always trusts, always hopes, always perseveres."

Note that 1 Corinthians does not say "love is blind"—you won't find that anywhere in the Bible. You also won't find "love is co-dependent" or "love accepts abuse" and certainly not "love blames itself for abuse". 1 Corinthians is describing the love of the strong. Love is the ability to see people for what they are and deal with them kindly and honestly without getting sucked into the drama. Love, as described in the Bible, never means feeling the need for people to be weaker than you and dependent. It never means clinging to someone else to make your decisions for you or to enable a long string of "I can'ts". Love in the Bible is intended to raise up other people and make them strong, independent, trustworthy and kind people too.

Note also that when Jesus commanded us to "Love your neighbor as yourself"—he did intend for us to love ourselves. It is important to remember your own needs for refreshment, rest, recreation and affirmation. We all count.

The fruits of spirit are gifts, we don't obtain them by working for them. But, all of these attributes also involve a choice. All of them will have a very beneficial effect on your life if you make the choice to seek them. Choosing love, joy, peace, patience, gentleness, goodness, faithfulness and self-control is not a natural choice, and it is not an easy choice. We are wired so that our initial reaction is going to be to grab what we need and hurry off, to love those who love us back—and often to love those who can do us some good—to fight when challenged, and to fly off the handle when we get angry. None of those reactions are constructive, and when those reactions develop into a pattern of behavior, those patterns will have a negative effect on your life.

So the choice of the upside is a continuous dance with our own nature. That is why a relationship with God is the most essential part of the equation. Self-discipline by itself will not get you to the upside. Trying to choose positive behavior patterns solely out of self-discipline, or a feeling of guilt or obligation, will eventually result in burn-out. In order to make the positive choice, you have to want to make the choices. Spending enough time cultivating a relationship with God will help you develop a greater capacity to desire more positive choices. Positive change flows out of positive patterns of behavior. The goal is for the positive behaviors to just seem like the obvious approach with no stress involved in the choice. It won't seem like a choice at all—that is what "going with the flow" means. The positive changes are the result of God's work in us changing our attitudes. We don't have to force choices out by willpower, cultural pressure or force of habit. So, how do we obtain the positive mental attitude?

All of us start out as young children with a lot of negative behaviors. We cry when we don't get our own way, stomp our feet, hit, scream. We grab things that aren't ours, demand immediate gratification of every desire, and generally act like we consider ourselves the center of the universe. As we mature, we learn more appropriate behavior patterns, but many of us don't change our basic opinion that we are, or should be, the center of the universe. A relationship with God, who actually is the center of the universe, tends to re-set one's perspective. We come to understand that we aren't the center of the universe. More importantly, once we experience the presence of God, we want more of the presence and start adapting our behavior in ways that increase the sense of presence.

This is the point where it many of us jump off the wagon and join the "church people"—talking funny and doing all the right things. This detour is usually unwitting and well intentioned, it is just the wrong move. The church people are the ones promulgating unreasonable expectations and often self-delusion. What happens is that people start off thinking they want a relationship with God. They have either taken a hit as a result of a bad life experience, or as a result of bad choices, or they are nice people who are motivated to live a good life and to help others. So they go to church. They end up around a lot of nice people with appropriate behavior. The church they go to is basically a club. It has a hierarchy, an "in-crowd", a set of priorities and its own behavior code. Its life is centered around its members and its primary function is the preservation of its internal community. God may or may not show up occasionally, but he is definitely not a member of the board. I think of these people as zombies, or as Jesus put it in Matthew 23:15, "sons of Hell". In that passage, Jesus is criticizing the Pharisees for their efforts to turn people into religious puppets He accuses the Pharisees of turning newcomers to the faith into "more of a son of Hell" than the Pharisees themselves. (The Pharisees *really did not like* Jesus.)

The zombies walk and they talk, but they aren't really alive. The new people don't realize the zombies aren't really alive, and they want to fit in. What they know of God is shaped by what they see around them. They believe that fitting in, going through the rituals, adhering to the behavior modes, is what God wants and what being a Christian means. Very often they feel as if they are the only ones who are unsure and often feel that they are not good enough to fit in with the Christians, or with God. So they adopt all the right behaviors and they say all the right things. When someone they love dies, and they feel sad and angry, they say their loved one is "in a better place" and that they were "ready to meet the Father". What they really mean is "this sucks and I miss them". They say the proper things even when their loved one was not at all ready to meet the Father and clung to life beyond all reason.

They say they "love their brothers and sisters in Christ" even when they are feeling wounded by being excluded from the "in" table at the church picnic, or by being told they aren't suitable for a leadership position at church. They listen to the soprano wars in the choir and say what a blessing the music ministry is. They get guilt-tripped into "serving" with the junior high ministry and go home with a headache after every meeting. They say they are engaging in "spiritual disciplines" in order to grow, but really they are just slogging through the motions feeling disconnected and confused. Eventually, they turn into zombies. The unfortunate part is that the people in churches make the choices to do things to fit in because they want to experience God. This is unfortunate because even though the fruits of the spirit are a choice, the kinds of choices you make just to fit in at church will not result in the fruits of the spirit growing in your soul. The choice to experience God is a different choice.

The choice to experience God is to choose to treat God as real and to seek his presence, and decide to trust that you will be okay with whatever happens. Choosing to act like a zombie is denying reality. It will never work with a real God. So, to connect with God, act like a real person and treat God like a real person.

When the water heater breaks, you swear a little. Then you turn off the water so isn't spraying all over the basement, and clean up what has already sprayed around. And while you do that you pray, "God, I have guests coming in three days and I had to fix the car three weeks ago and the emergency fund is pretty low. How am I supposed to do all this? What is the deal here? I thought you loved me! Why does this always happen to me at the worst possible time?" And you keep on ranting like that for a couple of hours, to your spouse or a few close friends or relatives—just not *at* other people or in front of the kids. Then you take a deep breath and say, "Well, whatever. God I need some help here." And then you talk to your spouse and check the bank account balance and the credit card balance, and head to the hardware store to look for a sale. And you buy the water heater you can afford instead of the one you want. Keep praying and you are very likely to find a sale on one that will work just fine. (Have it professionally installed. One of my favorite product liability cases was an improperly installed water heater that ignited and launched itself like a rocket through the ceiling above—fortunately no one was hurt.) For a few days you take cold showers. And eventually you have a new water heater and you find out you survived and it wasn't that big a deal after all.

When you find out that someone you thought was a friend has been saying unkind and untrue things about you behind your back, undermining you at work or school, or using a confidence to usurp an opportunity that was very important to you. You swear a little. You cry a little. You stomp around the walking path praying "God, how could they do this to me? I thought they were my friend and they betrayed me! How could you let this happen, I thought you loved me! No one loves me, my life is ruined! I will never have another opportunity like that. People will think I'm an idiot and no one will trust me again! I hate them! You should curse the ground they walk on! What am I supposed to do now?" And you keep on ranting like that for a couple of hours, just not in front of the kids, and only to a couple of very close friends or family. Then you say, "Well, whatever. God I need some help with this". And the next time you see your "friend" you say, "Help me understand what happened here, I thought we were friends." And you listen to the answer and you see if it makes sense or if they just had such emotional needs of their own that they couldn't care about anyone else in the middle of their own needs. And you forgive them, and you decide whether you are still going to be friends. Remember, forgiveness and remaining friends are two separate concepts. There is no need to include people who abuse or betray you in your friendship circle.

Keep praying, and you will find you can keep your voice soft and your mind clear. When you face the rest of the people involved in the matter, you keep your head up, speak civilly, and you don't mention your (former) friend's betrayal. When other people comment on it or sympathize with you, you say, "yeah, that sucked, but I'm moving on, I really don't want to talk about it." Keep praying; it is very hard to get those words out and to keep from expressing how you really feel about your former friend. Focus on new opportunities. Keep praying and you will find other opportunities and other, healthier, friends will come into your life. And you will find out you survived, and it wasn't such a big deal after all.

You get the picture: You go with the flow on the small things: the goldfish that dies the day after you buy it, the broken window, the burned roast for the dinner party. Then you go with the flow on the bigger things: the bad prom, bad breakups, the annoying neighbor, the expensive home repairs, the job relocations. Then you find you can go with the flow on the really big things: death, disability, job loss, poverty, natural disasters, divorce, abuse, wayward children, dependent parents, addictions—yours or a loved ones. Keep treating God like a real person, keep talking to him, he will talk back. You will not hear voices—if you do, go see a psychiatrist—right away. You will feel a presence, a warm connection, and a growing confidence that whatever it is, it isn't such a big deal and you will survive it. You will also feel a growing desire to spend more time with the presence, with God, to know more about him, to experience more of the peace and life than emanates from the connection to God.

123

You will find the relationship with God is something like the game of "warmer, colder" you played when you were a kid. In that game one player is blindfolded, spun around and released with the task of finding some object in the room that is described to them. The other participants guide them by saying "cold, colder, really icy" as they move away from the object. Or encourage them by saying "warmer, warmer" or "hot, really hot" as the blindfolded player closes in on the object. By following the directions from other participants, the blindfolded player eventually finds and grasps the object, identifies it and pulls off the blindfold in triumph. In the same way, when we talk to God, he guides us with an impression of his opinion—not audible but still perceptible.

When you call up the neighbor and say "your stupid brats just drove across my lawn on their snowmobiles. Were they raised by wolves?" The impression you get from God says "colder". When you call the neighbor and say, "I just watched your kids cut across my lawn to get from the cornfield to the street—I know they think it's frozen and won't hurt anything, but the flowerbeds are getting cut up, could you ask them to stop?" The impression says, "warmer, good job." Instead of turning your head when you walk past each other's houses and calling on the other neighbors to take sides, you can share a beer at the picnic and swap stories about your own teen-aged misdeeds.

When you hear there are going to be cuts at your job and you download all the customer information to a disk and take it home with you; and you stalk out with a few choice words and tell everyone you come in contact with how mismanaged the company is, the impression says, "Colder", don't you trust me?" When you put all your files in order, with all the contact information in place and a clear status and follow up directions for every file, and leave your contact information for any questions, the impression says, "Warmer, good job". Keep praying, your contacts are a lot more likely to call and say they really miss working with you, and to let you know of opportunities in the area. Your old co-workers and even your old boss will send you referrals.

As you see life work out and gain more confidence in your ability to survive, the positive choices come easier. You start to see those choices as only smart. You are able to look past the immediate problem to what life will be like when you have survived the crisis. Keeping your relationships intact becomes much more important than other aspects of the crisis. Another cup of spilled milk on the table becomes less important than your four-year old's self-confidence. Hearing the same story from your mother five times in an hour becomes less important than hearing the smile in her voice when she tells it. And

God says, "warmer"; and your child's dance is cute again; and your stylish mother's new fascination with garage sale t-shirts is funny. This is the upside.

While you need to use caution in not allowing "spiritual disciplines" to turn into mindless rituals and empty religion, there is a level of discipline and choice involved in obtaining the upside. You have to choose to talk to God. You have to choose to want to hear what he says. You have to choose to recognize that you are going to feel anxiety, and not to give into it. You have to remember to take a deep breath and not say the first things that come into your mind. But it is not these choices alone that result in the upside—it is that "warmer", "colder" communication from the presence of a real God that create the change.

It is also the little breaks you get along the way from the presence of a real God that gives you the confidence to believe that God is really real, interested in you, and that it will all be ok in the end. If you keep praying, you will find the parking places, the water heater sales, the referrals, the spilled milk that doesn't land on your cell phone, the electricity that stays on so your basement doesn't flood, the apartment you can afford. God shows himself in a little break when you need it most that is more than coincidence. You won't find some magic genie who hands you the winning lottery ticket—but you will find a warm parental presence who helps you over that last hill and shows you the gorgeous sunset at the end of a long day.

Sometimes magic does happen. I wrote the words above and went out pre-shopping for a car, intending to buy one in a few weeks. It had been a long four years since changing from a highly paid corporate position to a private firm with the need to grow a practice. I had gotten stuck in the real estate market in the middle of an effort to downsize, and had some expenses in connection with family matters for several years before I was downsized. I had made lot of adjustments and one of them was hanging onto my car twice as long as I usually do. It had held up well, but at nearly 215,000 miles, it was starting to do some funny things. The dashboard lights sometimes didn't come on, and the transmission was cranky in the morning. The time had come for a different car. I drive around 20,000 miles a year, so I wanted a low mileage, reliable replacement. My car replacement fund had been downsized as well over the past several years. I had done some research on-line and concluded I could only afford a low end sub-compact. I went to a local car dealer for that brand to see what it looked like. Turned out they were having a sale, advertised only by direct mail, that I didn't know anything about. They had an overstock of returned lease cars and were offering a special. They were charging whatever the original lessor still owed, less $1500. I left in a 2 year old car—the next model up from what I intended to buy-- with less than 20,000 miles on it and a clean CarFax report, for a price at least $1500 less than the on-line prices for that model—and right on my budget number. The salesman was a very nice Christian man visiting from an out of state branch office just for the sale. I was out of the dealership in about an hour, with no haggling. Magical. It was my mother's birthday, the first since her death, and I started the day with mixed emotions. It turned out to be a great day, and one in which I felt surrounded by God's love and presence.[27]

Experiencing the influence of the presence of God requires making space in your life for that influence. This is real and there is a strong practical aspect to a relationship with God. Attending to your personal health is important. It is much more difficult to open yourself to God's presence if you tired, too busy or strung out on caffeine and sugar (much less drugs or alcohol.) Respect yourself. Get enough sleep. Get some exercise, take a walk, or run, or play golf, or go the gym—but something you enjoy that rests your mind and exercises your body—and gets you out in the fresh air for a dose of sunshine whenever possible. We need that to be focused and feel open to new experiences.

Eat a balanced diet—remember your veggies. Your brain needs good nutrition to function properly, and blood sugar imbalances can make you moody and depressed. You can do this even on a limited budget. Walking is free and kale, one of nature's super foods, costs a dollar or less for a big bunch that, with an onion, will provide a healthy, tasty dish. Add some potatoes and a little bacon or ham and you will have a healthy, very inexpensive feast. Make a big pot and freeze it for lunch for the week; you will never miss McDonald's. Check out the web for fast, healthy, inexpensive food options. This is much easier than you think it is. I'm not suggesting you turn into a vegan and subsist on tofu

---

[27] My old car went to Willow's CARS ministry. Some wonderful volunteers with mechanical skills take suitable used cars, repair them and give them to struggling single moms and families (surprisingly they were even able to fix mine.) If the car isn't suitable for giving away, they sell it and use the proceeds to fund repairs of cars they give away; and repairs for single moms, homeless people and others in need who can't afford car repairs. It is a great ministry that makes a very real difference in people's lives. It was nice to be a part of it.

and sprouts—just that you think about what you are feeding yourself. You matter too—eat like a grown up.

Pay attention to your recreation and refreshment needs. Everyone needs some affirmation and some relaxation. You can't work all the time, and you can't take care of other people and their issues all the time. Read a book, meet some friends for a basketball game or over coffee. Window shop, scrapbook, listen to music or make some music with a guitar, spoons or water glasses. Putter around in the garden or in the garage. Do something that you enjoy that refreshes your mind. Many of us let television and the internet fill all our recreational space, but those things will almost never actually have the effect of refreshing your spirit. Watching a game or Skyping with friends, yes; Facebook posts for 300 of your closest friends or a police drama with dead bodies and guns—no. Try something else—anything else that you find refreshing. If you pay attention to your health, you will feel better, have more energy and be more open to new experiences. You will have more ability to make that initial positive choice to listen to God and try the positive approach in the face of anxiety.

Remember to thank God when the bills are all paid at the end of the month, when you are enjoying the neighborhood Christmas party, when your child walks across the stage with their diploma, or you look around at your clean, functioning home. Most of us already have a lot to be thankful for. Going with the flow includes taking a moment to appreciate the things God has already given to you.

Make some space in your life to hear God. God doesn't shout. 1 Kings 19:13 describes God speaking to Elijah in a gentle whisper. God will never demand that you listen to his cues. He will never impose his will on your life or his peace. If you want to hear God telling you "warmer, good job", you will have to listen, and create some quiet around you. You can't hear God's voice with headphones blaring music, even Christian music, in your ears.

The most common way we get sidetracked is busyness. There is a lot of stuff going on in our lives and it is important stuff. We have jobs to go to, families to feed, houses to clean and maintain, kid's activities to monitor, commitments we've made to the neighborhood and community. Those are all very good things and we should do them. But we create problems for ourselves when we let those activities get out of balance. We spend so much time and energy chasing our lives that we forget to live our lives. We drown in debt from all the things we decide we need that we don't use. We spend more and more time at work chasing achievement or placating the unreasonable expectations of others. We spend hours trying to keep up with hundreds of people on the internet that we never really talk to. We come home exhausted and camp in front of the TV watching violence or staged reality shows. We fill our lives with activity and noise from early morning until late at night. The truth is that we need some down time and some quiet, and that we classify some things as critical that aren't all that important.

Consider children's activities for example. Many children have activities or enrichment classes scheduled four or five days a week. They play soccer, they take music lessons, they are in scouts, they have play dates, they have tutoring sessions and homework. They spend hours surfing the net or playing video games. We drive through McDonald's to feed them on the way from science club to karate lessons. Those are all good things, but there are too many good things. We may have 2 or 3 children who are each involved in that many activities, not to mention our own list of good things we are engaged in. Our lives are out of control, and it leaves little time, room or inclination to hear the quiet impression of God's presence. We need to sift through all the good things that we do and eliminate a few to create some space and energy to enjoy the activities we keep, and to leave some space in our thinking to recognize God's presence.

Engaging with God at church through corporate worship is also important. That may sound like a contradiction to the way I have described church. But when the church stuff is real, when you meet someone who has been a Christian for years and is actually looking forward to meeting the Father, when you serve others at church in an area that uses your natural talents and passions, when you make some close friends who understand the desire to connect with God and share that with you, when you hear a well prepared message that illuminates truth, or participate in worship music that is heartfelt and well executed, your ability to engage with God is enhanced. Your mind is opened to things that you would not have thought of on your own, and you benefit from the education and experience of others. Good church can stretch you. You may have to try several, or a lot, of churches before you find one that is not overrun with zombies, but if you can find a church with living Christians it is a very positive thing.

While community with friends is a positive thing, and corporate worship and good messages are valuable; ultimately, a relationship with God is personal to you. To hear God saying "warmer, good job," you need to spend some time alone with him. Spending just 10 or 15 minutes a day praying and reading the Bible will make a big difference.

Try to apply this though the day. When the water heater breaks, take a few minutes to try to connect to God's presence and feel it say, "this isn't such a big deal, it will be fine". You can tell God he's nuts, it is too the end of the world, but his presence and unrealistic conviction that everything will be fine will still be comforting. To cultivate a relationship, you have to make time for it. God has all the time in the world for you. He is always there; it is up to you whether or not to cultivate a relationship with God.

The truth is that sometimes you have to work for joy and peace. You have to work to choose a positive attitude. Sometimes you don't really believe that God is there, that he loves you or that he can or would help you. Some days you have to cling to the belief that God exists and cares with the tips of your fingernails. Sometimes you firmly believe that the only sensible course of action in front of you is to eat a few TastyCakes, watch "Downton Abbey" and put a bucket of water by the door in case those brats come through on their snowmobiles again. If you just step forward into the flow, you will find that God is there, he does care, and he will help. If you make a habit out of stepping forward into the flow and listening to the cues—you will experience the upside. There are no shortcuts, magic wands or genies—just choices that you make.

Chapter Six
How Long Does It Take to Reach the Upside?

So, this sounds good in theory, but how long does it take and how do I know if I've reached the upside? Is there anything weird about all this? The answer is that the results are both immediate and permanent; continue to grow throughout your life, and you never arrive. You will never stop growing or being stretched. It isn't like climbing a mountain, you will not reach the summit. You will feel increasingly positive, strong, joyful and peaceful as you mature. The process is more like the growth of a tree—sometimes faster, sometimes slower, sometimes stressed, depending on conditions, but it never stops growing during its life. It isn't weird, but it may be little odd. What I mean by odd is that you will eventually find that you just aren't as worried about stuff as a lot of other people you know. That's odd, but in a good way.

Making a decision that you want to follow Christ's teaching and develop a relationship with God has an immediate result. As soon as you make the choice, tell God about it. Make a first attempt to "go with the flow" in his direction. You will start to feel a sense of connection to his presence and his love. It is life changing because you will never again doubt the existence or importance of God, and your outlook on life permanently changes. I experienced an immediate sense of connection and joy at age four that has never left. I know God is real. I can't adequately describe the transformation, but it was as concrete as turning on a light in a dark room. Not everyone experiences this in the same way. For some people it is more of a process. I have no explanation for that, except to suggest taking the experience as it comes. You will experience the connection.

Note that you won't experience a connection if your decision was just that you would like to check out what connection is like, to experiment with how relating to God would be, compare it your own way of living and see if relating to God is going to be worth it to you. If you are still in that mode, and are honestly trying to confirm God's character and existence with a desire to relate to God, God will show up enough places and times in response to an honest inquiry so that you will eventually have enough information to make that choice. If, on the other hand, your actual desire is more along the lines that you think it would be interesting to see God do some tricks, or you'd like a genie to make your life fit your expectations, don't expect to see that. God is God, not a magician who plays children's parties. You have to actually want, and commit, to doing things God's way for the rest of your life to experience a connection. A lot of people leave that part out. They say they want God in their lives, they want love, they want forgiveness, they want joy, but they forget this is a two-way street. God commits to us, he wants us to commit to him.

If you are living a pretty normal, healthy life, it may take some time to discover exactly how the connection with God is different from the way you would normally interact. This is subtle, and God is already a part of your life in some way. God is always a part of our lives, seeking after us even when we aren't looking for God. I became a Christian at a very young age, and there was a marked change in the level of connection with God when I decided that I wanted to be a Christian and follow after God. But God was a presence in my life from my earliest recollections. It was a few years before I identified the presence as God—it was just a kind presence that was there. (When you are a child, these things are normal. It didn't occur to me to ask anyone about it.) I heard the story of Samuel in a preschool Sunday school class. Samuel was a major prophet and leader in the Old Testament, his life is recorded in two books named after him, 1 and 2 Samuel. I Samuel relates how his mother had prayed for a child and promised to dedicate him to God. A few years after his birth Samuel's parents took him to the temple to serve. Eli, who was the chief priest at the time, took Samuel in and raised him. His parents visited Samuel when they came to Jerusalem for the festivals. (That part seemed bizarre to me, it still does. I don't think that was God's plan, I think they made that part up themselves. Misguided God-followers are not a new phenomenon.) A few years later, the Bible doesn't say exactly how old he was, Samuel had gone to bed and heard his name called. He went to Eli and said, "Here I am". Eli was confused. He told Samuel he had not called, and sent him back to bed. It happened a second time. Eli was still confused, and a little ticked off, and sent Samuel back to bed. It happened a third time. Eli determined that God was calling Samuel and told Samuel to return to bed and if it happened again to say "speak Lord, for your servant is listening." God called again, Samuel responded and that started a long career as a prophet of God and religious leader. Samuel was the last judge of Israel, and it is Samuel who appointed both Saul and David as King over Israel.

I did not hear voices, ever. Nothing like the movie "Poltergeist" has ever happened to me. But that story resonated with me and I concluded that the presence I sensed was God. I knew some Bible stories by then, and the kindness and love of God I had learned about matched the sense I had of the presence. I could look around and see the earth, and it just made sense to me that there was God. Since then I have learned many fact-based reasons for concluding there is a God and that his character matches the God described in the Bible. I have also learned that the question of belief is sometimes complicated and that there are unanswered questions and some things in the Bible that defy belief. But it still just makes sense to me that there is a God and that his presence is good.

I think my experience as a small child is more common that we might believe. I believe many of us sense the presence of God, we just don't identify the presence as God. When my great niece was small she loved the wildflowers (you can say "weeds") growing in my sister's yard. Not dandelions, in fact very few dandelions grew in her yard. But there were tiny blue flowers and tiny white flowers and a tiny yellow flower. I have no idea what they were—they were not your typical lawn weed— and they were very beautiful. Most people would have killed them off and went in search of sod. My sister and her husband care more about the people using their yard than a few weeds. We referred to them as God's flowers, and deemed them pickable (in contrast to the neighbors' roses and daylilies which were deemed off limits.) My niece once confided to me that she felt God put those flowers in the yard just for her. I agreed with her, and I think he did. Few other people would have appreciated them. She is older now and rolls her eyes just a little at the idea of God's flowers. She still connects with God through nature and is a delightful, kind person. (Okay, really she is the most terrific 16 year old on the planet, but you might think I was biased if I said that.)

I still encourage my niece that God sends those flowers especially to her, and I don't think I'm wrong. We can be too sophisticated for our own good. A friend of mine, a very sophisticated, very intelligent business executive has a small untamed area in her yard where wildflowers grow every year. The flowers that come up are different every year. This is odd for plants. Plants normally stay put and reseed themselves. One would expect the base plants to be the same from year to year, with perhaps a few volunteer transients. She has lived in that house for something around 10 years now, and never the same plants from year to year. She is convinced that God sends the flowers to her and looks forward every spring to seeing what will sprout that year. I think God does send her those flowers, a special treat for someone who appreciates his gift.

Another time I was at a 4th of July party to watch the local fireworks display--a very good one shot off over a lake—with a group of friends. It was a group of two or three extended families with several small children running around. One little boy was about 2. He blinked at the bright sparkling lights and flinched a little at the loud booms. He wasn't frightened, but he wasn't impressed either. We were all oohing and ahhing in appropriate fashion at the great display. Then he turned his back to the fireworks, pointed at the full moon and said "Moon!" We said, "Look over here, you are missing the pretty fireworks." He said "Moon!" more emphatically. That happened a couple more times and we chuckled a tiny bit that he didn't get fireworks. He looked a bit offended and said "Moon!" more emphatically—frustrated with his lack of words. Finally one of the older adults spoke to him, and said, "The moon is very pretty, and it is easier to look at and doesn't have all that noise, and doesn't fade away. God made the moon and it is better than the fireworks." He nodded happily, smiled, pointed up at the moon again with an enchanted look on his face and said "Moon!" He was right. The moon was more impressive than the fireworks, but we were too old to see it. We were wrapped up in our own world.

That little boy understood the presence of God. I think many small children understand the presence of God before they can articulate it, or really understand what it is. As we get older, we just get sidetracked by the people around us into focusing on the flash bang of all the fireworks instead of the moon and the flowers. I love fireworks and go to displays every chance I get—often three or four times around the Fourth of July and several other times during the year. But since that night, every time I see firework, I remember that the moon is a far prettier and a much more spectacular creation.

Another impediment to people feeling that they have had an experience of God, is expectation. They don't necessarily recognize God when he shows up. People expect some grand, epic event like one of the Bible prophets. They expect some grand revelation or world changing quest. People hear testimonies of others who came from very difficult circumstances, like addictions or abusive backgrounds, who had a dramatic breakthrough into something resembling normalcy; and they tend to expect some really dramatic change in their own life. The problem with those expectations is that most people aren't expected to go on grand, epic quests. The world doesn't need many grand, epic life changing quests. It really needs a lot of little changes brought about by caring people living positive lives. God mostly wants us to stay in our own environment and improve our own piece of the puzzle. Most of these people already lead normal, healthy lives and have good relationships with their friends and families. They don't need to make a 180 degree change in their behavior. In fact, that would be very damaging to their relationships. Their lives are going to change in more subtle ways. We shouldn't be disappointed by the lack of a grand "mission from God". If you think about it. The world would be a dramatically better place, and much more stable, if everyone just took better care of their own piece of the puzzle.

The final impediment people encounter in feeling they have an experience of God, is too much other stuff taking up their time and attention. God's presence is quiet and non-intrusive. He won't demand attention. If you are very busy, even with good, very healthy things, you may not give yourself the time and freedom to recognize a connection with God.

The recognition that God has become important to you can sneak up on you. I volunteer in the evangelism ministry at Willow, and they offer the alpha program several times a year. One man in one of my groups got a shocked look on his face in the middle of one of the discussion times. He said that he had been thinking he wasn't sure God existed and that he wasn't sure God related to us. For the prior two years he had been coming to church pretty regularly and enjoying the worship—and he had been thinking about church as a social experience—a time to interact with his wife and their friends. He had been praying but did not expect that there was a God listening or that God would respond in any way.

During one discussion he suddenly realized that a lot of his uncertainties were gone. He did believe in God and did believe that God cares for him, and had actually believed that for a number of months. He had not realized his opinions had changed until he participated in the discussion. The discussion didn't change his opinions; it gave him a chance to reflect and realize that his opinions had changed. That discussion process helped him to clarify what he believed. Several more people in the group had similar realizations. They had not been aware how much God was already part of their lives. They were expecting something else—some grand flash-bang fireworks, not a gradual transformation to feeling loved and secure with a more positive outlook on life and a greater ability to deal constructively with other people. Carving out some time from their normal, busy lives to think about their connection with God helped to solidify a relationship they were already building with God.

Many people process what they believe by talking through it. Discussion is a favorite tool of college educators for that very reason. Just like writing down your thoughts helps you to process ideas, talking through your ideas with others helps you to clarify in your own mind what you believe, and to examine where there are flaws in your thought processes. If you process ideas by talking through them, and aren't sure what you believe, I highly recommend the alpha course. It was started in England by Nicky Gumble, a wonderful communicator, as a way to help people process what they think about God and answer the questions they have about Christianity. Now alpha is taught all over the world. Check the alpha.org website, there is likely a class starting soon near your home or workplace.

If you have decided that you definitely want to be connected with God and to start living your life going with the flow, I recommend that you take the plunge and tell God that. Take the first few steps to move in that direction—for example, praying to God like he is real and is listening. Take a breath and a second to ask for patience before responding to your child, your spouse or your co-worker and consider what the truth really is the next time you get involved in an argument. That is the beginning. Then continue as we discussed in the last chapter. Go with the flow on a daily basis, carve out a little bit of time to seek connection with God, and the connection with flourish and grow.

The rate of growth is different for everyone. It depends on your own personality and how willing you are to take a chance on going with the flow. I became a Christian when I was quite young, so my growth has followed along with the natural physical and mental growth process. I can't completely separate the two, but I can see the results. I used to have a very volatile temper, now I don't. I used to be very impatient, now I'm not. A lot of things used to bother me because they weren't done well. I'm much more tolerant now than I used to be. I can look back now and see problems I caused for myself when at the time I felt completely justified in what I was doing. I know the improvements are the work of God in my life. I feel the "warmer/colder" response, and sometimes God just plain nags. I know it is God, because I don't care that much about spiritual growth, or the world outside of my family and friends on my own. I'm in the remedial class. It has taken a very long time, over 50 years, to get to this place. Others who decide to become Christians as adults, or who aren't so recalcitrant in the first place, experience faster growth.

Lee Strobel, for example, was an atheist into his thirties. He relates his conversion experience in A Case for Christ, Zondervan, first published in 1998. Lee's wife, Leslie, had become a Christian after spending some time talking to a friend. Lee describes Leslie as an already wonderful person, but still saw a marked change in her that intrigued him. She became healthier, happier, and freer. He let himself be dragged to church, and eventually decided he needed to make a thorough inquiry into whether God existed, whether Christ was the Messiah, and whether the whole relationship with God thing merited any consideration. Lee was an editor for the Chicago Tribune at the time with a background in investigative reporting (and a law degree.) Lee's conversion was not immediate. He took two years to do the research and approached the topic from an intellectual point of view. He came away convinced that it took more faith to refuse to believe than to believe. He concluded that the facts demanded the conclusion that God's existence; and Christ's death, resurrection and claim to be God's son sent to redeem us; was a reality and not a myth. A few years after that Lee became a minister. Now he is an author, speaker, and above all else, an evangelist—explaining to others the conclusions he drew. His growth has been amazing, but Lee has no fear of jumping in and going with the flow. He was a teaching pastor at Willow for several years. I've heard him speak a number of times and seen him in action. He is the real deal.

Erwin McManus is another example. His book, The Barbarian Way, Thomas Nelson, Inc. (2005) describes his conversion as a college student. Religion was not part of his life growing up, so he had no preconceptions about church or God. He dived right into the flow. He recommends that and contends it is the best way to see that God is real, that he has power and is just as willing to engage with us today as he was in Biblical times. McManus describes that kind of all-in faith as barbarianism. He recommends barbarian faith as the antidote to the sterilized world we often find in churches today. I think he is right. He describes one instance while he was still in college, not long after he became a Christian. A woman in the church group who led worship shared with him that she had lost faith, she did not believe God loved her anymore and she had decided to bag it and head back to her old life. Her old life was an unhealthy one that included drug abuse and unhealthy relationship patterns. Erwin tried to convince the woman that God did indeed love her and asked what would demonstrate that. She said, "well, make it snow". They were in North Carolina. He was appalled. Snow was clearly not possible. Then he heard himself promising God would make it snow for her. He just didn't know any better. Totally freaked out by then, he went home and prayed—fervently—for snow, until he fell asleep in the middle of his prayers. He woke up the next day, still freaked out that he had promised something impossible and that the woman would go off to her old life as a result.

He looked out the window—at snow, everywhere. It had snowed all night.

He has remained convinced that God wants us to expect him to show up in powerful, very concrete ways. That God wants us to have a barbarian's attitude toward Christianity. God wants us to have the kind of blind, concrete expectations the apostles had. McManus has followed that path. He is pastor of the Mosaic church in Los Angeles, as well as being an author, speaker and film maker. His life has shown amazing growth, and results too. I haven't met Erwin McManus, but I have heard him speak several times. He is a very open person, and I think he is the real deal as well.

Mama Maggie Gobran is the all-in version of a modern saint. She left a comfortable upper class life and a university teaching position to run a ministry helping people who live in the garbage dumps of Cairo. These people are the lowest class and have no prospects. Generations of them live and work at the dump. They collect garbage around town and make a living by gleaning other people's trash. It is one of the poorest places on the earth. Very few parents can afford the school fees and uniforms required for their children to attend school, so even small children work gleaning the garbage. It is a paradise for flies, rats and snakes. It smells just as bad as you imagine it does. Mama Maggie spoke at a conference I attended a couple of years ago, and she completely lit the place up. She was just wandering around chatting pleasantly with a manner that was so completely gentle and unaffected it is hard to describe. Sort of like your maiden aunt from Mars. Her perspective is that she kind of accidentally got into her ministry, helping out her own aunt. She just really wants to do what she is doing because she likes it so much; the people are so engaging and worthwhile. She thinks she's normal. She isn't really normal. She practically glows. I still haven't quite recovered from the experience, but I'd like to have that glow.

I can't say whether Lee Strobel, Erwin McManus and Mama Maggie are just extraordinary people, or whether their lives are the result of an extraordinary commitment to going with the flow and following God. I can say that the closer you draw to God, the more connection you will have, and the more growth will result. Matthew 13:3-9 records Jesus' parable of the farmer and the seeds. The farmer scattered seed and it fell on four types of soil: hard soil on a pathway; thin, rocky soil; weedy soil; and good soil. The seed on the first three types of soil didn't produce much wheat. The seed that fell on the good soil grew and produced fruit—but in varying amounts, some thirty, some sixty, some one-hundred times what was sown.

Later when Jesus is alone with the disciples, he explains the parable. People are like the soil, and our exposure to God is the seed. Some people pretty much ignore it and go on with their lives—the hard soil. Some accept it and seek to have God in their lives, but as soon as that life isn't what they expected, they give up on it—the thin, rocky soil. Others just get too busy—the weedy soil. And some, accept it, and try to adapt their lives to God—the good soil. The more they seek to follow God, the more benefit they receive. The speed and amount of our growth comes down to our commitment---the seed was the same for all the soil types. God doesn't change, if we want to experience the benefit of a relationship with God, we have to change.

It is important not to confuse growth with the initial commitment to follow God. We all mess up, and we are going to continue to mess up. The idea is just that when we mess up, we, like King David, say, "oops, sorry" and try to head back in the right direction. You don't have to be good at this to see results, just committed to the effort.

Unfortunately, the other factor that affects our progress toward the upside is stress. Go-to, strong people, even those who are a bit skeptical of the concept, will grow faster and see more results than others who may profess faith more easily, but don't take any risks. This is because the benefits of a relationship with God are tied to how much you rely on him and seek to be connected. James 2:18-20 says "...Show me your faith without deeds, and I will show you my faith by what I do. You believe that there is one God. Good! Even the demons believe that—and shudder."

Belief in God isn't the same thing as actually seeking to connect with God. Just as love is a verb, faith is a verb. "Going with the flow" isn't drifting along a creek at a theme park on an inner tube, it's more like white water rafting. You just try to stay away from the rocks and hang on. The more practice you have, the more comfortable you become with stronger rapids. An Olympic downhill skier navigates a miles long downhill course at 60 miles an hour on terrain so steep it would be hard just to stand still on it. That takes a lot of practice. I tried downhill skiing once on the bunny hill constructed at a local golf course. Small children were helping me and my knee hurt for a week. Commitment makes the difference. A relationship with God is similar. If you want to see God work, you have to do something.

Jesus describes this process in Matthew 7:24-27.

"Therefore, everyone who hears these words of mine and puts them into practice is like a wise man who built his house on the rock. The rain came down, the streams rose, and the winds blew and beat against that house, yet it did not fall, because it had its foundation on the rock. But everyone who hears these words of mine and does not put them into practice is like the foolish man who built his house on sand. The rain came down, the streams rose, and the winds blew and beat against that house, and it fell with a great crash."

Note that both men encountered the same circumstances, but the wise man who relied on God was safe, while the other saw his life crash in around him. The difference was in their own commitment.

Commitment is still a key component of progress toward the upside today. I am well acquainted with a few pastors. Two of my cousins are married to pastors, and I do some volunteer work with a few others. I've spent some time with missionaries and their families. I can tell you that professional Christians are normal people even though they sometimes do extraordinary things. The only difference between good pastors and the rest of us, is that good pastors really do focus on building a relationship with God more than the rest of us. (There is virtually no difference between a bad pastor and the rest of us.)

Good pastors are not focused on building a club for their members. They are not like the Pharisees of the Bible, basking in the praise of people based on their position. Good pastors are genuinely more patient and more concerned with others than the rest of us. The best ones don't even know that. They haven't noticed that they are patient and kind. They actually believe that the people they meet are interesting and likeable. I don't personally know anyone with Mama Maggie's glow, but it is clear to me that the more you cultivate a relationship with God, the more you grow in a positive way. I know I meet a higher percentage of interesting and likeable people, and fewer annoying, stupid people, than I used to meet. I don't think people have actually evolved in any meaningful fashion in the past 30 years. I don't feel at all like a different person. My life experiences are not different, but I experience life differently than I used to. That is what God does.

I live a very mundane, suburban life and would have to say that I just dabble in building a relationship with God. I have still experienced profound changes in my attitude. I expect that the difference in my experience from the experience of people like Mama Maggie, and others who do extraordinary things but will never be mistaken for saints, like Lee Strobel or Erwin McManus; is that their commitment level is much higher than mine. They are white water rafters and downhill skiers, I am not.

I gave up on that whole downhill ski thing. I occasionally cross country ski at the local golf course or forest preserve on a nice day. Illinois is very flat, that gets you out in the fresh air, but it isn't really challenging. My search for God is about at the cross-country skiing on a golf course level; and I enjoy those kinds of results. Many people who complain that they really don't feel a sense of connection with God are doing the equivalent of sitting at home watching television. The results are just going to be lower with lower levels of commitment.

So, if you want to experience more of God, do something more stressful. Start small, tell God you want to do things his way. Then remember to take out the trash and pick up your socks without being asked. Tell people you love that you love them. Show up for work on time and turn in your reports.

Eventually you will see results, but you may not really notice. You will most likely just feel less stressed and feel like the ups and downs in your life are speed bumps rather than mountains. Over time, you can look back and see that you really have changed, but that can take a number of years if you are living an ordinary kind of life. Don't bail, the change is happening. It is more like the moon, constant and quiet; rather than the fireworks we expect.

I think to see fireworks, you have to make more of a commitment. One of the fireworks examples in the Bible is Joshua. Joshua was Moses' second in command. For 40 years he played a supporting role under Moses' legendary leadership. Joshua was one of the spies that Moses sent to scout the Promised Land. Only he and Caleb came back saying that the Israelites could take possession of the land. The remaining 10 scouts said the people of the land were too numerous and too strong. Of all the adults living when that report was made, only Joshua and Caleb actually entered into Canaan. When Moses died, Joshua became the leader of the Israelites. Moses' shoes were not easy to fill. The move into Canaan meant war. Joshua was a popular leader, but not without opponents. God decided to show his support for Joshua as a leader.

When the people prepared to cross the Jordan River into Canaan, God showed up. The Ark of the Covenant was the symbol of God's promise to the Israelites that he would be their God, go with them and lead them to the Promised Land. The Ark was a gold-plated box topped by a golden angel. It was built at Moses' direction. It contained Aaron's staff that budded into life before Pharaoh and the tablets holding the Ten Commandments. The Ark was kept in the innermost area of the tabernacle tent, and God physically manifested his presence among the people by a pillar of fire at night and a pillar of smoke by day that remained positioned over the innermost part of the tabernacle tent that held the Ark. Whenever the pillar moved, the people would pack up and follow it, each tribe and family in its assigned order. For forty years the Israelites packed up and moved whenever the pillar moved, led by the priests carrying the Ark. Sometimes the pillar stayed in one place for a month, sometimes days, sometimes a year or more. The Israelites lived their lives waiting for the pillar to move and lead them into the Promised Land.

After forty years of wandering around a desert, the pillar was headed into Canaan—the Promised Land. Everyone was excited, and anxious. The Jordan River was in the way and it was at flood stage. The Jordan River is a small river, it is about 156 miles long and at its widest it is about 20 yards across. Much of the year it is shallow, ranging from 17 feet at its deepest to just a few feet deep. During most of the year crossing the Jordan is no big deal even though it has steeply sided banks and a significant current. However, at flood stage, the Jordan becomes much more formidable. The river fills the banks and has a very strong current. The Jordan is impassable when flooded, The Israelites were on the banks of the Jordan. It was flooded and the pillar of God wasn't stopping. The Israelites were a little freaked out.

God instructed Joshua to array the people in their usual order to cross the Jordan, the priests in front with the Ark, followed by everyone else. At dawn they set out. The priests stepped into the river. That actually meant jumping off the bank into a roaring current, not wading into a few inches of water. When their feet hit the water, the Jordan, stopped flowing from upstream, and in a reprise of the Israelites crossing the Red Sea leaving Egypt, the entire caravan of Israel passed over the Jordan River on dry land. They stacked up 12 large stones in the middle of the river to mark the occasion. Then the priests carried the Ark onto dry land, and the water roared back down the channel. The people living in Canaan heard about it and were completely freaked out.

The miracle didn't happen until the priests jumped into the flooded river. I don't think they really expected a miracle. I think they were just hoping to somehow swim the 20 yards. They probably thought they were going to die and just didn't want to appear afraid in front of everyone else. Groupthink was strong then too. Archeologists have found evidence of the Israelites at Gilgal, located just beyond the Jordan and the site of their first encampment according to the book of Joshua in the Bible, which also records the Jordan crossing. People dispute whether a miracle crossing actually occurred, just as they do with the Red Sea crossing, No one can really prove the crossings one way or the other today. But the point is that unless you jump in and take a risk, you won't see much happen. The less risk you take, the less results you see. Mama Maggie is a jump in the Jordan kind of person; I think that is where the glow comes from.

This does not mean you are supposed to quit your job, sell your possessions and move to a foreign country where you don't speak the language and open a soup kitchen. God wants people in that country to open the soup kitchen. God wants you to do something where you live. Start with your family. They are the hardest people you know to get along with. They know all your faults, they aren't impressed with you and they are still carrying a grudge from that time in the 4th grade. Take a risk, love them radically. If necessary, apologize for that time in the 4th grade. A relationship with God is about a radical attitude, not radical tasks.

When you have cleaned up your relationships with your family, move on to your co-workers and neighbors. After that move on to the people in your area who need someone to open a soup kitchen—or at least someone to drop off food for the local food pantry or to pull garlic mustard in the local forest preserve. If you have some time and resources left, see what you can do to help the under-resourced in other parts of the US, or in other countries.

Hold onto your temper in rush hour traffic and remember "a soft answer turns away wrath" and "Do not lie" when you are negotiating a contract. The more risk you take, the more you expose yourself to experiences that open your eyes and your heart to the world around you; the faster you will grow toward the upside. There is no need to create a to-do list or a five year self-improvement plan. Just keep an attitude of wanting to connect with God, follow his lead, be kind to those you come in contact with, and go with the flow. The current will start to pick up and you will get swept into the rapids soon enough. It will mostly feel like an adventure rather than a chore.

This is simple, but not easy. The challenges will be very real and sometimes daunting. Whenever you are faced with a challenge that feels overwhelming, remember Paul's words in Philippians 4:13, "I can do all things through Christ who gives me strength". "I can't" is always the wrong answer. "I can" should be your answer to holding your temper, telling the truth, helping out your parents, reading your Bible, praying, managing your money, keeping your promises to your spouse, listening to your children, showing up to volunteer when you said you would. "I can" should be your answer to a healthy challenge that piques your interest when your thoughts are saying, "I'm not good enough", "I could never learn to do that", "I'm not smart enough", "I'm not strong enough", or "The people there would never accept someone like me". You can do a lot of things with God's help. God wants us to leave our comfort zone, grow and improve and to take some risks. God wants us to maximize our potential. That won't happen sitting in front of the television or computer screen.

While "I can't" is never a good answer, "I don't need to do that" can be. Not all challenges are appropriate challenges. "This is an impractical, unworkable idea"; "This is going to result in me being completely overscheduled and impair my ability to fulfill my responsibilities to people I love; "This is going to impair my ability to take appropriate care of myself"; "This is a complete budget buster" and "This is completely outside of any talent area I have"; are often completely correct answers. We have not left the realm of reality.

"I can't do that" is also the wrong answer when you start to think you should be following a religious behavior code. In Colossians 2:16-17, Paul was advising Christians who were being criticized for not following the Jewish behavior codes, he said, "Therefore, do not let anyone judge you by what you eat or drink, or with regard to a religious festival, a New Moon celebration, or a Sabbath day. These are a shadow of the things to come; the reality, however is found in Christ." And verses 20-22 continue: "Since you died with Christ to the basic principles of this world, why, as though you still belonged to it, do you submit to its rules: Do not handle! Do not taste! Do not touch! These are all destined to perish with use because they are based on human commands and teachings."

Just say no to people in the church who say you can't go to a movie, or to a concert, or have a beer or a glass of wine, or associate with "sinners", or whatever other behavior codes are the norm at the church you attend. Jesus had the occasional glass of wine and he associated with sinners all the time. We are not meant to live in a social straightjacket. Christians can and should live normal lives, not bound up by pseudo-religious behavior codes.

143

One hopes, however, it wouldn't be too long before "I don't want to" becomes your answer to unhealthy living choices, like too much to drink or drugs. You don't have to drop all your friends and become a monk. If you have been going out with a group and ending up drinking too much, you can still hang out with your friends. Volunteer to be the designated driver, or have a beer at the beginning of the evening, one in the middle and drink club soda the rest of the night. Your pool game will improve. Your friends will be a little uncertain at first, but if you don't criticize them they relax pretty quickly.

"No thanks, I don't like the high" is a perfectly acceptable rejection of an offer of recreational drugs. "No thanks, I'm not in the mood", "You aren't my type" and "I don't know you well enough" are all perfectly fine answers to offers of recreational sex, although those answers may meet with a little more resistance than turning down other things. (God is actually serious about sexual morality. 1 Thessalonians 4:3-4 says, "It is God's will that you should be sanctified: that you should avoid sexual immorality; that each of you should learn to control his own body in a way that is holy and honorable". That letter was written during Nero's reign when sexual mores were much more liberal than now.) I know these answers work, I've done these things. I've never lost a friend over a healthy lifestyle choice.

If you have addictions, are prone to over-indulge or are involved in abusive behavior patterns, yours or someone else's, you will have to make more dramatic changes. God will help you with that if you ask. But, the focus of this book is not that kind of healing, it is about reaching the upside, starting from a normal, everyday kind of place.

God helps us modify the unhealthy behaviors we all have toward healthier alternatives. Remember, though, the prime directive is to love God and love others; not to conform to a behavior code. Christianity is intended for normal people, with normal lives, and God doesn't want us to give the church a bad name among the unconvinced by being weird or overbearing. 1 Thessalonians 4:11 says, "Make it your ambition to lead a quiet life, to mind your own business and to work with your hands, just as we told you, so that your daily life may win the respect of outsiders and so that you will not be dependent on anybody."

God is very practical. God wants Christians and the church to have a good reputation based on health and kindness—the upside. God wants the church to draw people to God because it is a demonstrably better way to live—not to drag them in kicking and screaming and subject newcomers to criticism and a lot of rules. Going with the flow does not involve standing on a street corner shouting and holding a sign. It does not require knocking on the doors of strangers to pass out oddly worded flyers. Going with the flow just means loving God, respecting yourself and loving others. Really, it is time that normal people took back the church from those bizarre people on the street corners. We can be involved and still be normal.

God's support for normalcy should not be mistaken for God's indifference to our level of commitment. God wants us to be wholly committed to making him a central part of our lives. The people we are familiar with who have done amazing things, like Mama Maggie, Mother Teresa, Billy Graham, Billy Sunday and others, dove in headfirst. God did too. God commits to us. God is intrepid. God likes commitment. God likes intrepid people. Commitment pays off in obtaining growth to the upside.

God does not like people to equivocate. He actually dislikes that more than people who are cold to the idea of a relationship with God. At least cold people have an opinion he can work with. Romans 12:11 encourages Christians to be "never lacking in zeal, but keep your spiritual fervor, serving the Lord". And Revelations 3:15-19, talking to Christians in the ancient church of Laodicea, says, "I know your deeds, that you are neither cold nor hot. I wish you were either one or the other! So because you are lukewarm—neither hot nor cold—I am about to spit you out." This passage is especially relevant to normal, middle class Americans because it continues by saying,

> "You say, 'I am rich. I have acquired wealth and I do not need a thing.' But you do not realize that you are wretched, pitiful, poor, blind and naked. I counsel you to buy from me gold refined in the fire, so you can become rich and white clothes to wear so you can cover your shameful nakedness; and salve to put on your eyes so you can see. Those whom I love I rebuke and discipline. So be earnest and repent."

God views being wrapped up in our daily lives without any thought about developing a relationship with God, or with people outside of our immediate sphere, as thoroughly repugnant—serious sin. You can't get to the upside without changing your point of view about what is important, and without taking some steps to put that into action.

For those of us living normal, comfortable suburban lives, it is challenging to think of ourselves as involved in serious sin—or even to view ourselves as rich and self-satisfied. Our lives have plenty of risk and there are lots of things we need and want. That is true, but from an objective perspective, comparing ourselves to the billions of others in the world, we have pretty nice lives. By any objective standard, if you have two or three televisions in the house, a couple of computers, two cars, take a vacation in the summer, and throw away food you bought and didn't get around to cooking—you're rich. If don't know the names of the people who live next door; your spouse bought your mother's birthday present last year; you snap at wait staff if they aren't fast enough; or if you think it is ok to text and drive: it's possible you are a little self-centered. Experiencing more love, joy and peace requires an attitude adjustment and a lot of little tweaks to our approach to life on a daily basis.

Remember, don't drink the Kool-Aid and turn into a zombie. This is not about doing a bunch of good deeds. Take it slow, ten minutes at a time if you have to, cheerfully making small positive choices. If you can't make a choice cheerfully, don't make the choice. Just keep a willing attitude and an open mind, and jump into the flow.

Once you make a sincere commitment to follow what God wants for your life, you may also find yourself drafted into some adventures you hadn't really considered. Often you may not see God in the flow for quite a while, you may not even notice that you are in the flow. You go along on a daily basis, believing you are just following your own ideas of something that sounds interesting, but eventually you end up in place that is clearly connected to some kind of service to God. One day you look back over a couple of years, and you see the path that got you where you are was long and circuitous and not really what you started out to do.

That's how I got to be a lawyer, I didn't even know a lawyer when I decided to go to law school—it just seemed like a good idea at the time. I was graduating with a degree in Economics, I didn't want to teach Economics, and did well on the LSAT; so I went to law school. I've enjoyed my jobs tremendously. After 37 years as a lawyer, most of it in a business environment, I now find that a significant part of my practice is representing churches and other not for profits. I particularly enjoy that part of my practice, but it was never something I set out to do. In a way, I feel like I was drafted, but it's been fun—and I did promise to do things God's way. So maybe I volunteered and I was just fuzzy on the details. Going with the flow is like that, the details are a little fuzzy and you end up in interesting places you didn't know existed. It is always an adventure.

Progress toward the upside is individual and unpredictable. There isn't one answer to how long it will take to experience the upside. There isn't one answer to what the upside will look like in your life. Some people experience thirty-fold growth, some sixty, some one-hundred. It is really up to you. The more focused you are on making God a priority in your life, and putting those priorities into action, the more growth you will see. You will be able to tell that you are starting to experience the upside when you start to enjoy life more, feel more energized, and meet more interesting people.

You will probably also encounter more people who are in front of you needing you to listen and be patient and kind when you don't have enough time and don't know them well enough to make the effort. When we commit to God that we want to do things his way, he gives us opportunities. Take advantage of them. God's opportunities are always interesting in a way you didn't expect. It may be necessary to take a few minutes occasionally and think about whether you are experiencing growth in order to tell whether you are moving toward the upside. Usually we get the moon instead of fireworks. The effect can be subtle or dramatic, but it is worth the effort.

Chapter Seven
How Do I know I'm Not Crazy?

I understand that talking about having a relationship with God is going to make some people think I'm a little nuts. I also understand that it is not politically correct to use words like "crazy" and "nuts", but really, that is what you are thinking.

There are several psychological disorders that cause people to believe that they have a special relationship with God. Some people believe they are God, some believe they are Jesus, or that they are God's prophet sent to reform the world and that only they understand God's true path. Such people have delusions and some even hear voices. It is very common for people with serious psychological problems to focus on religion. Those conditions are very real; and the people affected by them need our assistance and our respect as they deal with life issues created by their illness.

Richard Dawkins, a preeminent scientist and famous atheist, took the idea one step further. He wrote The God Delusion Book, Houghton, Mifflin Harcourt (2008) to voice his opinion that all belief in any God is simply a "virus of the mind" spread from generation to generation. The book set off a debate that continues today. The definition used in psychological circles for a delusion is the belief in something that is not true or inherently impossible, and continued firm belief in that idea despite compelling evidence to the contrary. Christians meet the test of firm belief and failure to be deterred in their belief. The question is whether God is real or not and whether Jesus is the son of God. If there is no God, then Christians are delusional, and Jesus was delusional for claiming to be the son of God. If God is real, then perhaps the belief that God is unimportant is the delusion.

While few people go so far as to say God is a delusion, very many sane, sophisticated people today don't believe that actual communication with God is a possibility. Sophisticated people say they believe in God generally, or in a life force of some kind, but often feel that an actual experience of God is not a realistic concept. Intelligent, sophisticated people are very suspect of anyone who claims to have a personal relationship with God. Frankly, even I evaluate those claims with caution.

Obviously I think God is real, and I believe a relationship with God is not only possible, but that it is necessary to reach one's full potential. I am also the first to concede that there is no concrete, foolproof, tangible proof of God's existence. (There is also no concrete proof that he does not exist.) We can only infer God's existence from the existence of the earth and his effect on it. There is no recording of God creating the earth. God does not tweet or show up on talk shows running for election. We do have solid historical evidence that Jesus existed. We have both Biblical and secular evidence that his followers believed he performed miracles, and we have their recorded testimony of his resurrection. No one ever claimed to find Jesus body—but no one photographed the resurrection itself. We don't have video recordings of the Roman soldiers guarding the tomb. We don't have an official Roman acknowledgement that Jesus rose from the dead as the Messiah (although we do have Pontius Pilate's official declaration that Jesus' crime was that he was the "King of the Jews", a Messiah claim.)

We have enough evidence for me to believe that God exists and Jesus was the long-awaited Messiah. Many would disagree with my conclusions. Over the course of history, many people have rejected the idea that God is real and that Jesus was God walking the earth to provide a means of repairing our relationship with God. Many would deny there is any need to repair our relationship with God.

The more sophisticated one is, the more likely one is to deny God's existence entirely or to sanitize the image of God into a kindly, arcane, distant, rather amorphous being in the sky. Sophisticated people attribute miracles, both modern and ancient, to coincidence. Sophisticated people simply focus on the interrelationship of human beings as the proper focus of religion among civilized people. But that approach is really a denial that God exists in any real sense. Ethics is far different than a living, breathing God. Yahweh is neither distant nor amorphous. Yahweh is an unstoppable, uncontainable, wholly involved, infinite life force with power that makes a tsunami look like a ripple in a bathtub.

If Yahweh is real, the sophisticated people have to be incorrect. But the psychological disorders are also very real; and our own thoughts are real. Sorting out whether God is saying "warmer," "colder" or you are, is not always simple and clear. Those people standing on street corners shouting that the end of the world is near are proof enough that not all perceived experiences of God are real. We need to reality test what we think we experience of God. Because God is real, real experiences of God will pass the tests.

First, it is important to remember that God loves everyone. God loves you, personally, as an individual, but he loves everyone else personally and as an individual as well. Just as a good parent can love each child for their own unique character and personality, God can love us all. Good parents love all their children whether they are world renowned superstars or the odd character who sits in the corner of the library—God also can, and does, love each of us individually. You can't earn God's love and you don't have to deserve it, he just loves you. You are special and unique to God, but none of us are God's favorite.

We don't have special powers and God does not need us in order to accomplish his plans. If we start to believe that we have the power to influence the universe, we need to reassess. There are no superheroes. We are all different, and all valuable in our own way. Paul in Romans 12:3-6 puts it this way: "For by the grace given me, I say to every one of you: Do not think of yourself more highly than you ought, but rather think of yourself with sober judgment, in accordance with the measure of faith God has given you. Just as each of us has one body with many members, and these members do not all have the same function, so in Christ, we who are many form one body, and each member belongs to all the others. We have different gifts, according to the grace given us." We are peers, with no reason to try to impress God or each other.

Lots of people, perfectly sane ones, lose track of this concept. We get caught up in working on a worthy cause to correct injustice, improve opportunities for the under-resourced, and make life better for humanity. Even more seductive, we get caught up in our missions to lead and teach others in churches and other ministries. Sometimes we just get caught up in our attempts to behave in the most upright way we can imagine. We start to think we can, or should, impress God, or that his love and approval are tied up in what we do. We often start to think we are necessary for God's work to be accomplished. We often start to think that we are more gifted, more concerned—better--than our peers. We end up arrogant, narrow minded and unkind. God is not leading that behavior, we are making it up ourselves.

We may not go completely off track into that kind of self-absorption, but may still end up overworked, burnt out and disillusioned because the problems are still out there and God does not seem close. Even Mother Teresa felt some of these emotions. In her private letters, published after her death, and against her wishes, she relates that for much of her life she did not feel a close presence of God. He seemed distant and unconnected. She chose to continue working and try to "love him as he had never been loved." Come Be My Light, Brian Kolodiejchuk and Mother Teresa, Image, 2009. The idea that Mother

Teresa, whom many of us would describe as the epitome of Christian dedication in our time, did not feel close to God is very disturbing. For some people it is a reason to believe that God is a myth or that we can't really have a relationship with God—that he is distant or uncaring.

No one can really know what was in Mother Teresa's mind or what she actually experienced. I think it is possible that she was exhausted from the work she put into loving and serving others in an extremely difficult environment. I suspect she was exhausted from seeing the human misery around her day after day, year after year and wondering why it did not seem to improve. But she felt enough of an experience of God to keep on working for decades to serve the poor and spread the word that God did indeed care for them. Some sense of presence or value kept her going, and no one can deny what she accomplished. It is truly amazing that she did not completely burn out and give up on her ministry. Despite some of her internal fears and loneliness, she convinced a lot of people that God did indeed love them and cared about their well-being. It is possible Mother Teresa was off on her own journey rather than something God wanted her to do, but I can't help believing that God was involved in her work and in her life. She never doubted it.

Sometimes we have to reality test our emotional reactions about God against normal emotional reactions to our life situation. We all let our view of how our life should be going control our opinion of what God should be doing. We may believe God is close to us and cares for us when things are going our way. We may believe that God is distant and uncaring when we experience difficulties and betrayal. In reality, we are never God's favorite, and we are always God's treasure. We have just confused God's plan and timing with our own. That is very easy to do.

Lots of people, perfectly sane people, have trouble distinguishing between God's plans and priorities and their own. All of us do that to some extent. We call many of the confused "Pastor". Professional Christians live in a confusing world. By professional Christian I mean people who are in full time ministry positions and the volunteers who have made the church their primary energy focus. Professional Christians are the ones who keep the doors open and churches running. It's an odd world. People in it have a lot of responsibility, not much money and fuzzy goals. They tend to become isolated in that world, both by choice and by the reaction of others. Some are good at making church and other charitable endeavors relevant and effective; many are not. There aren't many role models and there aren't many success stories. All of them, good and bad, have the same problem as Mother Teresa. They work long exhausting hours without seeing many results. Most churches have very small staffs, just one or two full time ministers and a small core of volunteers who try to do it all. The grind gets to them.

Many professional Christians start to think that they have to do more, be more, run more programs, try more things. They become more and more frustrated by the lack of real growth in the members of their congregation, and sometimes by the lack of congregation. They become more convinced that the next program, the next sermon series, the next fundraising event, the next project to help the poor, or help the sick, or help the elderly or take kids to camp or improve the building; is going to make their church turn the corner and become a vibrant, growing Christian community. The reality is that our personal growth is up to us. Our leaders aren't responsible for us. They don't have much control over our growth, even though they may feel responsible. And even though we may try to hold them responsible.

Another unfortunate truth is that, just as many people with psychological issues are drawn into psychology, some number of professional Christians are drawn into the church because of very high control needs or even psychological unhealthiness of some kind. Some church workers who confuse God's will with their own simply have issues. Their confusion doesn't result from anything God does. Their issues run a whole gamut. They may just be confused in their faith and searching for answers. They may have very serious psychological impairments. They may have unrealistic expectations and poor social skills from being isolated in "church world" too long. They may just be control freaks.

It is disturbingly common for church workers to display little evidence of any real connection with God. They are very troubled zombies. Some of them aren't really Christians at all, in the sense that they have only committed to the church and their agenda for the church, but never really committed to finding out who God is and developing a relationship with God. Or they may be Christians, in the most basic sense, but have never grown in their relationship with God in any way that influences their behavior. We call those people "unconverted" church workers. Unconverted church workers are a big problem. They create a lot of confusion among their congregations and among people looking at the church and wondering whether Christianity is real. Unconverted ministers attract a lot of attention from outside the church. People point at them as illustrations of the falseness of the God and the futility of religion. I think those of us in the church should pay more attention to the issue.

Unconverted church workers are a conundrum. They don't know they aren't Christians. Because they are leading the church, they never see examples of real relationships with God. As a result, it is nearly impossible to explain the problem to them. Anyone pointing out the issue is deemed to be a heathen in need of reformation. It requires exposure to good Christian leaders to open their eyes to new possibilities and the reality of a relationship with God. Willow holds a Leadership Summit every August. It is a two day conference devoted to leadership training for church workers and others, like the business community, who have leadership responsibilities. World class leaders like President Clinton, Gen. Colin Powell and Condoleeza Rice have spoken. President Clinton spoke while he President. Well known authors on the subject of leadership, like Jim Collins and Patrick Lencioni, speak every year, as do recognized, effective Christian leaders. A few pastors convert every year. A lot of people involved in ministry who were approaching burnout go away re-energized. The Leadership Summit and other conferences like it can be very helpful to bring the zombies back to life.

Fortunately, unconverted ministers are far less common than simple burnout. The frustration of church work, with its endless pace and few results, defeats a lot of people. For the most part, pastors and other church workers are deeply committed to their work. They want to see change. As Darren Whitehead, a former teaching pastor at Willow, described it, they echo Jeremiah's call that we may "see in our time" the kind of impact and dynamic presence of Yahweh reflected in the Old Testament; and the dynamic involvement and full on commitment reflected in the New Testament among early Christians. They long to see a modern church like the one described in Acts 2:42-47.

> "They devoted themselves to the apostles' teaching and to the fellowship, to the breaking of bread and to prayer. Everyone was filled with awe, and many wonders and miraculous signs were done by the apostles. All the believers were together and had everything in common. Selling their possessions and goods, they gave to anyone as he had need. Every day they continued to meet together in the temple courts. They broke bread in their homes and ate together with glad and sincere hearts, praising God and enjoying the favor of all the people. And the Lord added to their daily those who were being saved."

Church workers burn out trying to turn that description into a modern day reality. We should all try to give our church workers a break now and again to regain some energy—and some perspective.

That enticing Acts 2 description is of a very short lived situation. That description was accurate for only a few weeks or months immediately after the death of Jesus, and only for one congregation in Jerusalem. The new church was soon scattered and subjected to persecution, as recorded beginning in Acts 4. The 21 New Testament books that were written as letters to small church congregations spread around the Middle East are filled with discussion about various failings and quarrels of the new church. Even those first few weeks and months weren't idyllic. Lying, one-upmanship and bickering are recorded in Acts 5 and 6. The first martyr, Stephen, was stoned to death in Acts 7. Utopia never existed. We forget that.

Pastors also frequently forget that the United States is the richest country in the history of the world. Many churches, like Willow, are situated in financially fortunate areas. The pastors of those churches think they have an easy time of it compared to churches in China, or the Sudan, or other areas of the world where Christians are actively persecuted. Suburban pastors may believe they have an easy life compared to inner city ministries where the congregation lives with high levels of economic need and dysfunction. They expect to see compelling results in their congregation because they believe they have the easiest jobs. If they aren't zombies themselves, they feel like failures when they see so little change year after year. Like the rest of us, they want to see God create the kind of big, easily recognized miracles they've read about in the Bible.

To a certain extent, their frustration and confusion is a misunderstanding of the problem. Pastors in comfortable suburban churches do not have an easy job. In Biblical terms, financially comfortable, emotionally healthy people are the hardest case. They see little need for God in their own life and tend to reduce God to a kindly distant, amorphous being. For them, God and religion are the same thing and the real point is ethics. Church is a place to spend a few hours on Sunday engaged in polite rituals. Their responsibilities are limited to treating other people well and making appropriate donations to the poor. The dynamic, living, active presence of Yahweh in their lives is a foreign concept. In Matthew 19:24, Jesus commented on this attitude by saying: "I tell you the truth, it is hard for a rich man to enter the kingdom of Heaven. Again I tell you, it is easier for a camel to go through the eye of a needle than for a rich man to enter the kingdom of

154

God." America is a great place to live, but it is not Utopia in terms of people searching for a connection to God—that isn't something nice, normal people do here. The attitude of indifference to a real God common among nice, normal people is a source of great stress and confusion for ministers.

Good pastors get very frustrated dealing with nice, normal people. They keep feeling there should be more and they keep trying to create more. Even the most committed pastors, sometimes especially the most committed pastors, can lose track of God's quiet impression in their attempts to serve God. God's voice gets drowned out in the stress and busyness of their lives just like it does with the rest of us. The pastor's own ideas become "God's will". Sometimes pastors question the integrity, spirituality or commitment of the members of their congregation who don't fully commit to whatever the new "Great Leap Forward"[28] is. We can all succumb to this particular delusion, but professional Christians run a greater risk of damaging themselves and others by acting on it.

Pat Buchanan's declaration that God had told him to run for President is a very public example of this kind of inaccurate perception of what God wants. It is also the kind of thing that causes the general public to question whether Christians aren't all just a little "off" when they start talking about "following God's will" for their life, or "being led by God. Very nice, very well-meaning pastors and church workers sometimes unwittingly create the same sort of impression, just by trying too hard to do the right things instead of letting their normality show.

I can't blame people for reacting with skepticism, or worse, to claims that the speaker is "on a mission from God." I have that reaction myself. Some of these people are just plain weird. I think the solution is for normal people to get more involved in the church, rather than to abandon it and try to sort out how to relate to God by themselves. If a bunch of normal people each got involved in their local church, and didn't give in to the stilted strangeness; and if each person

---

[28] Great Leap Forward was a name the Chinese government used for its various development programs in the 1950's and 1960's. As documented in Bette Bao Lord's wonderful book, Eighth Moon: the True Story of a Young Girl's Life in Communist China", Harper & Rowe (1964) paperback issued by Avon Publishing in 1983, many of the programs were unsuccessful and some were profoundly detrimental. Each one was touted as the solution to the problem of not enough jobs, not enough food and not enough resources for the millions of rural Chinese looking for a better life. Still today, I am reminded of that book, fairly or unfairly, when I encounter anyone pushing any new program as the ultimate solution to a complicated issue. Real solutions to real problems are messy, slow and wound up in human relationships.

did a little bit of the work on a regular basis, no one would be burnt out—and the church would be a lot more normal. It is much easier to reality test whether or not a plan is your idea or God's when you are well rested and around normal people.

The tricky part of a discussion about people going off the deep end thinking they are on a mission from God for no particular reason, is that God does have a plan for each of us. God will provide a sense of his presence and a guiding nudge for our behavior. For most of us, including professional Christians, the nudge is to place a higher value on our fellow human beings. The nudges are much less task oriented than people imagine. In Ecclesiastes 5:18-20, Solomon sums it all up this way:

> "Then I realized that it is good and proper for a man to eat and drink and to find satisfaction in his toilsome labor under the sun during the few days of life God has given him—for this is his lot. Moreover, when God gives any man wealth and possessions, and enables him to enjoy them, to accept his lot and be happy in his work—this is a gift of God. He seldom reflects on the days of his life, because God keeps him occupied with gladness of heart."

In my life, I can tell when God is nudging because he always wants me to spend more time than I have, being nicer than I feel like being, to people I don't care that much about—when I am rushing around all wrapped up in some grand scheme I think is important. Many of the task oriented nudges that people perceive arise out of their own approval needs or performance needs. Many of them arise out of the task orientation of their community or their church. You can't fairly blame that on God. The Bible doesn't contain any performance-based standards. Solomon's admonition in Ecclesiastes 9:7-10 is probably the best definition of a great mental attitude and great mental health I have ever read.

> "Go, eat your food with gladness, and drink your wine with a joyful heart, for it is now that God favors what you do. Always be clothed in white[29], and always anoint your head with oil. Enjoy life with your wife, whom you love, all the days of this meaningless life that God has given you under the sun---all your meaningless days. For this is your lot in life and your toilsome labor under the sun. Whatever your hand finds to do, do it with

---

[29] Samuel Clemens, aka Mark Twain, cited this verse as his reason for wearing his trademark white suit.

all your might, for in the grave, where you are going, there is neither working nor planning nor knowledge nor wisdom."

God wants us to go with the flow, love people and enjoy life. That is the meaning of life, to worship God, acknowledge his presence and his authority, and just go with the flow, living the life God gave you, enjoying the gifts he has given you, and sharing them with others. That will never make you feel crazy.

God does assign game changing tasks to a few people—they are truly on a "mission from God"; but he doesn't assign anyone the job of trying to impress him. Titus 3:4-5 sums it up: But when the kindness and love of God our Savior appeared, he saved us, not because of righteous things we had done, but because of his mercy."

Moses was called to lead Israel out of Egypt, but Hebrews 3:23-29 points out that it was his great faith, not his great works; that was the foundation of his relationship to God. Number 12:3 describes Moses as a very humble man. The Israelites numbered over a million people when they left Egypt[30]. Moses was literally one in a million. Billy Graham and Dr. Martin Luther King are also one in a million leaders, and there are other heroes of the faith.

There are also heroes in secular contexts whose work has created a huge benefit for society. (Besides just ordinary good works and good science, God sometimes drafts people who aren't known as Christians to help out mankind in a one-in-a-million way. Jeremiah, an Old Testament prophet, describes Nebuchadnezzar, King of Babylon, as the "servant of God", Jeremiah 25:9. Jonas Salk, Rosa Parks and Rachel Carson seem like modern examples.) It is possible that you are one in a million too—it just isn't likely. God's paradigm is more of a "grow where you are planted" model. We are called to lead in a smaller arena. No need for some grand plan, just try being nice to your family, your co-workers, your friends—and your enemies. That last one will take all your attention. If you come up with a grand plan, think carefully about why you are pursuing the plan. If you want to prove to God or others that you are the best, it's probably your idea, not God's. Nothing wrong with grand plans, just don't blame them on God.

If it turns out you are one in a million, that fate will follow you around, no need to go looking for it. God will also provide for you in

---

[30] Exodus 12:37 records there were about six hundred thousand men, besides women and children. Many Egyptians also joined them in the exodus; and there were large herds of sheep, goats and cattle as well.

way that meets the task at hand. If you are one in a million, God will provide for that one-in-million task. Moses had help, Billy Graham has help—no one is called to go out and make themselves miserable and burned out trying to impress God.

As discussed earlier, nearly all of the people in the Bible who received specific task assignments were drafted, and they were not happy about it. Alternatively, like Queen Esther, they were just dropped into a situation without any thought at all about participating in a grand plan. They chose to participate once they were in the situation, but they did not seek out the assignment. If you approached God, jumping up and down, hand in the air shouting "pick me, pick me", it is likely that you are following a path of your own choosing, not one God sent you down. It isn't that God doesn't want people to willingly and happily follow the path; it is just that God doesn't shout and there aren't big arrows pointing the way. Jumping up and down shouting "pick me" will almost certainly drown out God's quiet presence. If that is you, just chill. God will involve you in his plan.

For most of us, God isn't asking us to change the world; he is just asking us to make our corner of the world more civilized. God isn't likely to ask you to stand on street corners shouting the truth to passerbys. God more commonly assigns small tasks to people than grand plans. God asks us to call a friend when they are feeling down, to donate to a worthy cause, to volunteer at church or in the community. God probably wants to you tell your friends and neighbors that God is real and loves them. God might actually want you to do something specific, but it likely involves holding your temper and being nice to the person down the street or sitting across from you at the dinner table—or even your enemy. For that matter, loving your enemy would be a one-in-a-million achievement if you could really pull it off.

There are a couple more reality tests. Since we should expect God to interact with us—all of us—even very normal suburbanites; it is important to be able to distinguish God's quiet presence and nudges from the general noise in our lives and in our thoughts. One of the primary hallmarks of God's voice, and one that easily distinguishes it from our own thoughts, or from psychosis, is that God's voice is always positive. Mentally ill people who hear voices hear negative voices. "You are no good". "You will never amount to anything". "What a loser you are." "Hurt that person—they are no good". "You are so much better than they are, they should all be doing what you say." Many of our own thoughts can be negative as well, "I'll never be able to do that". "They don't like me and there is no way I can ever be part of that group."

"This is too hard." By contrast, God's voice is always positive. "I love you". "You are my treasured child", "You are good enough, you are smart enough". "You can do this if you try hard". "Rest now and try again later when you are feeling refreshed. "Be kind to that person". "Hold your temper" "Be patient". "Don't be afraid". "Tell the truth, it will all work out". "Look at the beautiful sky today." "Did you see that beautiful bird fly past?" Try to take a breath and make some space in your life and your thoughts to perceive the positive messages God is sending to you. God loves you and he will encourage you in small, quiet ways.

Second, God will absolutely never nudge you to do something that harms yourself or anyone else. God's presence will never belittle you. God's presence will never belittle other people. God will never suggest that you lord it over other people. God does not like arrogance. At the Last Supper, recorded in Luke 22: 24-27, Jesus cautioned his disciples not to be arrogant in their leadership, but rather that "the greatest among you should be like the youngest, and the one who rules like the one who serves." If you feel that God is directing you to correct the faults of those around you and really show them what they should be doing—that is not God. If you feel the urge to go fix someone by making their faults clear to them or to other people, resist the urge. If correcting behavior is your job for some reason, i.e., you are that person's parent or manager (or close friend), keep the advice very quiet and as kind as you can manage.

God will convince those around us of their faults in good time. We are supposed to be demonstrating a genuine life filled with mental health, joy and love that makes people curious about what we have that they don't. We are supposed to focus on our own faults, not those of others. Note that this has to be genuine. God will never nudge you to lie by pretending to be perfect. God will never nudge you to lie by pretending to be worthless. "You shall not lie" is one of the Big Ten.

A third reality test for distinguishing whether God is involved with your inclination is that God nags. They don't tell you that in church, but it is clearly demonstrated in the Bible. One way to tell God's voice is its persistence. If you are experiencing a very persistent feeling about doing something kind and positive---that is likely God. If you are contemplating a positive action, and you encounter people who suggest it to you out of the blue, or you mention the possibility, expecting jeers, and people say "finally! I always thought you should be doing that" or "what a great fit for you!"---God probably has a hand in pointing you in that direction. If you think the idea is compelling and exciting, but ridiculous, impractical or just way too odd, but you can't shake the feeling that it is actually possible, and if whatever it is *were* achievable, that thing would be the most exciting thing you can think of to be involved with---that points to God. If whatever it is just seems inescapable, continuing to crop up in ways that are difficult to avoid— that is very likely to be God nagging. Give whatever it is a whirl and see where it leads.   No real point in trying to circumvent whatever it is. You can't outwait or avoid God. In Psalm 139:7-9, David says, whether in lament or great comfort, it's hard to tell:

> "Where can I go from your Spirit? Where can I flee from your presence? If I go up to the heavens, you are there. If I make my bed in the deep, you are there. If I rise on the wings of dawn, If I settle on the far side of the sea, even there your hand will guide me, your right hand will hold me fast."

God also has a sense of humor. If you find yourself saying repeatedly that "someone should do something about that---it's so unfair". Whatever it is will often wind up inescapably in your lap to fix.

Fourth, God' voice is very consistent. God will never nudge you to do anything that contradicts the Bible. The Bible is a very important resource in determining what God is really like and it is the baseline for testing whether one of these perceptions is really God. Start with the Ten Commandments. If you think God is telling you it is ok to have an affair with that person at work because your marriage is in a difficult place—that is not God. If you think God is telling you that you are too busy to visit your elderly parents and run a few errands for them, even if the other obligations are good things like serving the under-resourced— that is not God. If you think God is reassuring you that it is ok to cover up that dishonesty because the truth would be too hurtful to others-- that is not God. God will never tell you to be unkind, or dishonest, or that lashing out in anger is the appropriate course of action. In fact, God is annoyingly consistent. Hebrews 13:8 describes Jesus as "the same, yesterday, today and forever". In Malachi 3:6, the prophet quotes God as saying, "I the Lord, do not change. So you, O descendants of Jacob, are not destroyed." God does not change his mind. God really wants you to behave like an adult and to treat others kindly; and he *never* deviates from those nudges.

Along with God's persistence is God's practicality—a big part of the reality test. Using practicality as a reality test seems like an oxymoron, given all the flagrantly impossible miracles described in the Bible. But practicality is important. God recognizes that our lives are firmly rooted

160

in reality and God is, despite some very big plans, very practical. If you get nudged to do something, you will have the resources and talent available to do the task, even though you may be very stretched by the task. If God has a task in mind, it will be something that you have a natural talent for and enjoy doing.

God's assignment for you will likely be something that grows out of experience you already have. If you are feeling as if you need to "bear the cross" of your assigned Christian duties, you are in the wrong place or doing the wrong thing in the right place or you have allowed yourself to get too loaded down. God's plans are stretching adventures, not drudgery. You are likely already located where God wants you to be, and already interested in the issues he would like you to contribute to resolving. Take a look around and see what people need some attention in your small corner of the world. Try treating your enemies with civility and honesty—this even applies to political rivals. If we were all just showed love to our families, our neighbors and our co-workers, the world would be a very different place.

God probably doesn't want you to do something really strange halfway across the world, but he may ask you to do something a little bit odd in your own culture, particularly if you are one in a million. God asked Noah to build an ark; that was exceedingly odd. People jeered. We have a hard time believing it ever actually happened at all. Many people regard the ark as a myth. There are actually flood myths in a number of cultures from all around the world. In fact, there are more than 200 such myths in cultures from every continent. Every one of them has a higher power flooding the earth as a punishment for disobedience.

Some commentators, like Joseph Campbell, have concluded that the tale of Noah is so improbable that it too should be classified as a myth and we should reject the notion that there was ever a world-destroying flood.   I tend to think that if there are over 200 myths from every continent claiming that there was a world-wide flood, that there probably was a great, world wide flood of some kind. To me, the real question is whether any of the versions of the flood story provide any accurate information. The Biblical version is the only one that gives a detailed description in unembellished terms that purports to be actual history. Genesis 6 tells us the actual dimensions of the ark and that it was made of gopher (Cypress) wood. The myths from other cultures have a mythical tone about them, unlike the matter of fact tone in Genesis, although a few do provide some before and after context and details. As strange as it seems, I think the Biblical version is accurate, or essentially accurate—I can't quite believe two of every animal on the earth were on the boat. It was very odd for Noah to build an ark, but it was something God wanted him to do. He wasn't crazy. Sometimes God does want us to do something a bit odd, or at least out of our comfort zone.

On a more mundane level, Willow Creek recently opened its new 60,000 square foot Care Center to house its ministries to the under-resourced in a zip code listed among the wealthiest in the country. The $10 million building was fully funded by donations before construction began and hundreds of well-off people regularly volunteer there with the cheerful expectation and hope that many of the clients will become part of the church community[31]. That's odd, but it is a natural progression of the programs at Willow. The ministries aren't new, they have been in place for years and are well established. Many of those volunteers have been serving for years as well. There will be some expansion of programs and some new programs that will be starting in the new facility. Growth will be challenging, but it isn't a wholesale change or an impractical "Great Leap Forward"—it is organic growth. That's odd, but not crazy.

---

[31] Although Barrington and South Barrington are affluent, there are several communities within 30 minutes of the church that have significant populations of under-resourced people. Suburban poverty is often underestimated because it is less visible than urban poverty. The 2011 Report on Illinois Poverty, Social IMPACT Research Center (2011), Heartland Alliance for Human Needs and Human Rights. Project leaders: Jennifer Clary, Ellyn Drathring, Amy Rynall, Kristin Scally and Amy Terpstra, reports that between 2.9% and 4.7% (depending on the county) of the suburban Chicago metropolitan area population falls into the extreme poverty category with income of less than half of the national poverty level. Between 7.7% and 10.5 % fall below the national poverty level and between 11.1% and 16.4% fall below the "low income" standard. Willow has also been part of the Northwest Suburban PADS ministry for about 20 years. PADS provides a place to sleep, food and, at Willow, showers and laundry facilities, during the months of October through April to area homeless people. When the economy is good, the number of guests each week will range between 20 and 35, depending on the weather. When the economy is poor, the site maximum of 50 guests will be reached nearly every week. Willow is only one of 25-30 churches in its immediate area that hosts homeless people. Northwest Suburban PADS is only one of 7 or 8 PADS organizations just in the west and far west suburbs of Chicago. There are many more PADS organizations, and many more churches and many other shelters, providing homeless people with food and shelter every night during the cold months of the year. The Great Recession was not kind to a number of people. I have clients who are business owners, living in homes that were worth over a million dollars in 2005, that are now worth two-thirds, or half, of that; and whose incomes have dropped just as much or more. Several of them are teetering on the brink of bankruptcy, some have had to declare bankruptcy. Occasionally we even see a former pillar of the community at PADS. Some people who look wealthy get help from Willow's Care Center too. Financial need has many faces.

God's suggestions for you are also likely to be oddly kind. God may suggest you chair the local PTA, coach your child's soccer team, make some space for a drifting teenager in your family, refurbish the local playground, clean out brush in the local forest preserve, or host a neighborhood Bible study. God is very likely to want you to be involved in positive ways with your community. It may seem odd or difficult at first. New things always do. Involvement is odd in our culture today. Many of us have very few social relationships outside of our immediate families—there just isn't time. There can be time if being involved is a priority for you. If you feel a nudge to get involved, go ahead, be a little odd and help your community. But run it past the reality test first. Is it positive? Is it ethical and consistent with Biblical teaching? Is it within or at least within reach of, your skill set? Is it practical? Do you get positive feedback from people you trust? Odd is very different than crazy.

Finally, and this is a concept that people have had difficulty with for centuries, God's blessing and being in sync with what God wants for you in your life is completely unrelated to financial success and security. We all have a real tendency to feel that if we are doing well financially, if we are safe and secure physically, then God is blessing us. If we are struggling, then he is not. I often feel this myself. Certainly people who are truly poor, wondering where their next meal is coming from, and people who are trapped in an abusive situation, must wonder why God has abandoned them. He has not abandoned them, even if the rest of us have. God loves those people every bit as much as he loves me.

If you are evaluating a nudge from God based solely on the financial risk, you are not considering the whole picture. God will provide sufficient resources for his plans, but he doesn't promise that we will feel financially comfortable. God sustained Elijah, a one in a million Old Testament prophet, and his host family during a long famine, but they didn't have big stores of food. God supplied just enough oil and flour for each days' needs, but he did that every day for nearly 3 years. I Kings 17. God supplied the Israelites with manna every day for 40 years. But the manna fell each day and went bad if the Israelites attempted to store it overnight (except for the Sabbath.) Exodus 16.

God's presence is the blessing, not money. We have security, it just doesn't look the way we think it should. In Biblical terms, the neediest people are those who are financially comfortable and healthy, but busily engaged in their lives without a thought for God. James 2:5 says, "Listen my dear brothers: Has not God chosen those who are

163

poor in the eyes of the world to be rich in faith and to inherit the kingdom he has promised those who love him?" Sometimes it is when we don't know where else to turn and what to do next, that we are most confident of God's presence—holding your hand in the dark.

On the other hand, sometimes we talk about under-resourced people as if they are somehow ennobled by being poor—not true. Many under-resourced people are poor because they have dysfunctional behavior patterns. Under-resourced people in the US do not have the same opportunities as wealthier people. Their housing is worse, their schools are worse, their access to healthy food and to health care is worse. However they do have access to basic resources, including educational opportunities that exceed those available to many people, even many middle class people, in other parts of the world. Under-resourced people are not less intelligent or less industrious than wealthier people. Many times, the problem of poverty in the US is really one of attitude. People get caught in a cycle and believe they are unable to succeed, so they don't try. They cling to unhealthy patterns of behavior. Parents give their children drugs. Mothers encourage teenaged girls to have babies. Adults jeer at children who try to succeed in school. We act sometimes as if poverty is somehow fated and unchangeable. It is not. God is not cursing the poor. The poor are not noble victims. The reality is that poor people are just people with less money than the rest of us. God doesn't define or limit their financial status.

The corollary to this thinking is that being rich sometimes draws criticism, as if anyone who has money has somehow cheated their way to wealth. This is untrue and unfair. Most people with money have worked very hard for it and turn down many opportunities to waste it. Being rich is not bad; it is not unrighteous in some way. Being rich is a good thing. Having greater resources opens a lot of doors to enjoy life, and to do good things—besides offering some security and ease of mind. Many wealthier people in the US are wealthy because of positive choices they made. Wealthier people do have access to better opportunities, nice houses, good schools, access to a healthy diet and good health care. But, just like under-resourced people, the ultimate result is based on personal choices. Wealthy people have more opportunities to waste money, waste time and waste their health through poor choices. In the US, personal wealth is often the result of positive choices—hard work and discipline. Wealthy people are not smarter than other people, but they are frequently more disciplined than the average person. We sometimes act as if wealth is fated and unchangeable. It is not. The wealthy are not being blessed as God's favorites. The wealthy are not greedy, insensitive, ignorant pigs. The

164

reality is that wealthy people are just people with more money than the rest of us. Having things is nice, it just isn't the point of a relationship with God. It isn't even a side effect of having a relationship with God.

We could say the same thing of the middle class. In God's view, having money or not having money is a tangent to the real point. Being poor is not a curse from God. Being poor does not mean that person is any more or less connected with God than someone else. Being rich is not an anointment by God. Being rich does not mean a person is any more or less connected with God than someone else. Financial resources and financial security are not the point of a relationship with God at all. The real point is more love, joy and peace in our lives— stronger relationships and self-actualization. The real point is living with the connection to God himself. It is very hard for us to take money and security out of our thinking when evaluating a relationship with God, but it really is irrelevant. Potential wealth is just not part of the reality test at all.

Financial issues continue to be a huge sticking point for many people searching for a real connection to God. Many people have been turned off by their perception that the church is just after money. That is made worse by the fact that throughout history there have been religious leaders who really did just bleed people for money. Churches do need money to operate and very few churches, or other charities for that matter, are well funded. Many of them do sound like a broken record begging for money in an effort to stay afloat. When you start to feel that you are being dunned for money without good reason, but you are wondering whether you should give to the cause, evaluate the request fairly. Look at how the organization uses the money. Is the organization worthwhile and well-managed? Is the request reasonably related to your available financial resources? Do you believe in the cause and want to support it. If the answers to those questions are "yes"; seriously consider the request.

I've recommended tithing, or at least giving away some money, as one of the hallmarks of actually putting your belief into action, as well as a means of releasing the grip that money has on our thought processes. The discussion about tithing belongs in this chapter as well. Many people, even fellow Christians, will tell you that you are a little nuts for tithing. People believe that volunteering time is a perfectly fine substitute for tithing on your income or that taking care of your family is a perfectly fine substitute for tithing. Regrettably, while the Bible does make it clear that mechanistic tithing that is devoid of any real faith or commitment is not a substitute for actual commitment, the direction to tithe is very clear. Money has a unique place in our affections and the Bible doesn't provide any substitutes for giving some away[32].

The Bible is clear about our responsibility to support our family. If you have to choose between feeding your children or tithing, God would prefer that you took care of your family. But many of us equate our lifestyle preferences with necessities and decline to tithe in favor of lifestyle choices. God is serious about tithing. Remember that Jesus praised the poor widow for putting her pennies into the offering, and stubbornly insists in Matthew 6: 25, 32-33, that you

> "do not worry about your life, what you will eat or drink or what you will wear. ...For the pagans run after all these things and your Heavenly Father knows that you need them. But seek first his kingdom and his righteousness, and all these things will be given to you as well".

God wants us to trust him, not money. One of the fastest ways to actually see an effect in your life from a relationship with God is to turn loose of some of the money that you think you need.

Frankly, there is no escaping feeling a little nuts about tithing and you won't get much positive feedback when you ask for opinions, but try it anyway. Tithing is very freeing and it is amazing that you will find that you really can afford to do it. It is also amazing to see what happens when your money is put to good use for the benefit of others. In Luke 6:38, Jesus urges us to "Give, and it will be given to you. A good measure, pressed down, shaken together and running over will be poured into your lap. For with the measure you use, it will be measured to you". Paul said something similar in 2 Corinthians 9:6, "Remember

---

[32] The only explicit possible exception is taking care of your aging parents, and I think this passage likely relates to a vow to God in excess of the tithe. In Matthew 15:3, Jesus, chiding the Pharisees for hypocrisy said:

> "And why do you break the command of God for your tradition? For God said 'Honor your father and mother' and 'Anyone who curses his father or his mother must be put to death'. But you say that if a man says to his father or mother, 'Whatever help you might otherwise have received from me is a gift devoted to God', he is not to honor his father with it. Thus you nullify the word of God for the sake of your tradition".

this: whoever sows sparingly will reap sparingly, and whoever sows generously will reap generously."

These verses have been used to say that if you give money to the church you will receive monetary rewards. The Bible never really says that. The reward offered in the Bible is more joy, more love, more peace; not more money. God also promises to give us the material things we actually need, just not all the things we want.

As for those churches who beg for money but don't seem to do anything constructive with it, or the small minority of "religious leaders" who are frauds, charlatans or worse; the church is infected with humanity, just like any other human institution. Some common sense is required to sort out the good programs from the bad, but don't let that stop you. We don't stop going to doctors because some commit malpractice, we shouldn't give up on church, and certainly not God, because there are some foolish people and some bad people associated with church. If we all quit our jobs every time we encountered someone who was incompetent, dishonest, over-reaching, over bearing or self-aggrandizing, none of us would be working. That would be crazy. Those aren't good enough reasons to give up on God either.

Eventually, if you honestly pursue a relationship with God, you will start to feel a kind of connection with the presence of God. If may be hard to recognize, particularly when it is new and you don't really know what to expect. If you feel you have encountered God and aren't sure about it, it is a good idea to just take things slowly and see how they work out. Don't announce you are running for President because God told you to. Continue to read the Bible, to pray, to try to keep it in mind to be kind to people, and see how things progress. You will eventually notice that you feel more peaceful about everyday stuff. You like your family more, and the neighbors don't bug you as much. That is the presence of God working. You may call a friend from time to time and hear them say, "I'm so glad you called, I'm having a horrible day and you are just the person I wanted to talk to". That is God working.

If you are being drafted for some task, events will start to fall into place, and a sensible plan will emerge that excites you. Get feedback from some sensible people you know. Don't tell them you "think God is leading you" to do something. Just tell them that you were thinking of doing whatever it is, and ask what they think about it. Take a few small actions in the direction you are exploring, see how it feels and how it works out. If it is God working, eventually you will look back over the course of events and see that you landed in a place where you had a unique ability to contribute, and that you enjoyed yourself doing it. If it's your own idea, it will likely founder along the way before you get too deeply engrossed.

It will all feel a little odd, but in a good way—not in a crazy way. Romans 11:33-36 puts it this way: "Oh the depth of the riches of the wisdom and knowledge of God! How unsearchable his judgments and his paths beyond tracing out! Who has known the mind of the Lord? Or who has been his counselor? Who has ever given to God, that God should repay him? For from him and through him are all things. To him be the glory forever!"

And one final reminder that all this has to be real. We find that connection, go with the flow, and follow God's lead *after* we make a basic choice to make God our God and try to live out our lives his way. Our attitude changes first, we test it out in little ways, and as our thinking changes, our behavior changes. Just adopting a bunch of rules about how to behave will not work and will make you and everyone around you, a little nuts. Romans 12:1-2 (immediately following the verses quoted in the prior paragraph) puts it this way:

> "Therefore, I urge you brothers, in view of God's mercy, to offer your bodies as living sacrifices, holy and pleasing to God—this is your spiritual act of worship. Do not conform any longer to the pattern of this world, but be transformed by the renewing of your mind. Then you will be able to test and approve what God's will is—his good, pleasing and perfect will."

You may end up being oddly at peace with the world, but you won't be crazy.

Chapter Eight
The Big Question

So, then the big question is: "If Christianity is such a good thing, if a relationship with God has all these positive benefits, then why are Christians so not like that? Why are those people in the news waiving Bibles, forcefully asserting their Christianity and calling it a mandate to do things many of us feel are judgmental, negative and demeaning to their "brothers and sisters"? Why aren't Christians today more like the ones in Acts, or even like the ones during the first three centuries after Christ, when the church grew like wildfire, drawing people in by its extraordinary acts of devotion and social improvement[33]? That is a fair question. After all, if we can only know God by his effects, then the effects demonstrated by his followers should be evidence that the promises in the Bible are reality. The dichotomy between the church in the Bible and the one in Fairview Heights was troubling to me. I spent a great deal of time and effort over a number of years trying to reconcile that dichotomy in my own mind and to understand where and how the church went off the tracks.

The first century church described in the Bible was attractive. Acts 2 describes a church we would all want to be part of. People worked together, shared with each other and reached out to a confused and chaotic world. People joined that Acts 2 church by the thousands. As described in Acts 2:41, three thousand people joined the movement in just one day. Acts 2:46 adds that the new movement had found "favor with all the people. And the Lord was adding to their number day by day those who were saved." People willingly sacrificed their financial well-being, social standing and personal safety to join the church. The modern church seems bland with a lot of meaningless rules. How did this happen, if God is to be believed?

Part of the problem is one of perception. The early church had problems too. By Acts 6 there was a disagreement about ethnic discrimination in the distribution of food to needy widows. Paul argued with Barnabas about taking Mark along on a missionary trip and broke up their long standing partnership, Acts 15:39. Paul criticized Peter for his treatment of Gentile Christians, Galatians 2:11-14. Just weeks into the new church a couple named Ananias and Sapphira started putting on

---

33

The History of the Church, Eusebius, originally written around 330 AD, translated by GA Williamson and published in 1965, reprinted by Dorset Press in 1984.

airs and pretending to be holier than they were, Acts 5:1-11. The early Christians weren't always that much different than us. Peter and Paul were clearly devoted to Christ, accomplished amazing things and were widely honored and regarded with great favor, but they were still just people. They still had faults. The rest of the people in those churches were a pretty ordinary group, and they had the same characteristics and issues that we see in people in churches today. Most of Paul's letters discuss some kind of argument or contentious situation going on in the church he was writing to. The church has always been a messy place filled with people.

Also, the modern church isn't completely useless; we sometimes overstate its failings. Churches and faith-based charities are an indispensable part of our support system for their communities. Churches are also an indispensable part of our support system for the under-resourced. Slightly more than half of all charities are faith based in some way, either church congregations or a faith based agency. The Salvation Army operates between twenty and forty percent of the homeless shelters in the United States, depending on the area, and most of the local corps operate a church with regular services in addition to the social services they provide.

There are thousands of soup kitchens, food pantries, women's and children's shelters, homes for the aged and developmentally disabled, hospitals, 12-step and drug rehabilitation programs, prison ministries, low income housing programs, job training programs, programs to provide clothing and household items to the under-resourced and orphanages, that are operated by churches or faith based ministries. The social services network, as co-dependent, overwhelmed and under-funded as it is, would fail completely without faith based services. That is in addition to the children's programs, schools, and---sometimes---effective, interesting church services and week day activities that local churches manage to pull off. The church still covers a lot of ground today despite its many faults.

Part of the problem is one of implementation. The church has always attracted people who find creating a system of rules easier than developing a relationship with God—like the Pharisees. It is much easier to create a rule than try to relate to someone that you can't see or to deal with messy human behavior. Jesus was extremely critical of the Pharisees and Sadducees, the religious leaders of his day, for confounding people's desire to connect with God by interposing a lot of rules. The zombies have always been out there.

For example, by time of Jesus' ministry, the Law given to protect Israel as it wandered around in the desert, had turned into a complicated system of rules for what was unclean and clean. In the Old Testament "unclean" meant a simple direction to wash, or to quarantine something until it could be confirmed as harmless. By Jesus' time "uncleaness" had taken on a life of its own. Uncleanness was treated more or less like a virus, a living thing that contaminated all that it touched. The rules filled thick volumes, and Jesus ignored them. In Mark 7 when the disciples were criticized by the Pharisees for eating with unclean hands, Jesus said;

> "...Do you not understand that whatever goes into the man from outside cannot defile him; because it does not go into his heart, but into his stomach and is eliminated....that which proceeds out of the man, that is what defiles the man. For from within, out of the heart of men, proceed the evil thoughts, fornications, envy, slander, pride and foolishness. All these evil things proceed from within and defile the man." Mark 7; 18-19, 21-22.

Matthew 3:7 records that when Jesus saw the Pharisees and Sadducees coming to be baptized, he said, "you brood of vipers, who warned you to flee from the coming wrath." In Matthew 23:27, he said, "Woe to you, scribes and Pharisees, hypocrites! For you are like white-washed tombs which on the outside appear beautiful, but inside are full of dead men's bones and all uncleanness." Jesus did not appreciate the zombies giving people the wrong message about what relating to God is really like.

The Pharisees were not just religious leaders, they were also the political and social leaders of Israel. The Pharisees did not like the criticism. They were incensed by Jesus' dismissive attitude toward them and by his barbed criticism. Ultimately they decided to kill Jesus as a heretic. They missed the truth of who and what Jesus was—and they missed the upside—because they were focused on their own attempts to understand the infinite, all-powerful, Yahweh by confining him to a set of rituals. The rituals were originally intended to reflect the truth and to assist people to relate to God, but the rituals had taken on a life of their own.

The Bible calls people like this tares, or weeds. The parable of the tares is explained at Matthew 13:24-30 where he described weeds coming up with wheat in the Kingdom of Heaven crop. The parable concludes "Allow both to grow together until the harvest; and in the time of the harvest I will say to the reapers, 'First gather up the tares and bind them in bundles to burn them up; but gather the wheat into my barn.' "

Those are the zombie—the tares—the "sons of Hell". The simple, and very frustrating, truth is that these people do not know that they are a problem, and frankly, it isn't always clear who is right and who is wrong. Many of these people are extremely nice people who have worked hard and long to cultivate themselves in their image of the proper Christian. The problem is that a number of them have invented their own image of God and of what a proper Christian should be; or they may have adopted a behavior pattern that was modeled for them by other churchgoers. More importantly, they are relying on their own efforts at perfection. They are following rules, trying to be nice and to impress God by following the rules. That doesn't work.

Generally speaking, all that work makes them dull and cranky and they aren't very nice to be around. God does not like religious leaders or other people to invent rules, or create images of what they think he is like any more today than he did when Jesus criticized the Pharisees. Deuteronomy 4:2 records Gods direction: "You shall not add to the work which I am commanding you, nor take away from it, that you may keep the commandments of the Lord your God which I command you.

Jesus' harshest criticism was against church leaders who had a holier than thou attitude. God hates that. In fact, the first recorded instance of acting holier than thou in church, Ananias and Sapphira, resulted in their immediate death. Ananias and Sapphira were part of the Acts 2 church, and everyone was sharing and selling things to support the new movement. Ananias and Sapphira wanted the recognition that came from such sharing. They had a piece of land that they sold and then brought in part of the price, claiming it was the full price. And God struck them dead in the sanctuary within a few hours of each other, but not for keeping the money. As Peter said, "While it remained unsold, did it not remain your own? And after it was sold, was it not under your control? Why is it that you have conceived these deeds in your heart? You have not lied to man, but to God." Acts 5:4. The "holier than thou" attitude that we see in churches, the plaster saints who want to appear holy to impress people, do not represent God's heart and mind. They are deeply offensive to God. They aren't really very connected to God, which is why we don't see God's character displayed in them.

172

The other side of the problem is our own unrealistic expectations. We expect church leaders to be perfect, when they are just people like anyone else. We sometimes criticize too quickly. A town near me has a house walk in their historic district every summer. People who have restored the old homes open their homes to the public one weekend a year. It's fun to see the restorations and I've gone a number of times. One year a couple who were in leadership at Willow had opened their home on the walk. The husband led the budget ministry at Willow where I volunteered, and his wife had a counseling background and worked in Willow's compassion ministry. As I walked through the tour I heard several people commenting that it "was an awfully big house for a pastor" and something to the effect that he must really be raking it in at the expense of the congregation. Nothing could have been further from the truth. They bought the house as a fixer-upper and did much of the restoration themselves. He is the absolute embodiment of thrift. He packed a lunch every day, wore the same clothes for years on end, and had a tiny office about 6 feet square. The office had a small desk and one side chair that took up the entire space, nowhere even to stand. They are very generous, caring people, full of life and a pleasure to be around. The two of them raised 6 children, 3 of their own and the wife's younger siblings, beginning when her parents were killed in an accident just a year or so after their marriage. And I remember how happy he was explaining in a seminar about the time it had dawned on him that he could increase the money he gave to charity by the amount of the tax deduction he got for the gift. He thought that was normal.

On top of that, the house wasn't really big. It was beautifully restored and warmly decorated with family mementos, but about average size and not ostentatious at all. There were several houses on the tour that year that were larger and definitely more ornate. It was a completely unjustified criticism. But it wasn't an unusual thought for people to have.

People expect church leaders to be holy and they are suspicious of the motives of anyone who works for the church. But church leaders are really just ordinary people doing the best they can. Church leaders feel pressure to live up to the expectations, and that contributes to the problem of pretending to be holier than you are. It's an ugly cycle. If we want churches to be normal, we have to not only let our church leaders be normal, we have to expect them to be normal. We can't expect them to be perfect and saintly all the time and then criticize the church for being stiff and out of touch.

To complicate matters, mixed in among the tares and zombies, are some real, modern day saints. "Saint" is a hard word choice. I don't mean someone who could be canonized by the church, I just mean someone who gives Christianity a good name. Their behavior is impeccable, they should be annoying, and yet they are so filled with light you just want to be around them. My mother was the ordinary, suburban version of a saint. She was calm and kind and sparkly all at once. Imperfect, certainly, but still an island of peace in a chaotic world, and fun besides. Mama Maggie and Mother Teresa are the one-in-a-million version of a modern day saint. Those few "saints" among us really illustrate God's view of what Christianity is about. God's view of a Christian life includes a lot of joy, and a lot of love towards others. God thinks that kind of sainthood should be normal rather than extraordinary. God thinks we can all be that filled with light. The failures of Christians and the church are our failures, not God's failure.

We get to choose whether or not to follow God in a real way, to be a zombie or try to ignore the whole thing. People have always had that choice. After coming down from the mountain with the new law, and reading it aloud to the assembled Israelites, Moses charge to the Israelites was clear.

> "I call Heaven and earth to witness against you today, that I have set before you life and death, the blessing and the curse. So choose life in order that you may live, you and your descendants, by loving the Lord your God, by obeying his voice, and by holding fast to him, for this is your life and the length of your days, that you may live in the land which the Lord swore to your fathers, to Abraham, Isaac and Jacob to give to them", Deuteronomy 30:19-20.

The Israelites waffled over that choice for centuries, sometimes choosing the blessing and sometimes the curse. We are still waffling too.

Just in case anyone thought that direction was limited to the Israelites or to that specific set of laws, Revelations 22: 18-19, nearly the last words of the Bible, repeats the charge. It says, "I testify to everyone who hears the words of the prophecy of this book: if anyone adds to them, God shall add to him the plagues that are written in this book; and if anyone takes away from the words of the book of this prophecy, God shall take away his part from the tree of life and from the holy city." We all still get to choose today. We can't just ignore the issue. We choose by our actions. The church doesn't demonstrate the character of God very well because we are part of the church and we don't pay much attention to God. We need to choose to follow God, and choose to apply God's teaching to our actions if we want the church to have a better reputation.

A big part of choosing God is sorting through the religious noise we've created to get to the essence of what God is asking us to do. Just as the original Jewish law exploded into huge volumes of rules that controlled every aspect of life in ancient Israel, we have created a lot of religious trappings to "help people relate to God." We have books, movies, concerts, workshops and computer apps. Those are not bad things. They can be helpful and enjoyable. But God doesn't need that kind of help.

God wants us to follow a few simple directions. Luke 10: 25, 27-28 relates a conversation between Jesus and a lawyer (an expert on the Jewish law.) The lawyer asks, "Teacher, what shall I do to inherit eternal life?" Jesus turns the question back to him, asking what the law says about that. The lawyer was well-educated. He knew the proper answer. The lawyer answered Jesus by saying: "You shall love the Lord your God with all your heart, and with all our soul and with all your strength, and with all your mind; and love your neighbor as yourself." And Jesus responds, "You have answered correctly; do this and you will live." But that is too simple—or maybe too difficult--an answer for the lawyer, and he just can't let it go. He asks "And who is my neighbor?"— and gets embarrassed by the parable of the Good Samaritan—an outcast-- who helps out a Jew who has been assaulted by robbers and has been passed by and ignored by a Pharisee and—a lawyer. Everyone is our neighbor and God wants us to love them.

The lawyer had the same problem most of the rest of us have. God's direction is very simple. It is very clear. It is easy to understand. It is just really hard to actually *do*. We don't love our enemies as Jesus directs us in Matthew 5:44. No one loves their enemies. People who tell you they love their enemies are lying to you. So we look for a better explanation of what God actually means—because he can't mean what he said. Except he does mean it and he doesn't want anyone changing the message.

The simple answer is that we all get too wrapped up in trying to project the right image. God is perfect, we aren't. God only wants us to be attentive and willing. David was described as a "man after God's own heart" in 1 Samuel 13:14; and replaced Saul who had failed to obey God. David ruled for more than 40 years and he was far from perfect. He was a murderer, an adulterer and an exceedingly violent man. And he was pretty oblivious to his own sins. In the Psalms he repeatedly says things like

> "For thou has heard my vows, O God; Thou hast given me the inheritance of those who fear thy name" Psalms 61:5. "The Lord has rewarded me according to my righteousness" Psalm 18:20."

When David committed adultery with Bathsheba and had her husband killed, he prayed "Against thee and thee only have I sinned", Psalm 51:4—not really. And my favorite:

> "The righteous will rejoice when he sees the vengeance; He will wash his feet in the blood of the wicked. And men will say, 'Surely there is a reward for the righteous; Surely there is a God who judges on earth", Psalm 58:10-11.

David did not love his enemies. But, he was quick to repent when he finally noticed a sin, quick to praise God, and completely sure that God was God and he was not. In Psalm 50:1-2, David says, "The Mighty One, God, the Lord, has spoken, and summoned the earth from the rising of the sun to its setting. Out of Zion, the perfection of beauty, God has shown forth." In Psalm 36:5-9, he writes with stunning beauty,

> "Thy lovingkindness, O Lord, extends to the heavens, Thy faithfulness reaches to the skies. Thy righteousness is like the mountains of God; Thy judgments are like the great deep, O Lord, Thou preservest man and beast. How precious is Thy lovingkindness, O God! And the children of men take refuge in the shadow of Thy wings. They drink their fill of the abundance of Thy house; And Thou dost give them to drink of the river of Thy delights. For with Thee is the fountain of life; in Thy light, we see light."

In the Psalms, David begs for help, cries out for vengeance, vents his frustration and anger, apologizes abjectly and sings his praise and devotion to God. David treated God like a real person and craved his presence. David was certain that God was with him and cared about him as a real person. That is what God wants from us. If we did that, we, like David, would be more real. We would experience more of what God wants for us, and Christianity's reputation wouldn't be held captive by a relative few, confused people.

God can forgive us for any action. He forgave the Israelites hundreds of times for worshipping other Gods, and that included things like sacrificing babies to idols and perverted sexual rituals. God forgave David hundreds of times; he forgave James' and John's pride and Peter's abandonment, and he's forgiven me more times than I can count or even remember. What he can't forgive is being ignored.

People are insecure, they need acceptance and approval. People are imperfect, they make mistakes, they get confused. People in churches are no exception. We should not let this age-old failure of the human spirit, with its needs and sins, keep us from God. All of us are guilty of putting on a show sometimes to gain acceptance and approval. All of us are guilty of getting off track and doing something dumb or unkind. We don't let this universal failure keep us from participating at work, the local garden club, golf league, sports team, country club, PTA, neighborhood group or health club. It is annoying when people behave badly in those contexts, but we roll our eyes and move on. It may be hurtful when people behave badly in those contexts, but we aren't devastated. We shouldn't be devastated when we see bad behavior in a church either.

The church is always going to be imperfect and polluted by zombies, even at its best, but Christianity has changed the world. In Acts 6, the church leaders argued about how to distribute food to poor widows, but the accepted thinking in the secular world at the time was to let widows starve and get out of the way. Today we find that kind of policy shocking. It is the impact of the church over time that has revolutionized our view of acceptable behavior. Real life solutions are messy, slow and imperfect, but change does happen slowly. We can look past the failures of Christians and the church. We can recognize that their failures are also our failures. We can be part of the change. We can have the upside. We just have to start moving in that direction. We just have to say "yes" to God and see what happens next.

Chapter Nine
Conclusion

So, where do you go from here? First, stop ignoring God. Whatever you think about churches, or religion or other people, stop ignoring God. He is real, and that fact alone demands some attention.

Second, find out what God is really like. The best suggestion I can make is to actually read the Bible, as a whole, as a book of history and biography. We tend to just pick pieces of it out of context to quote as philosophy. When you read the Bible, you discover there is very little philosophy or religion in it at all. The Bible is mostly a compilation of biographies showing God's interaction with various people over centuries. Seeing his interaction with that many people over that long a time period gives you a good sense of his character and attitudes.

The four Gospels, Matthew, Mark, Luke and John, are particularly helpful in understanding God's character. The Gospels are four biographies of Jesus and are named after the authors. Two of the authors, Matthew and John, were apostles. Luke was a doctor who accompanied Jesus and the apostles on their travels and spent a great deal of time with Paul as well. Mark is another follower, a cousin of Barnabas, see Colossians 2, and the same Mark that Paul got fed up with and argued about with Barnabas. Mark is generally thought to have spent a lot of time with Peter, including much of the time Peter was imprisoned in Rome toward the end of his life. Scholars believe Mark included Peter's input in his biography of Jesus.

The Gospels give you a really picture of Jesus. Reading them is very helpful to cut through the noise churches create. I know. At one point, back in the little Baptist church, I was really fed up and wondering how anyone was supposed to figure out being a Christian. People I knew in church were really messy and strange, and I certainly had no delusions of sainthood. Remember I'm a lawyer and at that time I was working in a large, fast-paced corporate environment that was only concerned about profit. No saints in sight. I felt I had run into a dead end on how to navigate my very real life from a Christian perspective. Ethics weren't nearly enough to get me through the day. I hit on the idea of reading about Jesus, the one person in history who totally got his life right. I read all four Gospels through, 4 times straight. It changed my point of view.

Jesus loved his enemies. He was kind to demons and blessed the soldiers nailing him to a cross. He took care of his mom, treated other women with respect, was kind to children, liked parties, and was understanding of human failings. He healed the sick, fed the hungry and raised the dead. He was intrepid, blunt, high-energy, in your face, stubborn, and incredibly smart. And, as recorded in Luke 22:70, when they asked "Are you the Son of God, then?" He said "Yes, I am". I'm pretty sure what he really said was "Yes, YAHWEH", in full voice; because his listeners recoiled in shock, called him a blasphemer and crucified him.

At dawn the second day following the day of his death, he rose again, and spent the next six weeks visiting his followers. Jesus convinced his followers that he was alive, and encouraged them to persevere. And they did, starting the church and travelling widely around the ancient world. Thomas, whom we call the Doubter, travelled as far as India spreading the word that Yahweh walked the earth and called people to him. All of the apostles and early leaders, like James, Jesus' brother, spent the rest of their lives trying to convince others that Yahweh walked the earth, loved them and wanted to partner with them in their lives. Some were martyred just a few years later, John lived and taught for more than 70 years. All of them were eventually killed for proclaiming the truth that Jesus walked the earth and loved all mankind. The modern church can trace its unbroken history to the work of those few people. They made a difference. We aren't going to match that group of people, but we can make a difference too if we persevere.

Try to do what Jesus asks in Luke 10: 25, 27-28 "You shall love the Lord your God with all your heart, and with all our soul and with all your strength, and with all your mind; and love your neighbor as yourself." Surprisingly, this works, but it is a choice you have to make. After reading all 4 Gospels 4 times straight, I decided I could hold my temper long enough to talk to other people's lawyers without getting upset about it. I decided I could handle volunteering in church without openly rolling my eyes. (As I said, I have no delusions of sainthood. I set achievable goals.) I decided I could read my Bible most days, pray every day and make an effort to be nice to people even if they weren't the kind of people I wanted to be close friends with, and I made some close friends too.

I decided that Jesus really meant the things he said, as far-fetched as they sounded—like tithing or trying to make peace instead of indulging my temper. I decided to make more of an effort to actually do those things. I tried to apply those decisions to my actions ten minutes at a time because I needed to reconsider my choices that often in order to continue to make the positive choice. I messed up a lot. I still mess up a lot—but not as much as I used to. The more I actually turned belief into behavior, the stronger and happier I became. The annoying people started to be less annoying. The politics at work didn't seem all that important. I weathered storms better. I was less stressed out.

I got laid off from Sears in late1994. It was devastating, I was angry and upset and depressed. I felt God's presence during that time; it didn't help. I can't say I drew closer to God during that time. Maybe other people grow closer to God in a crisis, I was mostly just really mad. I ended up with a better job six months later, a week before my severance ran out. I negotiated purchasing and sales contracts for a global electrical equipment manufacturer. It was a great job, well paid and interesting.

I was laid off from that job 13 years later, in 2008. I was 53 and the economy was horrible. I was paying for my mother's assisted living and was an accidental landlord when my house failed to sell after I bought a condo with the intent to downsize. It was not a good time to be unemployed and over 50. Even though, objectively speaking, it was a worse situation than the change in 1994, I was a lot less upset. I was a little angry, and a little scared, but not devastated. I started my own firm, and then joined a local firm 9 months later. I'm not making anything close to the salary I was before, and I'm a little stressed out about that, but it's a nice place to work. I'm happy and the bills are all paid. Things work out. "Just go with the flow" works. I'm not likely to abandon the law for the slums of Cairo, but my life has changed. I am calmer, happier and more peaceful. Some people do great things for the church. I am not one of them. I'm pretty normal. That is my point, normal people can and should have a relationship with God that gives you peace and confidence and a willingness to engage with others as equals.

Don't let the church stop you. There are good churches, and the unfortunate truth is that it is very difficult to develop a relationship with God without being involved in a church. The teaching helps sort out some of the difficult parts of the Bible and gives you some historical context for the stories. Meeting with other people on a regular basis to focus on God for a time helps you to stay motivated. Good churches give us a regular time to break out of our routine and focus on relating to God for an hour or so.

Good churches also give you an opportunity to interact with people outside of your normal comfort zone. I went to South Africa on a trip with Willow. We were supposed to help out for a couple of days at a youth ministry conference. We did that, but it was a week-long trip. We spent a couple days at a game park and saw lions and giraffe, gnu, rhinos, and even hippos. At one point we were surrounded by a herd of elephants. It was great. We also went to church in Soweto and spent an afternoon in one of the settlements near Johannesburg where whole families live on a lot the size of my living room, in a corrugated tin shack the size of a walk-in closet. 50,000 people live on about 5 acres of land. I'd seen that kind of poverty before, but not walked around with chatty, happy, bare-footed 4 year olds saying "Don't touch that, it hurts" about the live high power lines running unprotected down the middle of the path. It was an eye-opener. Good churches rattle your cage sometimes.

Look for a church that insists you read the Bible for yourself, and encourages questions. Look for a church where helping others, particularly the under-resourced or the elderly, is a value. Look for a church where the leaders and most of the people are real and not pretending to be perfect. I like Willow, and I like big churches, but they aren't for everyone. Look around and find one that fits you. I've been to some really nice small churches where the teaching is good, the music is well done, and the people are friendly, accepting, and involved in the community.

Get involved helping other people in some way that interests you. One of the best ways to see change in your own life is by getting involved helping people. It helps to keep your own life in perspective. If you really can't stand to walk into a church, try a faith-based charity. Take some risks doing what you think God would want you to do supporting people and projects that help people in a constructive, effective way. See how it works out and take the next step toward God based on your experience. A relationship with God isn't a paint by numbers picture. Every life is unique. God loves you, and your picture will be unique.

If you don't like church the way it is, get involved and be part of the change. The church will only be different when people who go to churches stop pretending to be something they aren't. The church will only be different when normal healthy people don't bail because there are some weird, needy people there. Try being part of the solution. It's time normal people took back the church. The weird, needy people need to be there, they need help. If we are going to respond to God's call to love others, we need to be willing to contribute in some way to their healing; but let's stop abdicating responsibility for making church healthy and normal.

Be careful not to turn into a zombie. Don't get sucked into being one of those people who are endlessly running around doing good works and getting crankier by the day. That is not what God intends. Have some fun. Jesus did. Spend time with people you love. Do things you like. Dance. Sleep in. Spend some time outside. Look at the flowers, the birds, the trees and the weird bugs. Feel the rain and enjoy the rainbows. Get acquainted with God's creation.

If you are more contemplative, you might want to do some reading and see how other people have experienced God, but don't overdo it. A lot of books out there are very focused on spiritual behaviors or very esoteric theological discussions that are likely to either confuse you or lead you down the zombie path. I'd recommend a couple of short, clear books. The Practice of the Presence of God by Brother Lawrence Whitaker House (1983) is great. It is a collection of letters and writings by a monk living about 300 years ago. Brother Lawrence was just an ordinary monk, the cook among the group, but his descriptions of life with God are very moving even today. The book is very short and easy to read. Brother Lawrence sounds a lot like Mama Maggie—the book practically glows.

The second book is Life of the Beloved by Henri Nouwen, Crossroads Publishing (1992) with a subsequent printing in 2001. Henri Nouwen was a Catholic priest who published over 40 books and taught at Notre Dame, Yale and Harvard. He died in 1996. For the last years of his life, including the period in which Life of the Beloved was written, Nouwen lived and ministered as the pastor of Daybreak, an L'Arche Community for developmentally challenged adults in Toronto. The book reflects on the author's experiences and attempts to explain how God's presence and the feeling of connection with God has influenced his life. I re-read both those books from time to time, just for the sense of peace that oozes out of the words.

The Bible is really the best reference book. It isn't hard to understand if you get a modern translation like the New International version or the New American Standard version. Just skim over the parts about building the temple in the Old Testament and focus on the stories rather than the New Testament letters. Some of it is dense or boring and some of the letters sound like a bunch of rules. They really aren't but you need a firm grip on Jesus' teaching in the Gospels to understand the context of the letters. Don't worry about every little thing. You don't have to pass a test, just get a sense of who God really is. The stories give you examples and context that illustrate the points God is trying to make. Remember also that the Bible is about real people. Often the people in the Bible, even the heroes of the Bible, do stupid things. I find that reassuring.

As you actively seek to engage with God, you will change. God is real and he will influence your life. You can have more peace, more love for others and yourself, more joy in life, a more positive attitude, and more courage. Life can be sweeter. Why not take a chance. You have nothing to lose and the whole upside to gain.

www.ingramcontent.com/pod-product-compliance
Lightning Source LLC
Chambersburg PA
CBHW031512040426
42445CB00009B/194